AN
ECONOMIC GEOGRAPHY
OF
EAST AFRICA

BELL'S ADVANCED ECONOMIC GEOGRAPHIES

General Editor

PROFESSOR R. O. BUCHANAN

M.A.(N.Z.), B.Sc.(Econ.), Ph.D.(London)
Professor Emeritus, University of London

A. Systematic Studies

AN ECONOMIC GEOGRAPHY OF OIL
Peter R. Odell, B.A., Ph.D.

PLANTATION AGRICULTURE
P. P. Courtenay, B.A., Ph.D.

NEW ENGLAND: A STUDY IN INDUSTRIAL ADJUSTMENT
R. C. Estall, B.Sc.(Econ.), Ph.D.

GREATER LONDON: AN INDUSTRIAL GEOGRAPHY
J. E. Martin, B.Sc.(Econ.), Ph.D.

GEOGRAPHY AND ECONOMICS
Michael Chisholm, M.A.

AGRICULTURAL GEOGRAPHY
Leslie Symons, B.Sc.(Econ.), Ph.D.

REGIONAL ANALYSIS AND ECONOMIC GEOGRAPHY
John N. H. Britton, M.A., Ph.D.

B. Regional Studies

AN ECONOMIC GEOGRAPHY OF EAST AFRICA
A. M. O'Connor, B.A., Ph.D.

AN ECONOMIC GEOGRAPHY OF WEST AFRICA
H. P. White, M.A., & M. B. Gleave, M.A.

YUGOSLAVIA: PATTERNS OF ECONOMIC ACTIVITY
F. E. Ian Hamilton, B.Sc.(Econ.), Ph.D.

AN AGRICULTURAL GEOGRAPHY OF GREAT BRITAIN
J. T. Coppock, M.A., Ph.D.

AN HISTORICAL INTRODUCTION TO THE ECONOMIC GEOGRAPHY
OF GREAT BRITAIN
Wilfred Smith, M.A.

THE BRITISH IRON & STEEL SHEET INDUSTRY SINCE 1840
Kenneth Warren, M.A., Ph.D.

AN
ECONOMIC GEOGRAPHY
OF
EAST AFRICA

A. M. O'CONNOR
B.A., Ph.D.

Lecturer in Geography
University College, London
Formerly of
Makerere University College, Uganda

SECOND EDITION

LONDON
G. BELL & SONS, LTD
1971

Printed in Great Britain by
NEILL AND CO. LTD., EDINBURGH

Preface

The main incentive to write this book was provided by the remarkable dearth of literature on the geography of East Africa. I hope that it will play some part in filling the gap which this region causes on the geography shelves of libraries elsewhere in the world; but more particularly I hope that it will be of some help to all in East Africa who are interested in the tremendous contrasts of land and livelihood to be found within the region.

A further incentive was the lack of appreciation of the significance of regional differences within East Africa among those working in disciplines other than geography, and among those involved in administration and planning. For example, detailed analyses of the contribution of each sector of the economy to the national income are made in each country, yet virtually no attention is given to the geographical distribution of income. Such omissions are especially surprising and serious in view of the diversity existing within East Africa.

This diversity is so great that five years is a quite inadequate period in which to reach a full understanding of the economic geography of the region, and I trust that East Africans will forgive one who has arrived so recently for presuming to write about their countries. I have been hasty in writing mainly because there appears to be a pressing need among geographers for studies of East Africa, and among East Africans for studies of the geography of their region; I hope that this book does at least begin to satisfy these needs.

I have drawn heavily upon the few books that have been written on specific topics in the geography of East Africa, but the main published sources used have been government reports. Unless otherwise stated all works quoted as published in Nairobi, Dar es Salaam or Entebbe are published by the respective Government Printers. Other parts of the content of the book represent observations and enquiries made on my own travels in East Africa.

Consideration of cost has prevented the inclusion of photographs, and has limited the number of maps. For an excellent set of photographs, and for maps of such features as soils and vegetation, the reader is recommended to consult *East Africa: its Peoples and Resources* to which reference is made in Chapters 8, 15 and 16.

Much of this book will undoubtedly be open to criticism, and if readers would take the trouble to offer me such criticism I should greatly appreciate this. Indeed, if by its deficiencies the book stimulates others to improve upon it, it will have achieved one of its aims.

My thanks are due to many people who have helped me in the production of this book: to Makerere College Council for giving me the opportunity to live and work in East Africa; to the managers of the East African Teaching Materials Fund for a grant to assist me in making extensive travels in Kenya and Tanzania; to the government servants and others who have provided me with information; to the colleagues who have commented on parts of the manuscript, especially Mr. B. W. Langlands, and the students with whom I have had many valuable discussions; to Professor R. O. Buchanan for reading the manuscript and making many suggestions for improvement; to Mr. J. C. Sebunnya, draughtsman in the Makerere Department of Geography for his assistance with the maps; and most of all to my wife, for her constant encouragement.

Makerere University College, Kampala,   A.M.O'C.

December, 1965.

Preface to the Second Edition

In this edition an attempt has been made to take account of changes during the late 1960s. The text of every chapter has been revised, as have all the tables and most of the maps. Two very welcome developments of this period have been the increasing amount of research being undertaken by geographers in East Africa, and the growing awareness of the spatial dimension in economic planning in the region. Some effort has been made to reflect these, although to do them full justice would require an entirely new book.

All data are now expressed in metric units, since these have now been adopted throughout East Africa. The currency units employed are those of Kenya, Tanzania and Uganda, i.e. 20 shillings = £1 (now equivalent to £U.K. 1·16 or $U.S. 2·80).

The revision was greatly assisted by a return visit to East Africa in 1970 financed by a generous grant from the Hayter Fund. I am also grateful to Mr. A. Newman and Mr. T. Allen of University College, who re-drew the maps; and to all those who have made suggestions for improvement, once again notably Professor B. W. Langlands in Kampala and Professor R. O. Buchanan in London.

University College, London,   A.M.O'C.
February, 1971.

Contents

Tables

Maps

EAST AFRICA: Reference Map showing Administrative Divisions as at January 1971

In Kenya new regions were created in 1963 and re-named provinces in 1965. (Key to Kenya districts: 1. Kiambu, 2. Murang'a, 3. Nyandarua, 4. Nyeri, 5. Kirinyaga, 6. Siaya, 7. Kisumu, 8. Kakamega, 9. Bungoma, 10. Busia, 11. Trans-Nzoia, 12. Uasin Gishu, 13. Elgeyo Marakwet, 14, Nandi.) In Tanzania the present regions were created in 1963, mainly by splitting the former provinces. In Uganda the provinces were abolished in 1962, as was the Buganda Kingdom in 1967, but for some purposes the districts are still grouped as indicated. (The term 'Buganda' is thus still used for E. & W. Mengo, Masaka and Mubende.) For the location of towns see Map 16.

CHAPTER 1

Introduction

This book is concerned with how people in East Africa make a living. It examines the economic activities that take place in Kenya, Tanzania and Uganda, and especially their distribution. It also attempts to indicate the main factors affecting both the existence and the distribution of these activities.

A keynote of the geography of East Africa is the tremendous variety to be found within an area of $1\frac{3}{4}$ million square km.; but the contrasts in physical conditions and human activities show little relationship to national boundaries, and the three political units have much in common. All are independent countries, formerly under British administration and now members of the Commonwealth. The population of each is between 10 and 14 million, with Africans in an overwhelming majority but with other races represented. All depend on agriculture to provide a livelihood for most of the population, and all are poor, with an annual income per head of between £30 and £45. The main reason, however, for grouping together Kenya, Tanzania and Uganda as a region is that such a grouping is acknowledged by many of their 35 million inhabitants. Most people in Uganda, for example, feel a closer bond with Kenyans and Tanzanians than with their other neighbours in Sudan, Congo and Rwanda. The three countries share a number of common services, and are now partners in the East African Community.

An eminent geographer has recently written: 'It is harder to write a small book on economic geography than to compile a massive compendium. There are enough figures and examples available to fill volume after volume. Difficulty begins when selections have to be made.'[1] This is true even of the economic geography of East Africa, even though not all the figures that one would like to have are available. Most of this book is concerned with an analysis of the distribution of each economic activity, and may appear to be a mere compendium. In the last few chapters, therefore, the factors that have a particularly great influence on the pattern of activities receive special attention. Although such features as the physical environment and the distribution of population are discussed then rather than in this introductory section, the basic patterns of land and people are illustrated in Maps 1 and 2. It may also perhaps be helpful to sketch a background picture of both the regional diversity and the economic structure of East Africa, before embarking upon the close examination of the various ways in which its people make a living.[2]

REGIONAL SURVEY[3]

THE COASTLANDS

East Africa borders the Indian Ocean for about 1,300 km., and the coastlands form a very distinctive zone. There is a clearly marked coastal plain from Somalia to Mozambique, and nowhere do hills rise directly from the sea, although the plain is under 100 km. wide around the Kenya-Tanzania border. Winds from the ocean bring a high rainfall to most of the land fringing the coast, and this level and well watered land is generally quite densely settled. The rainfall drops sharply inland, however, and the land quickly becomes arid and sparsely populated. As one travels from the interior towards the coast, the change from scorched bush to clusters of huts beneath the coocnut palms is often very striking.

Some of the special characteristics of the coastlands stem from the fact that many people have approached them from the sea and have not penetrated far inland. Thus, although most of the population is African, there is a substantial Arab element; and in sharp contrast to the rest of East Africa the coast was visited by Europeans and Asians from the fifteenth century. Mombasa is an old town, although the other major coastal towns, Dar es Salaam and Tanga, are not. These three towns are distinctive in that through them passes most of the foreign trade of East Africa. This tends to quicken the pace of economic acitivity there, although in the whole zone the high temperatures resulting from the low altitude perhaps tend to slow it down.

The coastal zone includes the islands of Zanzibar and Pemba. Together they constituted a separate state for over a hundred years until they joined with Tanganyika in 1964 to form the new state of Tanzania. The islands are very small, and although they are densely peopled their combined population is only 360,000. Fifty years ago they were much more prosperous than the mainland, but their economy is now stagnant and the gap has been greatly reduced. After independence, a new difference arose as Zanzibar turned politically towards the East, and this distinction has remained despite the formal union with Tanganyika.

THE NYIKA AND SOUTHERN PLATEAUX

Away from the coast the land rises generally fairly gently to flat plateau country between 400 and 1,000 metres above sea level, known in some areas as the Nyika (Swahili for wilderness). This is an area of low rainfall, poor scrub vegetation and very sparse population, separating richer lands in the interior from the sea. In places it is broken by mountain ranges, notably the Usambara and Pare mountains and the Taita hills, where relief induces a higher rainfall and where more people have settled. Further south it is broken by a zone of lowland in the basins of the Ruaha and Rufiji rivers, where settlement is discouraged by periodic floods and by disease rather than by low rainfall. Water, often so scarce in East Africa, is there superabundant, and if it can be controlled this area offers promise for future agricultural development. In the far south of Tanzania the plateau reappears, but there also the rainfall exceeds 800 mm. in most years, and much of the land is under cultivation. The rainfall is unreliable, soils are poor, and the area is remote from the centre of economic life in Tanzania, so that although it is well-populated in parts, it is far from prosperous.

CENTRAL TANZANIA

The greater part of Tanzania consists of a plateau lying between 1,000 and 1,400 metres, with little to break a general monotony of relief. The mean annual rainfall is generally between 500 and 800 mm. but this rainfall is unreliable, while most of the land has infertile soils. Conditions are therefore difficult for agriculture, and the density of population rarely exceeds 10 per square km. Much land is under open woodland

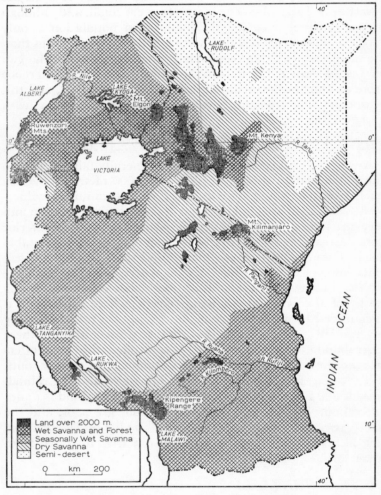

Figure 1. EAST AFRICA: Ecological Zones

This is a highly simplified representation, for the patterns of relief, climate and vegetation are all very complex.

vegetation, known locally as *miombo*, and cannot even be used for livestock because of the presence of tsetse-fly. This type of country covers a vast area, and the problems it presents as a home for man received much attention in the East Africa Royal Commission Report.[4] To the west it is broken only by the rift valley, occupied by Lake Tanganyika, which forms the boundary with Congo.

THE LAKE VICTORIA BASIN

The land falls slightly northwards from the central plateau of Tanzania towards the Lake Victoria basin, and the density of population increases greatly. The basin is one of the richest zones of East Africa, supporting over a quarter of the total population of the region. The country receives more rain and has more fertile soils than that to the south, and advantage has been taken of its agricultural opportunities. The land around the lake in some ways forms a single unit, although it is divided among all three countries, but there are contrasts between the northern and southern shores. Although the southern and eastern shores are wetter than the Tanzania plateau, the dominant winds across the lake take even more rain to the northern and western shores. Sukumaland, south of the lake, is densely settled by farmers who produce much cotton as well as annual food crops; but Buganda, to the north, gives an impression of greater prosperity, bananas and coffee providing a green landscape all the year round. Even in Buganda annual income per head is only about £50, but this is double that in most other parts of East Africa. Buganda, and especially the city of Kampala, is the focus of life in Uganda; but the economic core of the country, which the Lake Victoria zone represents, extends into the Eastern Region, where it includes the towns of Jinja and Mbale.

Further east the Lake Victoria basin continues into Western and Nyanza Provinces of Kenya, which are very densely populated, though the physical environment is less favourable than that of southern Uganda. The poor, rocky land of Bunyore and Maragoli, for example, supports over 400 people per square km. Thus, while Buganda is a zone of immigration, people migrate from Nyanza to other parts of Kenya. West of the lake the zone of high rainfall and perennial crops continues

B

from Buganda into Bukoba District of Tanzania, but there it becomes very narrow. A short distance west of the lake there is another belt of dry and sparsely settled country.

NORTHERN UGANDA

Northwards from Lake Victoria the land takes on a poorer appearance as rainfall decreases from 1,300 to 800 mm. a year, as soils become less fertile, and as population becomes sparser. North of Lake Kyoga rainfall increases again, although the land is very flat, but is more seasonal than in Buganda. The cultivation of annual crops supports a population of 20 to 40 per square km. in many areas, but a large tract in the west is so sparsely occupied that it has been possible to schedule it a National Park, where the interest of wild animals is paramount. The plateau is bounded on the west by the valley of the Nile, beyond which lies West Nile District, which is more densely settled but suffers from its remoteness from the remainder of Uganda.

THE ARID NORTH-EAST

Nowhere does rainfall deficiency determine the character of the landscape more than in the northern half of Kenya and the adjacent part of Uganda. Around Lake Rudolf the mean annual fall is only 150 mm., and this supports hardly any vegetation. Even where rainfall is much higher, notably near the residual mountains that rise sharply from the pene-plain surface, it occurs as occasional cloudbursts so that little water sinks into the soil. The very sparse population of this zone is almost entirely dependent on livestock, which somehow find enough grazing to sustain themselves. This semi-desert area occupies more than half of Kenya, yet less than 1 per cent. of the country's population lives there. It extends eastwards into Somalia and south-eastwards almost to the coast.

THE KENYA HIGHLANDS

South of the semi-desert zone a mass of tertiary to recent volcanic rocks stands up as highlands, culminating in the 5,200-metre peak of Mount Kenya. From there land over 2,000 metres extends 500 km. westwards almost to the shores of Lake Victoria, although it is broken by the north-south rift valley, the floor of which in places lies 1,500 metres below the land to either side. In this highland zone heavy rainfall and fertile volcanic soils provide excellent conditions for agriculture, and much of the land is under cultivation. The eastern part is occupied mainly by the Kikuyu and related tribes, and some areas are so densely settled that severe pressure on the land is felt.

Extensive stretches in the highlands, expecially in the west, were not apparently occupied in the early part of this century, and these were settled by Europeans who established large farms capable of yielding a high income. Since independence, many settlers have left, and some of their land has been used for African resettlement schemes; but large European farms still produce a very distinctive landscape in many areas. There has been a burst of economic activity in the African settled areas of the highlands in the past ten years, and in every way the highlands are now the economic heart of the country. This is epitomized by the location there of Nairobi, the capital of Kenya and largest city of East Africa, with a population of 450,000.

KILIMANJARO AND ELGON

Two outliers of the volcanic highlands, although covering a small area, are of great importance. Astride the Kenya-Uganda border stands the cone of Mount Elgon, and just across the Tanzania border the massive extinct volcano of Kilimanjaro rises higher than any other African mountain, to almost 5,900 metres. The southern slopes of both mountains, and also of Mount Meru 80 km. west of Kilimanjaro, have a high rainfall and fertile soils, and are very thickly settled up to a height of about 2,000 metres. The Chagga people are renowned in East Africa for their intensive banana and coffee cultivation around Mount Kilimanjaro, and a similar economy is found on the slopes of Meru and Elgon. The densest rural population in Uganda is to be found in the valleys cutting into Mount Elgon.

THE SOUTHERN HIGHLANDS

The southern highlands of Tanzania are as extensive as the highlands of Kenya, but do not reach a comparable altitude.

They are not volcanic and have less fertile soils, but they receive ample rainfall, although distance from the Equator is such that this falls mainly in a single wet season. The physical

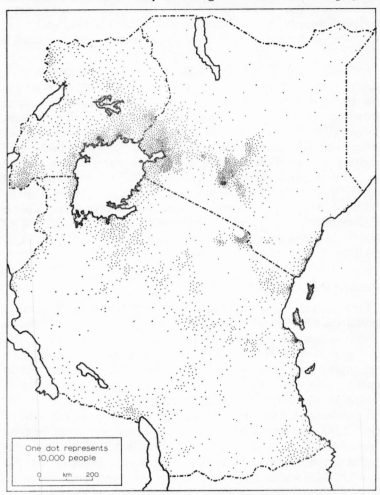

Figure 2. EAST AFRICA: Distribution of Population

This map is based on data from the Kenya 1969, Tanzania 1967 and Uganda 1969 censuses, but it also owes much to P. W. Porter, 'East Africa—Population Distribution', *Annals of the Association of American Geographers*, Vol. 56, No. 1, 1966, Map Supplement.

environment is quite satisfactory for agricultural settlement, but
the opportunities are not fully used. There is a dense population
around Tukuyu, but elsewhere, as around Njombe, much land
is unoccupied. Some European settlement is found, notably
around Iringa, but the southern Tanzania highlands provided
less attraction than Kenya with its cooler climate, better soils
and greater accessibility. No railway serves this area, and
improvements in road transport are only slowly overcoming
the problem of isolation from the rest of East Africa.

THE WESTERN HIGHLANDS

A broken highland zone extends from southern Tanzania
to western Uganda. In north-western Tanzania the uplands
are sparsely inhabited, but in south-west Uganda the population is extremely dense and terraced hillsides rising to 2,500
metres form a very distinctive landscape. One feature which the
zone shares with the southern highlands is a feeble development
of commercial acitivity, partly because of inaccessibility. Here,
even more than elsewhere, this survey must suffer from over-
generalization, for the west is characterized by extremely sharp
local contrasts. A view from the volcanic craters of north-west
Ankole across the dry flat floor of the rift valley to the 5,000-
metre, snow-capped, non-volcanic peaks of the Ruwenzori
would make this abundantly clear.

THE EAST AFRICAN ECONOMY[5]

The first and most important thing to note about the
economic life of East Africa is the poverty of the region. If the
world may be divided into highly developed, prosperous
nations on the one hand, and underdeveloped countries caught
in a vicious circle of poverty on the other, East Africa falls
quite clearly into the latter category. The standard of living of
most people in the region, by any criteria, is extremely low,
and in desperate need of improvement. Economic development is taking place, but no more rapidly than in the more
advanced countries of Europe and North America: the gap
between these and East Africa therefore shows no sign of
narrowing.

The best available indication of relative wealth and poverty is provided by the official estimates of the Gross Domestic Product of each country (Table 1), although there are clearly some aspects which cannot be measured statistically. These

TABLE 1

GROSS DOMESTIC PRODUCT OF
SELECTED AFRICAN COUNTRIES, 1968–69

G.D.P. (£ million)

	Population (million)	Total	Monetary	Non-Monetary	Per Capita G.D.P. (£)
1968					
Malawi	4·3	87			20
Ethiopia	24·2	502			21
Ghana	8·4	656			78
Zambia	4·0	401			100
Kenya	10·6	442	333	109	42
Tanzania	12·6	370	259	111	29
Uganda	9·2	322	222	100	35
EAST AFRICA	32·4	1134	814	320	35
1969					
Kenya	10·9	476	363	113	44
Tanzania	13·0	391	278	113	30
Uganda	9·5	357	250	107	37
EAST AFRICA	34·4	1224	891	333	37

The data are drawn from a variety of publications from the United Nations and from national Statistical Offices.

figures suggest an income in East Africa of £37 per head. This is even lower than in most other parts of the continent; and in Ghana, Ivory Coast and Zambia income per head is more than double that in East Africa. There are only eight independent African states for which the official estimate is lower than that for Tanzania. By contrast most countries in western Europe have a Gross Domestic Product exceeding £700 per head.

The situation is broadly similar in all the East African countries, but the small differences between them are of some significance. Kenya has a higher figure than the others mainly on account of large-scale enterprise undertaken there in both agriculture and manufacturing. Some of this is in the hands of foreign companies, and all is controlled by a very small sector of the population. The differences among the three countries are, in fact, much smaller than the regional variations within each, which will be discussed in subsequent chapters and summarized in the conclusion to this book.

This rather static picture must be qualified, for the patterns are constantly changing. In general the early 1950s witnessed a rapid increase of income through high prices for most cash crops: agricultural income rose sharply and this stimulated other forms of development. The period between 1959 and 1963 on the other hand was one of relative stagnation as exemplified by the small amount of building then taking place in most towns, although there were marked regional variations. Fortunately, the next six years brought improved economic conditions almost everywhere. Exact comparisons of the growth in per capita income are hindered by changes in the methods of calculation, but over the 15 years from 1954 to 1969 Kenya appears to have experienced the most rapid growth and Uganda the slowest. Fluctuations in world prices and deteriorating terms of trade have hit Uganda hardest, and the growth of the national income has in some years only just kept pace with the rise in population.

The economy of East Africa is still based on peasant agriculture, as it was a hundred years ago, although this now includes an element of commercial production almost everywhere. Over 80 per cent. of the population live and work on their own farms of less than 5 hectares, normally growing their own food and selling some produce to satisfy their cash requirements. The importance of agriculture to the people of the region is even greater than this, for large-scale mixed farms and plantations provide the chief source of paid employment. Over 85 per cent. of the exports of the region are agricultural products, even though export crops occupy only a small proportion of the cultivated land.

During this century other economic activities have been established, and these are now increasing in importance. Mining, manufacturing and trade will all receive attention in later chapters; but none of these approaches agriculture as a source of income in East Africa. One illustration of the importance of the farm to most of the population is provided by the fact that those who have sought work in the towns rarely lose contact with their home areas. The man often leaves his wife on the farm while he goes to a job in the town, though he may be away a year or more. Even when the whole family become urban dwellers, they often retain a stake in the land at home and hope to return there eventually.

The significance of agriculture in East Africa stands out clearly in Table 2. Again there are important differences

TABLE 2

INDUSTRIAL ORIGIN OF THE GROSS DOMESTIC PRODUCT IN AFRICAN COUNTRIES, 1968

Percentage contribution to G.D.P.

	Agriculture Forests, Fish	Mining	Manufacturing	Trade and Transport	Others
Malawi	38	0	8	15	39
Ethiopia	58	0	8	11	23
Ivory Coast	41	0	9	23	27
Zambia	9	33	10	20	28
Rhodesia	16	9	19	21	35
Kenya	35	0	11	19	35
Tanzania	41	2	7	21	29
Uganda	52	1	7	17	23
EAST AFRICA	42	1	8	19	30

within the region, for industrial development has made more progress in Kenya than elsewhere: and again there is a sharp contrast between East Africa and some other African countries. But the composition of the economy is not untypical of the continent as a whole, for many African countries have an economic structure broadly similar to that of East Africa.

No distinction has so far been made between subsistence and commercial production. Table 1 indicates the contribution of each in East Africa, but the figures must be treated with reserve. All figures for subsistence crop production are estimates, while for activities such as fishing only rough guesses can be made about the proportion of production that enters trade. Similarly food crops sold locally may be recorded as falling within the subsistence rather than the monetary economy.

The main criticism to which the official figures are open is in their assessment of the value of subsistence production. That of food crops is based on prevailing market prices, but the fact that little of each is sold suggests that their value to the farmer is greater than the market price. A 20 per cent. increase in the size of the banana crop in an area where few are normally sold may cause such a glut that a 50 per cent. reduction in its local market price results: on the present method of assessment the total value of the crop is then reckoned to be less than before, although it is larger in size and the area obviously cannot be any worse off. It may be impossible to devise a better method of assessment, but it should be recognized that the value of subsistence production in East Africa may be understated in the official figures.

The relative importance of the subsistence and monetary sectors varies among the East African countries. The latter accounts for three-quarters of all income in Kenya, but for only two-thirds of the total in Tanzania. In all three countries there are great differences from place to place in the extent to which commercial production has entered into local life. Thus in Uganda subsistence production is thought to be worth about £15 per head each year in both Buganda and Kigezi, but commercial enterprise brings a further £20 per head to rural households in Buganda, compared with only £3 in Kigezi.

It is unwise to draw too sharp a distinction between the two forms of production for they are closely interlocked. Complete local self-sufficiency is rare, as most people need cash for paying taxes if for nothing else; yet subsistence production forms the chief occupation of most people even when they have been growing cash crops for many years. Several African countries have a 'dual economy' in the sense that an alien commercial economy has been established beside an African economy aimed primarily at subsistence. But in East Africa commercial production has been integrated into the local economy to a large extent. The theme of a dual economy is often stressed in accounts of development in Zambia while discussions of the Congo economy often refer to the 'traditional areas' and the 'non-traditional areas' as quite distinct units. In these regions over 85 per cent. of all commercial production was once under European control. The equivalent figure for East Africa was always under 40 per cent. In this respect, therefore, the structure of the East African economy differs greatly from that of some other African countries. A closely related characteristic of East Africa is the small number of people in paid employment. Even in most underdeveloped countries more than 30 per cent. of the adult male population normally work for others. In East Africa only 15 per cent. do so, and the proportion is hardly rising at present. This is another respect in which Kenya differs somewhat from Tanzania and Uganda, but even in Kenya only 20 per cent. of all men are wage-earners.

Finally, the dependence of East Africa on overseas trade might be noted here, although the topic is discussed further in Chapter 14. The commercial economy developed on the basis of primary production for export and consumption of imported manufactured goods. This is a very unsatisfactory state of affairs, and since independence the production of goods for sale within the region has been expanding rapidly, yet foreign trade is still more important in the economy of Kenya, Tanzania and Uganda than in that of most countries.

REFERENCES

1   H. Boesch, *A Geography of World Economy*, Van Nostrand, Princeton, 1964, p. 5.
2   The historical background has not been sketched here as several books are available on this subject, e.g. B. A. Ogot and J. A. Kieran (eds.), *Zamani: A Survey of East African History*, East African Publishing House and Longmans, Nairobi, 1968.
3   The best available study of the regional geography of East Africa is the school text: G. M. Hickman and W. H. G. Dickins, *The Lands and Peoples of East Africa*, Longmans, London, 1960.
4   *East Africa Royal Commission 1953–1955 Report*, H.M.S.O., London, 1955. This is still one of the most useful documents on East Africa for geographers.
5   Many aspects of the economy of each country are discussed at length in the International Bank for Reconstruction and Development reports: *The Economic Development of Tanganyika*, Dar es Salaam, 1960; *The Economic Development of Uganda*, Entebbe, 1961, and *The Economic Development of Kenya*, Nairobi, 1962. These reports were also published by Johns Hopkins University Press, Baltimore. Also useful is P. Selwyn and T. Y. Watson, *Report on the Economic Development of the Zanzibar Protectorate* Zanzibar, 1962. Changes in the economy since the early 1960s are fully documented in the development plans of each country (Nairobi, 1966 & 1969; Dar es Salaam, 1964 & 1969; Entebbe, 1966).

The most valuable references of all are the national atlases of Kenya (Nairobi, 1962), Tanzania (Dar es Salaam, 1967) and Uganda (Entebbe, 1969). See also L. Berry (ed.), *Tanzania in Maps*, University of London Press, 1971.

CHAPTER 2

Agriculture

Agriculture is so important in East Africa that its general characteristics should be considered before each major crop is examined. Many farming systems exist within the region, but certain broad categories may be distinguished. The most widespread is the cultivation of annual crops on very small farms, each plot being rested after a few years of cropping. Where the physical environment is particularly favourable perennial crops may be of greater importance, although some annual crops also are always grown. This may perhaps be termed 'peasant agriculture' whether perennials are grown or not, for the farmers generally have no mechanical equipment and employ no labour, but are dependent on the efforts of themselves and their families. The extent to which cash crops have been incorporated into this type of farming varies greatly from place to place, but nowhere are they grown to the exclusion of subsistence crops.

A very much smaller area is occupied by large farms, many of which are run by Europeans in the Kenya highlands. These are strictly commercial enterprises, and little of the produce is consumed on the farm. Whereas on small peasant holdings animals are rarely integrated into the farming system, many of these are truly mixed farms. Others are plantations concerned with large scale production of a single crop. Both the large mixed farms and the plantations provide a very distinctive landscape and a sharp contrast with areas of peasant agriculture.

Over vast tracts of East Africa none of these types of agriculture is important, but rather a pastoral economy prevails. These tracts are very sparsely populated, however, and the number of people who depend mainly on pastoralism for their livelihood is relatively small.

In all three countries small farms producing annual crops occupy the largest area of cultivated land, but there are sharp contrasts in the extent to which the other systems are also found. In Kenya large mixed farms and plantations are both of great importance. In Tanzania there are few of the former, but just as many of the latter, and also some areas of small farms largely dependent on perennial crops. This last form of agriculture is of most importance in Uganda, where there are few plantations and no large mixed farms. An attempt has been made to indicate the distribution of these types of farming on Map 3.

SMALL FARMS PRODUCING ANNUAL CROPS

Many characteristics of peasant agriculture in East Africa are common to large parts of the continent.[1] The traditional agricultural system, concerned entirely with the production of food crops, was generally shifting cultivation. How far this may be considered to continue today depends on what is meant by the term. Lord Hailey speaks of 'Shifting cultivation, which involves at intervals the movement of whole villages to a new site.'[2] De Schlippe describes it thus: 'When a piece of land becomes exhausted by cropping, it is left alone and goes back to natural vegetation. The cultivator chooses fresh bush, which he clears for his new fields and even for his new dwellings. The memory of the old cultivations becomes lost.'[3] This type of farming is not common in East Africa today. Over most of the region shifting cultivation is practised only in the sense that the farmer cultivates a plot for a few years and then allows it to rest while he tills another patch. The plots are not often clearly defined, and when one is abandoned it soon merges into the surrounding bush, but the same land is usually brought back into cultivation after only a short period under 'bush fallow.' Conditions vary greatly from place to place, and there is a gradual transition from true shifting cultivation to a system of rotation which differs from that found in Europe only in that the land is occupied by natural rather than planted vegetation during the resting period.

The most common practice is to clear a patch of land, with the help of burning, and to cultivate this for about three years until yields show signs of declining. The land is then allowed to revert to bush for anything from two to twelve years while other land still within reach of the homestead is used. In these

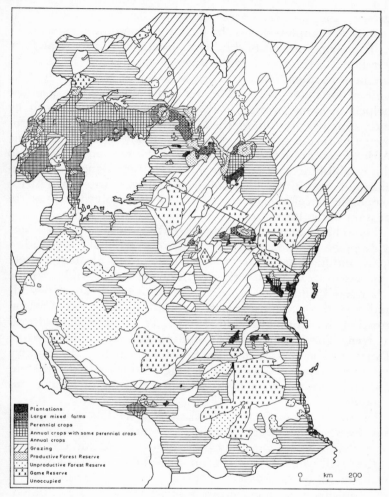

Figure 3. EAST AFRICA: Dominant Forms of Land Use

conditions the settlement normally remains fixed. Just as the length of the fallow period varies, so does the size of cultivated area. When there are no field boundaries it is unrealistic to speak of the size of the farm, but the general pattern is for each family to have between 1½ and 3 hectares under crops each year. The figure depends on climatic and soil conditions, the crops grown, the farmers' perception of the likely return, the techniques employed and the degree of population pressure.

The abandonment of shifting cultivation in its extreme form is related to the increasing density of population. Pressure on the land in much of East Africa is too great to permit it to lie unused for many years. The adoption of cash crops has also helped to create a more stable type of agriculture, both by increasing the pressure on the land and by encouraging governments to take a greater interest in peasant farming. In some African countries the dual nature of the economy has led to the establishment of commercial agriculture alongside a little-changed traditional agricultural system. In East Africa economic development has more often involved change in peasant agriculture itself.

Something approaching true shifting cultivation is most widespread in Tanzania, large parts of which still have land to spare and have no well-established cash crops. In such densely populated areas as western Kenya or eastern Uganda, on the other hand, plots can be rested for only a very short period; and even throughout northern Uganda the adoption of cotton growing has brought added stability to the agricultural pattern. The continuance of shifting cultivation in parts of Tanzania also reflects soil conditions, for much of the country has very poor soils, needing a long resting period, whereas this is not necessary in most agricultural areas of Kenya and Uganda.

In most places each family works its own holding individually, but in some localities certain tasks are undertaken communally. Men are generally responsible for the initial clearing of the land, while the cultivation of food crops is still normally in the hands of the women. Generally the only equipment is a hoe, and the area under crops is accordingly severely limited. Plots under a single crop, or under two or more interplanted crops, are rarely as much as ½ hectare in extent. Tractor-hire services have been established in some places, but are still of small importance. Few farmers can employ paid labour to cultivate a larger area. Little attention has been given to increasing yields by using manure or fertilisers, in some areas because the return resulting is too low, in others because farmers lack the necessary knowledge or capital. Some of these characteristics are inter-related: women's responsibility for food crops discourages the employment of labourers whom the men would have to pay, and also hinders the spread of new techniques while the low educational level among women continues.

This general picture of peasant agriculture needs qualification for each district. There are significant local differences in the techniques used in cultivation. Ploughs drawn by oxen are widespread in Teso and adjacent parts of Bukedi and Lango Districts of Uganda, but almost unknown elsewhere in the country. Part of the explanation must clearly lie in the strong pastoral tradition of the Iteso. This integration of livestock with cultivation is unusual even though most cultivators also keep cattle, and even in Teso it does not constitute mixed farming. This is developing most noticeably in Kenya, among the Kikuyu, who seem more keen than most tribes to develop new farming techniques, stimulated perhaps by pressure on the land. It has also long been a notable feature of Ukara Island in Lake Victoria.

It is not possible to discuss the innumerable local variations in the agricultural calendar, but one feature which must be noted is the contrast between areas where two crops a year are taken from the same land and those where only a single crop is obtained. This contrast is very clear in Uganda, where two harvests are taken in the south, but where the concentration of rainfall into a single wet season allows only one in the north. Cultivation of two crops a year is an essential element in supporting the high density of rural population in districts such as Kiambu and Murang'a in Kenya.

In most of East Africa the pattern of peasant agriculture is changing only slowly.[4] In parts of Kenya, however, rapid changes are taking place. Land consolidation has greatly altered the landscape in many districts, producing for the first time a pattern of fields and hedges. Private ownership is giving farmers an incentive to take care of their land and even to invest money in it. The transformation in some Kikuyu areas has been such that it has been termed an agricultural revolution.[5] In Tanzania the government has plans for equally rapid change, but of a very different character. Rather than encouraging individualism, the policy of 'Ujamaa', propounded in the 1967 Arusha Declaration, stresses corporate activity, and envisages the resettlement of much of the dispersed rural population in villages and the working of their land collectively. It is considered that this will aid the incorporation of new techniques such as mechanization, assist marketing and permit the provision of more social services. The results of the implementation of this policy during the 1970s will be awaited with great interest.[6]

SMALL FARMS PRODUCING PERENNIAL CROPS

The areas where peasant farmers are mainly dependent on perennial crops are distinctive in several ways. In some of these areas shifting cultivation has probably never been practised: there is certainly a long tradition of cultivating the same land generation after generation in Buganda and Bukoba, on Mount Elgon and Mount Kilimanjaro. Some land is planted with annual crops and is allowed to rest periodically, but it rarely reverts to bush before being used again. The distribution of this type of agriculture is severely limited by physical conditions, for continuous cultivation is possible only where rainfall is high and soils are fertile.

The main perennial food crop is the banana. This is not very demanding on labour and gives high yields per hectare, so the farmers generally have the time and the land to plant a cash crop, usually coffee. This brings sufficient income to set these people apart from most peasant farmers in standards of living. Even where perennial cropping is well established most farmers are far from prosperous, but they have generally replaced thatched huts by more substantial houses with iron roofs and can afford to send their children to school.

In Buganda, and also near the coast where coconuts are of great importance, some African farmers own large blocks of land and hire labourers to cultivate it. A few of these farms are indeed plantations, but many occupy 5 to 20 hectares, and are really intermediate between peasant and plantation agriculture.

LARGE MIXED FARMS

Over much of the Kenya highlands, and small parts of Tanzania, the type of agriculture practised differs very greatly from that just examined, and the distinctive agricultural system produces a completely different type of landscape. Most of the farms are between 200 and 800 hectares, and virtually all were established by Europeans, although 30 to 40 per cent. are now African-owned. Most of the farmers grow a variety of crops and keep more than one type of livestock. Crops and stock are generally closely integrated, with some crops grown for fodder, and some manure applied to the land. Many such farms differ little in their organization from those in north-west Europe.[7]

Specific combinations of crops and stock vary greatly from place to place, but a typical farm might have 100 hectares under crops, 50 hectares under planted grass and 200 hectares under natural pasture for 200 cattle. Such a farm would represent an investment of about £20,000, and from it the owner would obtain an annual gross income of £10,000, of which £2,000 would be net profit. This is ten times greater than that obtained by even the most progressive peasant farmers, and seen thus the dual nature of the agricultural economy is apparent.

Large mixed farms of this type occupy an extremely small part of the land under crops and pasture in East Africa, but they contributed 8 per cent. of the value of agricultural products sold within the region in 1969. They are heavily concentrated in Kenya, and although the area under this form of agriculture has recently shrunk, they still provided 20 per cent. of the farm produce sold there in 1969. There were then about 1,200 large mixed farms in Kenya occupying a little over 500,000 hectares. In Tanzania there are under 400 such farms, occupying 150,000 hectares, and in Uganda there are none.

The concentration of these farms in Kenya is related to physical, social and political conditions. At the time of European settlement Kenya had much the largest area of unoccupied land with a climate suitable for the types of crops and animals familiar to the settlers. The only other areas with similar conditions were in the north and the southern highlands

C

of Tanzania, both of which have some farms of this type. Elsewhere the land was either lower, and more suited to tropical plantation crops while less attractive for European settlement, or was already occupied by African farmers. The pattern also reflects positive encouragement of such settlement by the Kenya government: in Tanzania official support was less strong, while in Uganda such settlement was actively discouraged.

Among the recent changes in East African agriculture, one of the most significant is the withdrawal of many European farmers from the Kenya highlands.[8] In some areas this has merely meant the transfer of ownership to African individuals or co-operative groups; but elsewhere the large farms have been used for settlement schemes and subdivided into peasant holdings, varying in size from 4 to 15 hectares. This process began in 1960, and by 1970 about 1,000 European farmers had been replaced by some 50,000 families on 500,000 hectares.

It is still too early to judge the effect of resettlement on agricultural production, although it is already clear that there are cases of both increased intensity of land use and at least a short-term decline in productivity. The effect on the spatial pattern of large-scale agriculture is quite apparent, however. Those farmers occupying land scheduled for resettlement who wished to remain in Kenya generally took over farms elsewhere from others who were leaving, so large farms continue to occupy continuous blocks of the Kenya highlands, but these are less extensive than in the past. The distribution of areas experiencing resettlement was a matter of government policy, based largely on proximity to areas of land hunger in peasant agriculture. Thus large farms have entirely disappeared from the Kinangop plateau, just west of the over-crowded zone of Kikuyu settlement, but still occupy all the land on the Uasin Gishu plateau around Eldoret.

PLANTATION AGRICULTURE

There is no clear cut division between the types of farm already considered and plantations, or estates as they are more often termed in East Africa. Coffee, for example, is grown on all scales from $\frac{1}{10}$ hectare to 500 hectares, and producers may undertake various degrees of processing. Plantations may perhaps be distinguished as enterprises which specialize in a single crop, have at least 20 hectares under that crop, and undertake at least the first stage of processing it. By this definition they occupy 600,000 hectares in East Africa, rather less than 5 per cent. of all the land cultivated in any year. Despite their small extent they account for one-third of the value of all cash crops, for they produce almost all the sisal and sugar of the region, most of its tea and some of its coffee, wattle and coconuts.

Most of the large estates are owned by British companies, such as Brooke Bond Liebig Ltd., which dominates the Kenya tea industry, and many of the smaller ones by European individuals. Others are owned by Asians, whose role is especially great in the sugar industry; while an increasing proportion are under government control. The existence of enterprises of this type is related to certain characteristics of the crops for which the region offers suitable environmental conditions. Sisal, sugar and tea can all be processed economically only on a large scale, and in each case there is a strong incentive to link cultivation closely with processing. All are either extremely bulky when harvested, or suffer from any delay between field and factory.

Although there have been strong economic arguments for establishing plantation agriculture in East Africa, it has not met with government approval everywhere, and this has limited its extent. In Kenya and Tanzania European companies and individuals have generally been encouraged to undertake this form of development, but in Kenya the establishment of estates by Asians was for many years hindered by the government. The vacillations of the Uganda government on this matter, and their consequences, have been described by C. C. Wrigley.[9] In general, plantation agriculture has been discouraged in Uganda, and largely for this reason it is now less important than elsewhere, occupying only 40,000 hectares, compared with 200,000 hectares in Kenya and 300,000 hectares in Tanzania.

The distribution of plantations has also been greatly affected by the density of African population in each part of the region. The large area occupied by sisal estates in Tanzania reflects the vast amount of apparently unused land that the Europeans found there. In Uganda the area of cultivatable land never used by peasant farmers is far smaller, especially in the more accessible parts of the country.

In contrast to the large mixed farms, plantation agriculture continues to expand, although more slowly than in the past. Estates now often have difficulty in obtaining more land, but sometimes, as in the Tanzania sisal industry, land is already owned but not yet brought into cultivation. Resettlement in the Kenya highlands has not in general affected plantations, for these could not be taken over by peasant farmers as easily as the mixed farms. In some places new estates are still being established, notably for tea cultivation, but the total area of crops on estates is certainly increasing more slowly than the area of cash crops on peasant farms.

THE DIVERSITY OF CROPS

East Africa is best known overseas for its coffee and perhaps cotton, but the primary object of agriculture in this region is the supply of food, and most of the cultivated land is planted with food crops to supply local needs. Only if the farmer has land and labour to spare after providing food for the family is a cash crop planted to provide for its other needs. Since the cultivation of food crops accounts for most of the work done by over 80 per cent. of East Africans, it must be reckoned the most important economic activity in the region. The precise area under food crops in East Africa is not known: such data as are available suggest that rather more than 80 per cent. of the land under cultivation in the three countries carries staple food crops.

The range of food crops is very wide, including grains such as maize and millet; root crops, notably cassava and sweet potatoes; bananas, which replace grains and roots as the starchy staple in some areas; and beans and groundnuts, which add protein to the diet. Numerous fruits and vegetables are widely grown, but on too small a scale to receive attention in this study. Among these are oranges, mangoes, pawpaws, pumpkins and tomatoes. No major food crop of Africa is entirely absent, although yams, so important in West Africa, are of little significance.

In addition to tropical crops some food crops of temperate lands are also represented, so that the diversity is greater than in any other region of Africa. Among the factors favouring this, the diversity of climatic conditions found within the region is probably the most important. There are zones with temperatures suitable for wheat and potatoes, and others where cassava and sesame flourish; the rainfall is high enough for any crop in some areas, but adequate only for sorghum in others. Various other contributory factors will appear as each crop is considered.

Not only are numerous food crops grown in the region as a whole, but even on each farm, and indeed in one field. On one occasion the writer counted twelve growing together in a field in western Uganda. Commonly two or three are interplanted, while many different fruits and vegetables are normally grown just around the house. Thus considering the main crops individually might give a distorted impression of East African agriculture if no attention were given to food crop production in general terms.

The great variety of crops grown both within each district and on most farms reflects the strong tradition of self-sufficiency and official policies encouraging this. The lack of specialization and trade in foodstuffs means that most people must grow several crops if they are to enjoy a varied diet. Certainly the Baganda are 'banana people' and the Kikuyu are 'maize people', but both, like people anywhere, desire some variety, and the farmer himself traditionally provides this, as well as the basic staple.

Some crops are indigenous to East Africa, but most have been introduced. Bananas probably came from the east, while maize, cassava and sweet potatoes certainly came from the Americas, though all have now become 'traditional' crops. The form of production differs from one crop to another, as does the proportion entering trade. Millet, sorghum, bananas, cassava, sweet potatoes and beans are grown almost entirely on peasant farms, and the whole production is frequently consumed on the farm. Rarely are they grown specifically for cash sale. Groundnuts and rice are also grown only on peasant farms, but rather more of these is produced for sale. Maize is grown on large European farms as well as on peasant holdings, although the latter account for far more of the production. While even maize is grown primarily for subsistence, substantial quantities enter trade, and it provides the main income for many African as well as European farmers.

The small proportion of food crop production entering trade distinguishes East Africa from some other parts of the continent.

TABLE 3

CASH CROPS OF EAST AFRICA

AREA, 1969 ('000 HECTARES)	Kenya	Tanzania	Uganda	East Africa
Cotton	60	440	850	1350
Coffee	80	130	320	530
Sisal	100	280	0	380
Cashew nuts	20	200	0	220
Sugar	30	20	20	70
Tea	30	10	10	50
Pyrethrum	30	20	0	50
Cloves	0	30	0	30
Tobacco	0	10	10	20
VALUE OF EXPORTS AND LOCAL SALES, 1969 (£ MILLION)				
Coffee	17	13	39	69
Cotton lint	1	13	15	29
Tea	12	3	5	20
Sugar	4	4	6	14
Sisal	2	9	0	11
Cashew nuts	1	7	0	8
Cloves	0	8	0	8
Tobacco	0	3	2	5
Pyrethrum	3	1	0	4

The data are drawn from many sources and vary greatly in reliability. Adequate statistics are not available to draw up a comparable table for staple food crops.

The local market for food crops is very small, as so many people satisfy their own requirements. There are fewer people in employment, and a smaller urban population to be supplied, than in most countries to the south. In addition, rural trade is less developed than in West Africa, and there are no regular movements comparable to that of kola nuts there. Many rural weekly markets exist, but it is unusual to find large quantities of staple foodstuffs on sale. Lacking adequate data one may easily underestimate the importance of sales of food crops in

East Africa, but without doubt cash is obtained by farmers mainly from other crops.

The variety of cash crops must also be stressed, for twelve of them bring over £1 million a year each to East African farmers. Some are produced for export and others for local consumption: some are annuals while others have a life of over fifty years. Cotton is grown entirely on small farms, but sisal is a plantation crop. Cashew nuts demand high temperatures, found only near the coast, whereas pyrethrum is confined to the cool highlands. This variety is a great advantage in view of the economic dangers of overdependence on a single primary product, although the advantage would be greater if the region formed a single political unit.

The cash crops differ so greatly one from another that in most respects they must be considered individually. The relative importance of each is indicated, as far as available data allow, in Table 3. The pattern for East Africa as a whole is quite different from that for any other region, while it also differs sharply from that existing 30 years ago. The table also shows marked differences between the three countries. All the generalizations so far made about East Africa hide considerable local variations. There are marked contrasts, for example, in the relative importance of food and cash crops. In south-western Uganda and in the southern highlands of Tanzania virtually all cultivated land is under food crops; but in parts of Buganda cash crops occupy almost half the farmland. Even the Baganda have not turned to cash crops so thoroughly that they must buy food, as have some peasant farmers in Ghana, but Zanzibar and Pemba must import much of their food requirements, for cloves and coconuts grown mainly for cash dominate their agriculture.

The distinction between food and cash crops is clearer in Uganda than in Kenya or Tanzania, for food crops enter least into trade there. Sales of food crops are probably even less important in neighbouring Rwanda, but they are far smaller in Uganda than in most African countries. Thus McMaster devoted little attention to sales in his book on food crops in Uganda,[10] and was criticised by a reviewer from West Africa on this score.

Most sales of food crops take place in Kenya, both from

European farms, and from African farms all over the country. Kenya has a relatively large number of people in paid employment, who provide a market, and other cash crops have been little developed on peasant farms there. In this respect, as in many others, Tanzania lies between the other two countries, and there are especially sharp contrasts between different parts of that country.

REFERENCES

1   A general review is W. B. Morgan, 'Peasant Agriculture in Tropical Africa', in M. F. Thomas & G. Whittington (ed.), *Environment and Land Use in Africa*, Methuen, London, 1969; a fuller examination of certain aspects is W. Allan, *The African Husbandman*, Oliver & Boyd, Edinburgh, 1965. Various East African farming systems are described in D. J. Parsons, *The Systems of Agriculture Practised in Uganda*, Uganda Department of Agriculture, Kawanda, 1960; and H. Ruthenberg (ed.), *Smallholder Farming and Smallholder Development in Tanzania*, Weltforum Verlag, Munchen, 1968.

2   Lord Hailey, *An African Survey*, Oxford U.P., London, 1957, p. 820.

3   P. de Schlippe, *Shifting Cultivation in Africa*, Routledge & Kegan Paul, London, 1956, p. 37.

4   An excellent outline of agricultural change is D. N. McMaster, 'East Africa: Influences and Trends in Land Use', in R. M. Prothero (ed.), *A Geography of Africa*, Routledge & Kegan Paul, London, 1969.

5   E.g. D. R. F. Taylor, 'Agricultural Change in Kikuyuland', in Thomas & Whittington, *op. cit.*, p. 463. See also E. S. Clayton, *Agrarian Development in Peasant Economies*, Pergamon, Oxford, 1964; and J. C. De Wilde, *Experiences with Agricultural Development in Tropical Africa*, Vol. II, Johns Hopkins Press, Baltimore, 1967.

6   Various forms of new settlement are discussed in R. W. Kates, J. McKay and L. Berry, 'Twelve New Settlements in Tanzania', *University of East Africa, Social Science Conference 1968/9, Geography Papers*, pp. 63–100. On current policy see Tanzania, *Second Five-Year Plan 1969–1974*, Dar es Salaam, 1969, Ch. 1 & 3. On Tanzanian agriculture development in general, see R. Dumont for Tanzania Government, *Tanzanian Agriculture after the Arusha Declaration*, Dar es Salaam, 1969.

7   R. S. Odingo, *The Kenya Highlands: Agricultural Geography*, E. A. Publishing House, Nairobi, in the press.

8   The expansion and contraction of European farming are the subjects of W. T. W. Morgan, 'The White Highlands of Kenya', *Geographical Journal*, Vol. 129, Part 2, 1963 pp. 140–155; and N. S. Carey-Jones, 'The Decolonization of the White Highlands of Kenya', *Geographical Journal*, Vol. 131, Part 2, 1965, pp. 186–201. Progress in resettlement to 1969 is covered in Kenya, *Development Plan 1970–1974*, Nairobi, 1969, Ch. 8.

9   C. C. Wrigley, *Crops and Wealth in Uganda*, E.A.I.S.R., Kampala, 1959.

10 D. N. McMaster, *A Subsistence Crop Geography of Uganda*, Geographical Publications, Bude, 1962.

CHAPTER 3

Crops Grown Primarily for Subsistence

In this chapter the distribution of some of the major food crops is examined. None are grown exclusively for subsistence, but only a small surplus over domestic requirements is normally sold. Several crops discussed in the next chapter are also chiefly subsistence crops, but all are frequently regarded as a source of cash income.

For all food crops the available data are estimates and liable to serious error. Sometimes, therefore, the pattern discussed may be that in the records rather than that on the ground; but most data reflect reality sufficiently closely to be of value. In Uganda assessments of crop areas are made annually for each locality, though major discrepancies were found between these and the results of an agricultural census undertaken in 1963.[1] No such records are kept elsewhere, but in Kenya a sample census of African agriculture was taken in 1960/61, and the results are used here.[2] The last published acreage estimates for Tanzania were made in 1948, but Ministry of Agriculture files contain recent estimates which have been incorporated in this study.

Apart from official reports, the literature on East African subsistence crops is scanty. The subject has been studied in detail only in Uganda, for which country the present discussion rests heavily on the valuable work of D. N. McMaster.[3] For Kenya and Tanzania there is little other than an occasional reference to food crops in anthropological studies of particular tribes.[4]

MILLET AND SORGHUM

Millet and sorghum are the traditional grain crops of East Africa, and formed the basis of the agricultural system in most areas until new crops spread from the Americas. They are

29

still the staple food crops over much of the region, although in many places they have been displaced by maize. The term 'millet' is used for a variety of grain plants, and usage differs from place to place: in Sudan, for example, the term is used for the crop known in East Africa as sorghum. The table below may assist in identification.

ENGLISH	LATIN	SWAHILI
Finger millet	*Eleusine coracana*	Wimbi
Bulrush millet	*Pennisetum typhoideum*	Mawele
Sorghum	*Sorghum vulgare*	Mtama

Nowhere else in Africa are all these three plants important. Finger millet spread from Ethiopia into East Africa, which is now the main area of production. Bulrush millet is characteristic of the sudan zone of west Africa; and sorghum is a major staple in southern Africa, although it is widely grown elsewhere and in fact stands fourth among the world's cereal crops. East Africa thus forms a meeting point of zones in which each is important.

The three crops together occupy about 2½ million hectares, or between a quarter and a third of all cultivated land in East Africa, although they are often interplanted with other crops. As they are traditional staple foods, this degree of importance is perhaps to be expected; but it also reflects their suitability to the environmental conditions of many areas. Bulrush millet and sorghum both tolerate poor soils, and both require less than 350 mm. of rain in the growing season, and finger millet is little more demanding in either respect. All benefit from constant high temperatures, and thrive in all but the highest, and the driest, parts of the region. They each yield a fairly nutritious grain, easily stored and easily prepared for use either as food or as drink.

However, these crops have certain disadvantages which contribute to their replacement by others where physical conditions permit choice. Yields of finger and bulrush millet rarely exceed 1,000 kg. per hectare, and they require much more labour for a given amount of food than bananas or maize. The main disadvantage of sorghum is its taste, and it might have disappeared from East Africa in face of competition from more palatable alternatives but for its tolerance of drought and its relatively high yields. It grows where the rainfall is too low for finger millet; and in areas of moderate rainfall it gives 50 per cent. more grain per hectare. Sorghum is more satisfactory for beer-making than for food, and in many places it is now used entirely for this purpose.

The distribution of millet and sorghum cultivation within East Africa is indicated on Map 4: the patterns differ sufficiently for each to be examined separately. The area planted annually with either finger or bulrush millet is about 1 million hectares in Tanzania, ½ million in Uganda and ¼ million in Kenya. In Uganda bulrush millet is unimportant, but in Tanzania and Kenya it occupies more land than finger millet.

Over most of Tanzania millet, sorghum and maize together from the staple foods, and in 1948 millet was the leading crop in the centre and west. It has since increasingly been displaced by maize, but it is still the most important crop in most of Singida and Tabora Regions. Finger millet is also widely grown in Mara Region, east of Lake Victoria, while bulrush millet is important in the adjacent northern part of Sukumaland. In these areas the climate is marginal for cultivation, and many crops do not thrive, while in parts of Sukumaland soils have been so overworked that they will support only bulrush millet. These are also districts where the spread of new ideas has been limited, and where traditions remain strong. This factor also favours millet cultivation in Mbeya Region. The parts of Tanzania in which little millet is grown include the coastlands, Kilimanjaro Region and Iringa Region, in all of which rainfall is sufficient for maize or bananas and outside influence has been considerable.

Some finger millet is cultivated in every district of Uganda, but the greatest concentration is found in Teso in the east, where it occupies 40 per cent. of all land under food crops. It is almost as important in Lango and Acholi, although the intensity of production is lower as the population is less dense. Much is also grown in densely-populated Bugisu and Bukedi Districts, although it accounts for only 20 per cent. of their food crop area. Millet does better than most crops on the light soils of the east and north, and does not suffer from the clearly-marked dry season. It is popular food there, and fits well into a rotation with cotton. In Buganda and the west, where the physical environment suits a wider range of crops, millet is unimportant. In Buganda there is little evidence that much interest was ever taken in millet, but in the west preference for bananas has only recently led to a reduction of millet cultivation.

In Kenya millet has been replaced by maize to a much greater extent than in Tanzania or Uganda, and a social stigma against it has developed, especially among Bantu tribes, but increasingly among the Luo also. This in part reflects the strength of alien influences in Kenya, the forces assisting a breakdown of traditions, and also government encouragement of maize cultivation. In Central Province where population pressure favours a higher yielding crop, and where the rich soil and high rainfall would be rather wasted on millet, very little is now grown. Yet 'statements made by old men and women bring out clearly that in pre-European days the staple crop was bulrush millet'.[5] Bulrush millet is still important on the plains east of Mount Kenya in Embu and Meru, while some is grown further east in Machakos and Kitui. These areas are hotter and drier than the highlands of Central Province, have poorer soils, and are more sparsely populated. Some finger millet is grown in the Taita hills, but little of either type elsewhere in the coastal region. The leading area of production in Kenya is Nyanza Province, where new crops have spread only slowly and millet still occupies one quarter of the food crop area. In this area of high rainfall and moderate soils finger millet is the variety normally grown. It is also important in Western Province, although nowhere there is it the leading food crop today. Huntingford gives finger millet as the principal crop of the traditionally pastoral peoples of the rift valley, notably the Nandi and Elgeyo,[6] but these groups have largely replaced it by maize.

Sorghum probably occupies about 1 million hectares, fairly evenly divided between the three countries. Much is grown interplanted with other crops, including finger millet, in case these fail as a result of poor rains: and much is also grown in dry or infertile areas. Yet production is higher than that of either finger or bulrush millet, since sorghum gives higher yields per hectare.

Map 4 shows the very uneven distribution of sorghum cultivation in Uganda. Much is grown in Teso and Lango

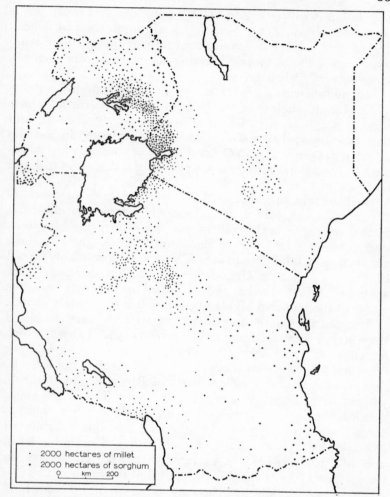

Figure 4. EAST AFRICA: Millet and Sorghum Cultivation
This and the two following maps depend on a variety of sources,
and represent an estimated annual average for the period 1965–1969.

along with finger millet, but the crop is more important in
Karamoja where it is planted on 90 per cent. of the cultivated
land. Apart from pastoralism, sorghum production is the only
important economic activity of the district, although the

population is so sparse and yields are so low that much less is produced than in Teso. Sorghum is also important in Kigezi, despite very different environmental conditions, occupying more than half the cropped land in some areas. Elsewhere in Uganda very little is grown.

Sorghum is widely grown in Nyanza and Western Provinces of Kenya, although it is the leading crop only in the lakeshore zone of South Nyanza which is dry yet poorly drained, and therefore unsuited to maize. Hardly any is planted in Kericho and Nandi Districts, or in Central Province; but the crop makes a small contribution to food supplies in the dry areas of Kitui and eastern Machakos.

In Tanzania sorghum is the chief food crop in much of Mtwara Region, and is extensively cultivated near the coast further north. It is also widely grown for beer, if not for food, over the centre and west of the country, although it nowhere occupies more land than maize. The crop is more widely spread in Tanzania than in Uganda or Kenya, but there are large areas, including Tanga and Kilimanjaro Regions and the whole of the southern highlands, where it is very rarely grown.

The distribution of sorghum thus appears more localized than that of many food crops. It is grown mainly in areas which are either suffering from pressure of population on the land, or marginal for any cultivation. Kigezi and Nyanza fall into the former category, as do most parts of Rwanda and Burundi, where sorghum is of great importance. The high yields obtained encourage people to plant sorghum where land is scarce, while it will grow even on land that has been almost worn out by years of continuous cultivation. Karamoja, Kitui and Mtwara provide one example from each country of an area with such poor rainfall and soils that the range of possible crops is very small: the capacity of sorghum to withstand drought and to grow in infertile soil certainly favours its cultivation in such areas.

The proportion of the total production of millet and sorghum entering commerce is extremely small, for most town-dwellers prefer to buy maize, bananas or cassava. There is some local trade in which merchants buy the crop in times of glut for resale in times of scarcity: and small movements take place between one rural area and another, since harvest-time varies over the region, and since some areas are short of grain for beer making. For example, some millet is regularly sent from the plains of Bukedi to the hills of Bugisu in Uganda. There is even some trade among the three countries, Tanzania supplying millet and sorghum worth £100,000 a year to Kenya in the late-1960s. As official policies favouring local self-sufficiency are relaxed some increase in trade may be expected, although the greater part of the crop will continue to be consumed by the growers, and although production will probably continue to shrink in face of competition from more popular crops.

BANANAS

Bananas (*Musa spp.*) are the second traditional staple food crop of East Africa, taking the place of millet in some of the wetter and more fertile districts. They are sometimes referred to as 'plantains' since they are eaten cooked rather than raw, but the varieties grown are not those to which botanists generally apply the term 'plantain'. The banana probably originated in Asia, but it has been cultivated in East Africa for many centuries, and can certainly be considered a traditional crop.

The plant is a perennial which is propagated from suckers, bears in just over a year, and remains productive for up to 50 years. Labour requirements are low and evenly spread through the year, and this contributes to the popularity of the crop. In comparison with grains yields are heavy, averaging 6 to 10 tons per hectare each year. On the other hand the food value of the banana is lower than that of most other food crops. Bananas do not store easily, but if planting has been properly planned they may be picked during any month as required. Different varieties are suitable for boiling, for making beer and for eating raw, although the last is of small importance. The leaves and stems have many uses, including thatching, wrappings and cordage. One powerful factor encouraging banana cultivation today is a strong social attachment to it, especially among the women, who are generally responsible for the crop. Where it dominates peasant agriculture it has almost become a way of life, as rice is said to be in much of Asia. On the fringes of these areas it often carries prestige, and is gradually being adopted, sometimes at the expense of more nutritious foods.

The banana is more demanding than most food crops in its ecological requirements, and this limits its distribution. For successful cultivation annual rainfall should exceed 900 mm. and should be evenly spread over the year, with under 25 mm. in not more than two months. The crop also requires warmth, and thrives in East Africa only below 2,000 metres. Yields are closely related to the fertility of the soil, which should be both deep and well drained. Partly because of the strong social attachment to the banana, it has been taken to, and even beyond, the ecological limits of successful cultivation in some areas.

Even though bananas can be grown only in small parts of East Africa, there are about 1 million hectares under the crop, and production exceeds 8 million tons a year. Most are grown in small plots, but there are some extensive groves, especially where much land is privately owned. Over 90 per cent. of the production is consumed on the farms, and sales take place only locally.

Two-thirds of the land under bananas is in Uganda, where they form the staple diet over a large area. One authority states that production is higher there than in any other country in the world:[7] yet Uganda is sometimes omitted entirely from lists of producing countries, since no bananas are exported.[8] They are the leading food crop throughout Buganda, where they occupy a quarter of the cultivated land and almost half that under food crops. Their distribution within Buganda is closely related to that of population, which in turn reflects that of rainfall. In general the rainfall and the amount of banana cultivation both decrease away from Lake Victoria, and in the north and the west of the Region, where under 1,000 mm. is received, the area planted is small. Between these dry areas there is a wetter zone in Mubende where more bananas are grown, but partly because of poor soils they are less important than near the lake.

The banana zone extends eastwards into Busoga, where bananas account for one-third of all land under food crops: but further east, in Bukedi, they give way to some extent to millet. There soils are poorer, a dry season is more marked,

and strong winds tend to damage banana plants. McMaster
notes the relatively small importance of the crop in the parts of

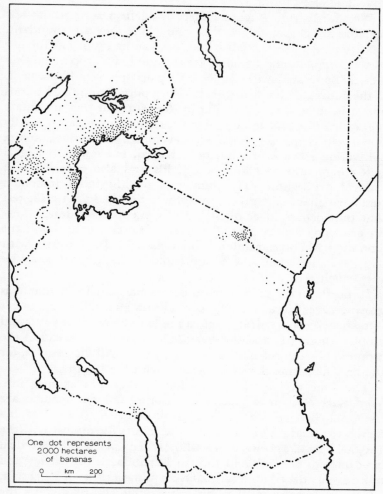

Figure 5. EAST AFRICA: Banana Cultivation

Bukedi occupied by non-Bantu.[9] In Bugisu bananas again
come to the fore, occupying half the food crop area. High
rainfall, fertile volcanic soils, the need for a high yielding crop
and the need for one which does not encourage erosion on the

D

steep slopes all contribute to this. As the population is extremely dense, the intensity of production is greater than anywhere else.

Westwards from Buganda there is again a zone where few bananas are grown, followed by one where they are abundant. In eastern Ankole rainfall is too low for the crop, but further west it is higher, and bananas are the dominant crop in another densely populated area. Indeed, they occupy over 70 per cent. of the cultivated land in Ankole either pure or in mixed stands and it is obvious to a traveller in the area that they dominate the agricultural scene even more than in Buganda, especially since cash crops are so poorly developed. Intensive banana cultivation extends into northern Kigezi, but southern Kigezi is too high and cool for good yields and also experiences a marked dry season. The data used by McMaster indicated that few bananas are grown in Toro, but revised figures suggest that they occupy over one-third of the cultivated land. Few are grown on the dry rift valley floor, but they are the dominant food crop wherever rainfall is high enough. In Bunyoro, with its sparse population, the area planted is small, but it could be very much greater.

In northern Uganda only an occasional patch of bananas is grown. Over large areas the annual rainfall is adequate, but it is too heavily concentrated into a single wet season for perennial crops. Another factor discouraging a northward spread of the crop may be the occupation of the north by Nilotic peoples, for the banana seems closely associated with the Bantu.

The zone of banana cultivation in Buganda extends into West Lake Region of Tanzania. Around Bukoba bananas are the unchallenged staple food crop, occupying most of the cultivated land. This small area accounts for almost half the 150,000 hectares grown in the whole of Tanzania. The physical environment is similar to that in Buganda, with heavier and more evenly distributed rainfall than in most parts of Tanzania, while the area is settled by a tribe closely related to the Baganda. Some bananas are also grown in the well-watered parts of Kibondo and Kasulu Districts to the south-west, bordering on Burundi.

A second major area of production is on the slopes of Mount Kilimanjaro and Mount Meru, where conditions are similar to those on Mount Elgon in Bugisu District of Uganda. A high and well-distributed rainfall, volcanic soils and a dense population all encourage the crop. Throughout the zone between 1,000 and 1,800 metres on Mount Kilimanjaro, bananas occupy twice as much land as any other food crop. The total area planted is rather less than in West Lake Region, but as yields are higher production may be greater. Bananas are also important in the Usambara mountains, around Lushoto, but in most of Tanga Region rainfall is inadequate.

The only other area where bananas form the staple food crop lies in the extreme south, between Tukuyu and Lake Malawi. The few figures available suggest that this area has the highest rainfall in East Africa, while both the volcanic soils around Tukuyu and the alluvial soils by the lake are very fertile. The population is very dense, and land must be kept in permanent cultivation. It thus appears that wherever in Tanzania physical conditions are suitable and the land is densely settled bananas have been adopted as the staple crop.

By contrast bananas are nowhere the dominant crop in Kenya, and the total area planted is only 70,000 hectares. They are of greatest importance in Western Province, especially in Bunyore and Maragoli, which have high rainfall and very dense population: but even there they occupy less than 10 per cent. of the cultivated land. Some bananas are grown throughout the lower parts of Central Province and, some are produced near the coast and along the Tana and Galana rivers, but they play a very subsidiary role in the agriculture of both areas. Many of the bananas grown in the central highlands and near the coast are of the yellow type for eating raw, and are sold in Nairobi and Mombasa. It is difficult to understand why the crop is less important in the wet areas of Kenya than in Uganda or on Kilimanjaro. The Kikuyu, for example, are a Bantu people, like the Baganda and Chagga, and bananas thrive in much of the country they occupy. A full explanation could only be a matter of speculation or of intimate knowledge of the people's culture history.

Only in a few areas are many bananas grown for sale. Kampala was once supplied from its immediate vicinity but, as the town has grown, supplies have come from further afield. Many farmers in the recently-settled area of Bugerere now grow bananas as their main cash crop, and some individuals are thought to make £500 a year from them. In eastern Uganda, Mbale and Tororo provide markets for some surplus bananas from Bugisu: and in the west they form a cash crop around Fort Portal and in north-west Ankole, the fishermen of Lake George and Lake Edward being important buyers of bananas or banana beer. In many other areas many bananas surplus to subsistence needs go to waste for want of a market. Total sales to urban dwellers in Uganda in 1959 were estimated at only 50,000 tons, although sales within the rural population probably exceeded 150,000 tons. Although grown primarily for subsistence bananas are also an important cash crop on the slopes of Kilimanjaro, bringing half as much cash as coffee to some areas.[10] Certainly many more are sold there than around Bukoba, where the total production is comparable.

Several factors discourage a greater production of bananas for sale. Their value to weight ratio is very low, partly because over half their weight consists of stalk and peel; they do not keep well; and they are clumsy to transport. The market is small not only because so many people can grow their own bananas, but also because the tribes for whom they are the staple food form a very small proportion of the population in employment who must buy food. The first three factors prevent any export of bananas from the main producing areas, which all lie far from the sea. The coastal zone is better placed for exports, but physical conditions are less well suited to bananas there. They are among the leading exports of Somalia, but a guaranteed market in Italy at inflated prices is responsible for this.

The main commercial outlet for bananas is probably beer. A third of the planting is of varieties suitable for brewing, and the problems noted above do not apply to beer. It is of higher value for its weight, and keeps much better if given the chance. Bananas make a large contribution to the £6 million worth of beer produced annually in rural areas of Uganda: and in certain places, such as north-west Ankole, three-quarters of peasant cash income probably comes from sales of banana beer.

One prospect of making bananas of greater commercial importance involves the use of the leaves, which can be made into a fibre with characteristics similar to manila hemp. As yet, however, no plans for development of this nature have been made.

CASSAVA

Cassava (*Manihot utilissima*) is the most important root crop in East Africa, and is very widely grown. Both sweet and bitter varieties are grown in Africa, but the former is much the more important in this region. The crop gives a high yield, suffers little from disease, survives locust attacks, withstands drought better than most, and presents no storage problem since it may be left in the ground up to four years until required. It is therefore highly regarded as a famine reserve crop, and is often planted for use when other crops are in short supply. Its food value is low and it is not very palatable to most people, and consequently it forms the chief food staple in few areas. It is very easy to grow, but less easy to prepare for use, and therefore more is planted than is harvested.

The plant was brought to Africa from South America, probably by the Portuguese, and did not reach East Africa until the nineteenth century. It is thus nowhere a traditional crop, and its present importance largely relates to government pressure after 1920 aimed at tackling the problem of recurrent famines. It is still unpopular in some areas where its production is enforced by local bye-laws, but generally its value is now appreciated and it is planted from choice. As cassava will tolerate very poor soils, as well as drought, it can often be grown on poor land unsuitable for other crops, or as the last crop on land due to be rested.

The total area under cassava in East Africa is probably almost ¾ million hectares, and it is among the four most widely grown food crops. It occupies at least 400,000 hectares in Tanzania, 200,000 in Uganda and 100,000 in Kenya.

Within Uganda the greatest concentration is found in West Nile and Madi Districts, where cassava occupies one-third of the land under food crops. It is also important in Bunyoro and Toro, while a substantial amount is planted in Acholi, Lango, Teso and Bukedi. Only in Buganda, Bugisu, Ankole, Kigezi and Karamoja is it of little importance.

The concentration in West Nile is surprising since cassava was not known there before 1920, but several conditions favour the crop. In the uplands population pressure is such that soils are worked until almost exhausted, yet a high yielding crop is required. There is much labour migration from the district, and cassava can be planted and left unattended for a year or more while men are away. Proximity to areas of Congo where the crop is important may be significant in West Nile, Bunyoro and Toro, although its cultivation did not spread from there.[11] Cassava is also a suitable crop for the parts of these districts on the rift valley floor, where rainfall is low, soils are sandy, and the chief occupation of many people is fishing which leaves little time for cultivation.

In Buganda and Ankole the incentive to plant cassava is small since bananas, which are much preferred, can easily be grown: and in southern Kigezi the climate is more suited to sweet potatoes than to cassava. In much of eastern and northern Uganda unreliable rainfall and poor soils have encouraged many local authorities to insist that each taxpayer shall plant some cassava to ensure minimum food supplies, although millet is the main staple. In much of Karamoja, however, rainfall is inadequate even for cassava.

Cassava is much less important in Kenya than in Uganda. It is prominent in Western Province near to the Uganda border, and in parts of Coast Province, and some is grown in Kitui and Machakos Districts. Elsewhere only an occasional patch of cassava can be found. Almost everywhere other foods are preferred, and in most agricultural areas climatic and soil conditions are sufficiently favourable for these. Much of central Kenya is in fact too high and cool for cassava, while much of the country is too dry. Little official pressure to plant cassava has been applied, partly because opportunities of buying maize in times of local food shortage are greater than in Uganda or Tanzania. Only in Machakos and Kitui and near the coast, where soils are poor and rainfall is adequate for cassava but irregular in its timing, have sustained efforts been made to encourage the crop.

Cassava cultivation has developed only recently in most of Tanzania, as in Uganda and Kenya, although it was grown near the coast before the period of European administration. But much of the country suffers from poor soils and unreliable rainfall, and famines were once frequent. Government pressure to plant cassava has therefore been even stronger than in Uganda, and it is now planted as a famine reserve in most districts, and is the second food crop in several. Official policy favouring local self-sufficiency in foodstuffs has encouraged the relatively even spread of the crop over the country: but emphasis on this has now been reduced, and some local specialization has begun, involving substantial sales from some areas.

The strongest official pressure was imposed in the Sukuma and Nyamwezi areas south of Lake Victoria, and cassava is very important in these areas. Its role is also great in the far south, around Lake Malawi, where a dense population requires a high yielding crop but the rainfall regime limits the range of possible crops, and where labour migration is substantial. Much cassava is grown all along the coast, and it is the main staple on Mafia island, around Bagamoyo and north of Tanga, where it appears to be well-liked. On Zanzibar and Pemba islands it occupies more land than any other food crop, and is second only to rice as a staple food. Production rose sharply during the Second World War, when rice imports were cut off. Cassava is favoured by the islanders' concern with their cash crops and wish for a food crop which requires little attention. It also suits coral soils which will support few other crops, and meets much of the needs of the dense population from a small area of land. The main settled parts of Tanzania where little cassava is grown are Kilimanjaro and the southern highlands, which in some respects resemble the Kenya highlands.

Since cassava is often planted only as a famine reserve and much is never consumed, markets have frequently been sought for it. though with little success. The urban population shows little interest in it, and the demand outside the towns is very limited. There is no trade comparable to that in Congo, where much cassava is moved from Kasai Province to supply workers in Katanga. Overseas markets exist, especially in Europe, where cassava is used to manufacture starch, tapioca and animal feeding stuffs. The price offered, however, is only about £18 a ton at the East African ports, and at that price cassava is not an attractive export crop. Transport costs make exports from inland areas quite unprofitable, and they are confined to Mtwara Region of Tanzania, which lies beside the coast and has few other sources of income. Between 15,000 and 20,000 tons is generally shipped out of Mtwara annually, some in the form of cassava flour and some as dried root.

The crop would be of more value to East Africa if used locally for starch and tapioca manufacture. This has now begun in Lango District of Uganda, but on only a very small scale. The experience of West Africa, where several attempts to establish such production have failed, is rather discouraging: and cassava is likely to remain predominantly a subsistence crop in East Africa for the foreseeable future.

SWEET POTATOES

Sweet potatoes (*Ipomoea batatas*) are the second major root crop of East Africa. This crop, like cassava, came to Africa from South America, but it was well established, especially in Uganda, before the Europeans arrived. Its food value is as low as that of cassava, but it is now a traditional and popular food in many areas. It is the most heavy yielding of all East African food crops, 8 tons per hectare being normal; but it is more demanding than most in terms of soil and climate, and gives these yields only where annual rainfall exceeds 1,000 mm. It cannot be stored in the ground since it is attacked by insects, and it is also affected by locust attack. It has therefore been encouraged as a famine reserve crop much less than cassava, and the area planted is considerably smaller.

The crop probably occupies about $\frac{1}{4}$ million hectares, of which almost half is in Uganda. There, few farms in the well-watered areas are without a patch of sweet potatoes. They are always the responsibility of the women and are generally grown on mounds in a plot of $\frac{1}{10}$ hectare or less near to the house. Even though the plots are so small, there is often some surplus available for sale, and sweet potatoes are regularly found in urban and rural markets. Nevertheless sales represent only a very small part of total production.

The broad distribution of the crop is related in part to physical conditions, for the high rainfall and fertile soils of much of Uganda provide a more suitable environment than the drier country with poor soils which occupies most of Tanzania. It may also have been influenced by the agricultural systems existing when the plant was introduced, being more attractive to people familiar with a planted rather than a sown crop, the banana, than to those dependent on millet and sorghum. The latter, who formed the majority in Kenya and Tanzania, preferred maize among the introductions from America.

Within Uganda sweet potatoes are very widely distributed, and only where annual rainfall is below 900 mm. are they of no significance. Yet in no district do they occupy over a quarter of the land under food crops, and in none are they the main staple. Over most of the country they are the second or third food crop and the distribution of cultivation matches closely that of population. The greatest intensity of production occurs in southern Kigezi, where pressure of population on the land demands a high yielding crop and sweet potatoes have become even more important than sorghum. They are preferred to sorghum, and the dry season hinders banana cultivation, while cool conditions suit sweet potatoes better than cassava. The damp margins of the many swamps in southern Kigezi provide particularly suitable conditions for sweet potato cultivation.

The presence of many swamps and much land around them with damp heavy soil, has encouraged many farmers in Eastern Region also to plant sweet potatoes. They are especially important in southern Teso, where the dense population requires a high yielding crop, but rainfall is too seasonal for bananas. A further concentration of production occurs around Kampala, where pressure on the land is great, and where the urban population provides a market for any surplus. Loads of sweet potatoes on the backs of bicycles are a common early morning sight on the roads leading into Kampala.

Some sweet potatoes are grown in most parts of Tanzania, although they are rarely a major crop and probably occupy no more than 80,000 hectares in all. Their role in the local economy is largest in Mwanza and Shinyanga Regions, where the rainfall regime permits only annual crops but pressure on the land is great. While cassava is also grown, sweet potatoes are preferred, especially in Shinyanga. They are also important in West Lake Region and in the Usambara and Mbulu mountains, but over most of the country low rainfall and poor soils discourage the crop, except within damp valley floors. Sweet potatoes could be grown along the coast, but they are of very little importance there. The crop has always been officially encouraged in Tanzania, but no pressure has been exerted as for cassava cultivation.

In Kenya also sweet potatoes are of minor importance, occupying only about 60,000 hectares and accounting for 3 per cent. of all cultivated land. The main areas of production are the overcrowded parts of Kiambu, Murang'a and Nyeri Districts. Maize is much preferred there, but farmers with little land must plant a higher yielding crop in addition, and in cool highland country with fertile soils sweet potatoes do better than cassava. In Nyanza and Western Provinces they are of little significance, although they could easily be grown. Neither the Luo nor the Baluhya appear to like them as food, in contrast to most Uganda tribes. Throughout Kenya people show a clear preference for maize and grow sweet potatoes only when maize cannot supply all their requirements of starchy food.

OTHER ROOT CROPS

Yams are a traditional root crop in some of the wetter parts of East Africa, but they have been largely replaced by crops which require less labour[12]. In Kiambu and Murang'a Districts of Kenya, for example, yams have declined greatly in importance: but in Meru District, where new ideas have penetrated less deeply, they still occupy 20,000 hetcares. Some yams are still grown in Coast Province, but they are a very minor crop there. Some are also grown in many parts of Uganda, notably by the Bagisu on Mount Elgon, and by the Bakonjo on the slopes of Ruwenzori, but in neither Uganda nor Tanzania do they make a large contribution to food supplies.

The colocasia, like the yam, is an important crop in West Africa, where it is often known as the coco-yam: but it too plays a very small role in East African agriculture. Its cultivation is largely confined to small patches on swamp margins in Buganda and Toro, and in the Kenya highlands.

English potatoes are now more important than either yams or colocasia, but as many are grown for sale they will be considered in the next chapter.

BEANS AND PEAS

A variety of pulses is grown in East Africa, and they make an important contribution to food supplies, providing the chief source of protein for many people and being complementary to the staple foods discussed so far. So many types are available that a pulse crop can be grown in all agricultural areas, and they fit very well into the agricultural system since their nitrogen-fixing properties help to restore soil fertility. They are generally interplanted with other crops, and so official planting figures may exaggerate their importance: but these suggest that together they rank second only to maize in Kenya and rank third in area among food crops in Uganda.

In Kenya pulses are most important in the central highlands and in Machakos and Kitui Districts. In Machakos they account for 40 per cent. of the area under all crops, and together with maize form the staple foodstuffs of the district. They are second only to maize in area throughout Meru, Embu, Kirinyaga, Murang'a and Kiambu Districts, most plots having these two crops interplanted. Further west pulses are widely grown in South and Central Nyanza and Kakamega, but are of little significance in Kericho, Nandi, Busia and Bungoma. They are also unimportant in Coast Province, except in the Taita hills.

Beans are generally the main component, with chick peas in the central highlands and pigeon peas in Machakos and K'tui as subsidiaries. Field peas are particularly important on land above 1,800 metres, while cow peas become dominant near the coast. This pattern is clearly related to climatic conditions, for cow peas and pigeon peas require higher tempeiatures than most beans, while chick peas and field peas thrive best in cooler areas. A useful attribute of pigeon peas is their tolerance of poor soils such as those of Machakos and Kitui.

The contrasts in overall importance of pulses within Kenya are not easily explained. In Machakos and Kitui the range of possible crops is very limited: in the central highlands it is greater, but the shortage of animal protein in diets there encourages high consumption of pulses. In much of the west the ratio of livestock to people is higher, and both there and by the coast fish are an important source of protein. While these considerations may affect the distribution of pulse cultivation its proper understanding would require further study.

Pulse crops are very evenly spread over Uganda, occupying about 10 per cent. of the food crop area in most districts. The wide distribution is related to the existence of a type suitable for most environments found in Uganda. Beans are the most important pulse crop in most districts, but especially so in the well-watered Lake Victoria zone. Cow peas are particularly important in Teso, for few other crops can be grown in the small and unreliable second rains there. In Lango and Acholi, where rainfall is concentrated into a single long wet season, pigeon peas form a suitable crop, for they require several months of rain after planting, but can then withstand long periods of drought. As in Kenya, field peas are confined to cool highlands, and are important only in southern Kigezi.

In Tanzania pulses are as evenly distributed as in Uganda, and in no agricultural areas are they entirely absent. They are of major importance only around Bukoba, where beans rank second only to bananas as a staple food, perhaps because of the severe shortage of meat there. There are lesser concentrations of production further south, in Kibondo and Kasulu Districts, and around Mwanza. Cow peas were once widespread, but have generally been replaced by other crops, and are now important, as in Kenya, only near the coast. The Mporotos and Livingstone mountains, in the far south, are further highland areas where field peas are grown, settlement there extending above 2,500 metres where the range of possible crops is small.

Seed beans are produced for export on large-scale farms in Arusha Region, serving markets once supplied by Hungary; but although flourishing the industry is small. Production is about 4,000 tons a year, compared with some 200,000 tons of pulses grown on peasant farms in Tanzania.

The pulse crops are to some degree commercial crops, for more of the production is sold than of any previously discussed. Nevertheless they are rarely grown specifically for sale, those sold being generally just the surplus above domestic requirements. This is confirmed by the variation in the volume of sales from year to year. If 80 per cent. of the crop is required by the producers for their own food supplies in a good year, there will be none available for sale when yields are 25 per cent. lower.

More pulses are sold than millet or cassava mainly because a larger market exists. Beans are an important item of diet for most town dwellers and for employees on estates and elsewhere, normally supplementing maize. Pigeon peas and chick peas find markets in towns as they are staple foods for the Asians, while some high quality field peas and beans from the Kenya highlands are taken by the small local canning industry. These sales, which sometimes involve movements between the three countries, are encouraged by the higher value to weight ratio of pulses than of most food crops.

The value of pulses also permits exports even from inland areas, and overseas markets exist, especially in Europe, for large quantities of these crops. Exports from Tanzania and Kenya exceed 20,000 tons, worth £1 million, in both 1968 and 1969, both countries providing equal shares. The price obtainable does not make pulses as attractive as cash crops such as cotton, especially as far inland as Uganda: but it is sufficient to encourage sales from many parts of Tanzania where no major cash crop has been established. Among the crops discussed in this chapter pulses are certainly those which offer the best prospect of increasing cash income among East African farmers.

REFERENCES

1   Uganda Department of Agriculture, *Annual Report*, and Uganda, *Report on Census of Agriculture*, Entebbe, 1966, now supplemented by Uganda, *Report of Annual Agricultural Statistics 1968*, Entebbe, 1969.
2   Kenya, *Sample Census of African Agriculture 1960/61*, Nairobi, 1962.
3   D. N. McMaster, *A Subsistence Crop Geography of Uganda*, Geographical Publications, Bude, 1962. Other useful material on crops in Uganda may be found in A. R. Dunbar, *The Annual Crops of Uganda*, E. A. Literature Bureau, Nairobi, 1969, and J. D. Jameson (ed.), *Agriculture in Uganda*, Oxford U.P., London, 1970.
4   E.g. studies of the Kipsigis and the Ukaguru in J. H. Steward (ed.), *Contemporary Change in Traditional Societies*, Univ. of Illinois Press, Urbana, 1967.
5   J. Fisher, *The Anatomy of Kikuyu Domesticity and Husbandry*, D.T.C., London, 1962, p. 231.
6   G. W. Huntingford, *The Southern Nilo-Hamites*, International African Institute, London, 1953, pp. 22, 71, 81.
7   N. W. Simmonds, *Bananas*, Longmans, London, 1966, p. 276. This book gives much attention to East Africa.
8   E.g. F. A. O. *Production Yearbook*, Rome, Annual.
9   D. N. McMaster, *op. cit.*, p. 47.
10 R. S. Beck, *Economic Survey of Coffee-Banana Farms in Machame, Kilimanjaro District*, Dar es Salaam, 1963.
11 W. O. Jones, *Manioc in Africa*, Stanford U.P., 1959, p. 288. Chapter 9 provides a full discussion of cassava cultivation in East Africa.
12 B. F. Johnston, *The Staple Food Economies of Western Tropical Africa*, Stanford U.P., 1958, p. 142. This study is very useful for comparisons with equatorial and western Africa.

CHAPTER 4

Crops grown for Subsistence
and for Local Sale

MAIZE

Maize is 'now more widely distributed in Africa than any other food plant',[1] although it is not indigenous but was brought from America. In East Africa it is as important as in the countries to the south and more important than in West or North Africa. It is now the leading food crop of the region, having replaced millet as the dominant subsistence crop over most of Kenya and much of Tanzania, and providing the staple diet of most people in paid employment almost everywhere. Maize is planted on at least 2 million hectares of land annually, and 3 million tons is probably harvested.

Maize was already the staple food in parts of East Africa by 1900, but its importance has greatly increased during this century, and is still increasing. Most people grow the crop primarily for their own needs, but many now plant more than they will require, and some depend on maize as their chief source of cash. The movement of people into employment has provided a market, and in most places any surplus can be sold. In addition, maize was adopted by European farmers in Kenya, although production on large farms there reached its peak in 1929 and now represents only 3 per cent. of the East African total.

The distribution of maize cultivation within East Africa is uneven (Map 6). The crop probably occupies about $1\frac{1}{4}$ million hectares in Kenya and $\frac{3}{4}$ million hectares in Tanzania, but under $\frac{1}{4}$ million hectares in Uganda. In Kenya it is planted on half the cultivated land, although other crops are often interplanted with it, but in Uganda it occupies only 5 per cent. of the cropped land. The distribution of production differs little from that of planting, although average yields may be slightly higher in Kenya and Uganda than in Tanzania.

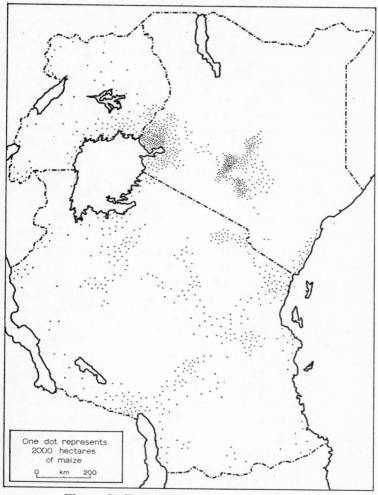

One dot represents
2000 hectares
of maize

0   km   200

Figure 6. EAST AFRICA: Maize Cultivation

Maize can be grown in almost all the settled parts of East Africa. It tolerates a wide range of temperatures so that it is found both at the coast and at altitudes over 2,000 metres; most varieties require only 500 mm. of rain in the growing season and some will survive with only 400 mm.; and it will grow on many types of soil. Both climate and soils affect the yield, but even in poor conditions this is higher than that of most grains. In good conditions yields often exceed 1,500 kg. per hectare without fertilisers. Maize is very easy to grow, suffers little from disease, and is attacked less by birds than other grains. It does not store very well, but can be milled into flour which keeps better. Most people in East Africa like maize better than the other staple foods of the region, although most Baganda, Wachagga, Asians and Europeans are among the exceptions.

These features all contribute to the importance of maize in East Africa, but some factors favour it more in some places than in others. The most important has been the attitude of governments. Much assistance has been given in Kenya, where the authorities have always approved of maize cultivation and have tried to ensure an adequate supply for those who do not grow their own food. An elaborate marketing system exists, and the Maize and Produce Board offers prices higher than those prevailing elsewhere. In Uganda the Department of Agriculture has discouraged maize cultivation because of fears that a crop giving such poor ground cover assists soil erosion. There is no guaranteed market for surplus production and prices at local markets are generally low. The significance of this was shown in 1953, when the Uganda Government did buy maize at high prices. The result was a great increase in planting and a trebling of sales, so that for two years the railway was moving accumulated stocks to Kenya.

Differences in official policies influence the distribution of production for subsistence as well as for sale, but they do not entirely explain it. Although the Uganda Government has discouraged farmers from growing maize for their own use, it cannot prevent their doing so. The greater importance of maize in Kenya also reflects local dietary preference, for people in Uganda have shown less interest in changing from their traditional staples, bananas and finger millet. External contacts have been stronger in Kenya than in the parts of Uganda dependent on annual crops, and this may have assisted the adoption of maize there. High humidity, and consequent difficulty in drying the crop, may be a further factor discouraging it in Buganda and Western Uganda.

In most respects Tanzania falls between Kenya and Uganda. Maize has been readily accepted into the diet, yet it has not ousted millet and sorghum as far as in Kenya. Government has not tried to restrict maize growing, but neither has it given as much positive encouragement as in Kenya. The market provided by people in employment is larger in Tanzania than in Uganda, but smaller than in Kenya.

The distribution of maize cultivation within Kenya closely resembles that of population, since maize is the staple crop of most farmers. It occupies more than half the cultivated land throughout Central and Eastern Provinces, although it is less dominant in relatively isolated Meru District than else-where. The volcanic soils of central Kenya are very favourable through their fertility and their resistance to erosion. The resulting high yields have been of great benefit in this densely settled area. Maize is equally important, however, in the less fertile districts of Kitui and Machakos.

Maize is also planted on over half the cropped land in each district of Nyanza and Western Provinces. In Kipsigis country, north and east of Kericho, it is almost a monoculture, providing the chief source of cash as well as food for most farmers. In Nandi District, where millet was the main crop until recently, but where there is no long tradition of any cultivation, the 1960/61 agricultural census recorded a cultivated area of 17,000 hectares, of which 14,000 were under maize. In Western Province maize is less dominant, but the intensity of production is greater, as Map 6 shows, for population is much denser there. In Bungoma District and adjacent parts of Kakamega it is certainly the chief cash crop, as well as the staple food.

Maize is less important in Coast Province, where physical conditions are rarely ideal, and where government officers have offered less encouragement. Yet even there it is the main food crop, and its cultivation is increasing steadily. The only areas of peasant agriculture where little maize is grown are those over 2,300 metres, where it ripens extremely slowly, and those with either infertile and poorly-drained soils or with rainfall barely adequate for any cultivation. Thus it gives way to potatoes in the highest areas, and to sorghum in the lakeside locations of Nyanza Province and in eastern Kitui.

Maize production on the large farms in Kenya is heavily

E

concentrated in Trans-Nzoia, but it is also important in Uasin Gishu and Nakuru Districts. In Trans-Nzoia physical conditions suit maize better than any other crop. As much of the land lies around 1,800 metres temperatures are rather high for wheat, while the dry season is too severe for most perennial crops. Even there, high guaranteed prices have been a vital factor in making maize a worthwhile crop for commercial farmers; and when the price fell in 1964 some land was turned over to wheat. Maize is also the leading crop in north-west Uasin Gishu, but on the higher land around Eldoret wheat is more important. The only other important area of production on large farms is around Rongai in Nakuru District between the high country west of the rift valley and the dry valley floor. The distribution of large-scale production of this bulky crop has been strongly influenced by accessibility as well as by physical conditions since most is sold, and all the major producing areas are within easy reach of railway stations.

The distribution of maize sales in Kenya is very different from that of production. Areas of small-scale farming supply little more to the Maize and Produce Board than large-scale farming areas, despite their far larger production. The pattern of recorded sales from peasant farms does not match that of cultivation, for Nyanza and Western Provinces usually account for two-thirds of the total, and Meru, Embu and Machakos Districts provide most of the remainder. In Nyeri, Murang'a and Kiambu the whole production is generally consumed on the farms or sold locally. Pressure of population on land is there very great, and although much is under maize there is no surplus for sale to other districts.

No data are available on the distribution of maize cultivation in Tanzania, and the pattern shown on Map 6 represents only a rough estimate. The crop is of greatest importance in the southern highlands, probably occupying more than half the cultivated land in Iringa and Mufindi Districts. Even in high country more suited to wheat or potatoes, such as the Mporoto mountains, maize is the most popular crop. It is also the staple food crop in Mbinga, Songea and Tunduru, but towards the coast millet and sorghum become more important. Maize is the leading crop in most of Morogoro Region, where rainfall is satisfactory and alien influence considerable, and also in

Mpwapwa and Kondoa Districts of Dodoma Region; but over much of central Tanzania soils are too poor and rainfall is too low for good yields, and millet and sorghum are giving way only slowly to maize. The places where it occupies the largest share of the land under food crops are in Tanga Region, where much is grown by sisal estate labourers or their wives. Maize is also an important crop in Arusha Region, although rainfall severely limits its extent there. It is least important in Coast and Bukoba Regions, most people preferring rice in the former and bananas in the latter.

The pattern of recorded sales fluctuates very greatly, but Arusha and Iringa Regions usually provide the largest quantities. They are well placed to supply the markets of the main towns and the sisal estates, much maize moving from Arusha to Tanga Region and from Iringa to Morogoro and Dar es Salaam. Much is also sold locally within Tanga and Morogoro Regions, maize being a major cash crop, for example, around Kilosa. The main producing areas in which sales are least important are Mbeya and Ruvuma, where there is little local demand and other markets are very distant.

Although the contribution of Uganda to East African maize production is small, some is grown in most districts, The crop is most widely grown in Buganda, Busoga, Bugisu, Sebei, West Nile and Kigezi, although only in Sebei does it occupy more than 10 per cent. of the cultivated land. The last four districts are all on the periphery of the country, and McMaster suggests that the weaker influence of the Uganda authorities there and the importance of maize across the borders have contributed to the pattern[2]. The crop also seems to be associated with immigrant groups, both near the borders and in Buganda and Busoga. In the latter areas some maize is grown for sale to those in employment in and around Kampala and Jinja.

Movements of maize between the East African countries are small, and are in fact mainly illegal, since they are of maize grown outside Kenya but sold within that country at the high fixed prices prevailing there. If free trade in maize were permitted, there might be a large flow from Uganda to Kenya. The East Africa Royal Commission observed that it is in Uganda 'that the greatest opportunity lies for specializing in maize production as a contribution to the economies of all three territories'.[3] But for this commodity the common market is not allowed to operate. Neither the Kenya nor the Uganda government considers that the development of such trade would be beneficial, though their reasons for discouraging it are very different.

Much maize was produced for export overseas in the 1920s. This trade was hard hit by the Depression and has never revived, but since the Kenya Government fixes prices at a level high enough to ensure adequate supplies even if the harvest is poor, there is usually a surplus which has to be exported. The average volume sold overseas annually between 1966 and 1969 was 120,000 tons, worth £2 million. This maize is generally sold at a loss to the Marketing Board, for world prices are too low to make maize a profitable export crop for East Africa. The situation may soon change, however, for improved storage facilities should make it unnecessary to guarantee that production matches demand even in bad years, and so permit the payment of less inflated prices. This would mean that either fewer surpluses would be produced, or perhaps with new high-yielding varieties maize could be grown for export at competitive prices, as the 1970–74 Development Plan anticipates.[4]

WHEAT

Unlike all other East African staple food crops wheat is grown primarily for sale, mainly on the large farms. It was introduced into East Africa in the late nineteenth century as a peasant crop in Tanzania, but it has never become popular on small farms. Almost 200,000 hectares are now sown with wheat, and production is about 250,000 tons a year. Large farms in Kenya provide 80 per cent. of the total, similar farms in Tanzania 5 per cent. and small farms the remainder.

Wheat has the merit of thriving in cool highland country where few other crops flourish. It suffers much more severely from rust disease anywhere below 1,500 metres than at higher altitudes, and is usually grown on land above 2,000 metres. It requires only 400 mm. of rain in the growing season, and this is received in all areas at such altitude. Yields are greatly affected by soil fertility, and the volcanic soils of the Kenya highlands suit the crop admirably. The existence of European settlers there has been an essential factor in the importance of wheat, for this crop benefits much more than maize from large scale cultivation. For small patches of land, to which labour rather than capital is applied, maize is more appropriate.

Almost half the wheat of Kenya is grown on the Uasin Gishu plateau, where it occupies over half the land under crops. Around Moiben the figure rises to 80 per cent. This area stands 2,200 metres above sea level, has fertile volcanic soils, and has remarkably level land which provides suitable conditions for mechanized cultivation. Mean annual rainfall is only 1,000 mm., and under 750 mm. falls in some years, which limits the range of possible crops. The main Kenya-Uganda railway and a good network of feeder roads provide adequate transport facilities.

Other important areas of production are in Nakuru and Nyandarua Districts, notably around Molo and Njoro and between Gilgil and Thomson's Falls. These areas also lie above 2,200 metres, yet receive under 900 mm. of rain, have fertile soils, and are served by railways. Minor wheat areas are found around Nanyuki and in Trans Nzoia, at the foot of Mount Kenya and Mount Elgon respectively.

In Tanzania wheat is grown mainly in Arusha and Kilimanjaro Regions; but much less is produced than in Kenya, for the highland area is much smaller and there are fewer large farms. There are particular concentrations on the western slopes of Mount Kilimanjaro and around Oldeani, even though the latter lies 170 km. west of the Arusha railhead. These areas have volcanic soils, but the cultivated land lies below 2,200 metres and the wheat suffers from rust, as well as from droughts and bird attack. Some wheat is grown on small farms in the north, and the southern highlands is another area of peasant production. Wheat is the staple food of some 50,000 people in Njombe District, and some is grown in Mbeya and Songea Districts. Most is consumed by the growers or sold for local milling. Commercial wheat production has been tried near Iringa, but the land there is rather low and has poor soils. There is higher land with fertile soils in Mbeya Region, and although this lies far from all potential markets wheat is being established on state farms in Sumbawanga District.

Even in the most favoured parts of East Africa production costs are much higher than in Canada or Australia, and wheat cultivation developed only behind a high tariff on imports.

Until 1939 imports were required, but wartime shortages stimulated increased cultivation, although guaranteed prices were essential to this. The East African customs union greatly assists Kenya wheat producers. The largest demand is within Kenya, with its substantial urban population; but a quarter of the Kenya production is usually exported to Tanzania and Uganda. This trade was worth over £1½ million in 1967 and 1968, and wheat is thus among Kenya's major exports. There is no prospect of profitable overseas exports, however, unless growers' prices are drastically reduced, while in the 1970s Tanzania aims to achieve self-sufficiency.

RICE

Rice is far less important in this region than in West Africa, but it is the staple food in a few areas and is slowly increasing in importance. It is grown entirely on small farms, generally on land where natural flooding takes place rather than by artificial irrigation. Land suitable for greatly increased cultivation is available, for the swampy lakeshores offer excellent conditions, while large areas could be irrigated. The food value of rice is higher than that of most starchy staples, yields are higher than those of most grains, and the land best suited to rice is often unsuitable for either crops. There is already a substantial market within East Africa, and much rice is now imported.

The chief factor discouraging more rice cultivation is the amount of labour required, ideally over 150 man-days per hectare, compared with about 50 for other grains. In addition, new techniques have to be learnt, and production is largely confined to a few tribes which have mastered these. The work may be not only long and difficult but also unpleasant if it involves spending hours in swamps abounding with insects and with the snails which carry bilharzia.

Of the 60,000 hectares under rice in East Africa about 85 per cent. is in Tanzania, notably near the coast. Around the Rufiji river rice occupies more land than any other crop, and the zone of production extends in each direction along the coast and also inland into the Kilombero valley. In parts of the south, notably Mtwara District, rice is the second food crop, while around Dar es Salaam the urban market has stimulated production for sale, although it is not fully exploited. Along much of the coast farmers must depend mainly on rainfall and suffer from poor soils; if population increases and if floodwaters are harnessed for controlled irrigation the opportunities for increased production are far greater in the valleys of the Rufiji and its tributaries.

Rice is more important as a staple food in Zanzibar than on the Tanganyika coast, and some requirements have to be imported. Production in Zanzibar and Pemba is about 20,000 tons a year, from 8,000 hectares, compared with imports of 15,000 tons. Local production developed during the war, when supplies from south-east Asia were cut off, and has been maintained with the help of government encouragement. The main demand is on Zanzibar island, but more rice is grown in Pemba, which has higher rainfall and more fertile soils.

Rice is the staple food of some Nyakyusa, who occupy the fertile plains at the north end of Lake Malawi. Rainfall there is extremely high, while numerous rivers flow down from the Rungwe highlands, and in spite of inaccessibility sales from Mbeya Region are increasing. Rice is also grown around Kigoma, beside Lake Tanganyika, and in several parts of Tabora Region, although those areas have lower rainfall and poorer soils. Rice is of increasing importance on low lying, ill-drained land in Mwanza and Shinyanga Regions, encouraged by population pressure there. Some is also cultivated on the plains below the Pare and Usambara mountains, mainly for cash, but most farmers do not consider the labour involved worth while.

Rather less than 8,000 hectares of rice is planted each year in Kenya. It is the staple food in the Tana and Umba valleys near the coast, where flood waters from the rivers are available, but the population there is small. About 1,000 hectares are under rice on the Kano plains in Nyanza, but land tenure problems and the unpopularity of the work hinder plans for large irrigation schemes. The recently-established Mwea-Tebere irrigation scheme east of Mount Kenya has been much more successful. Yields there exceed 4½ tons per hectare, and the area is providing a substantial supply of rice for Nairobi.

In Uganda wartime shortages of rice led to the planting of over 25,000 hectares by 1945, but today the figure is only 3,000 and rice is an important crop only in Bwamba, a small area of hot, wet country west of the Ruwenzori. There is much land suitable for rice in Uganda, notably on the swampy margins of Lake Kyoga; but few farmers are interested in rice as food and cotton provides a cash income with less effort. Rice is unlikely to be widely grown until increase of population forces farmers to bring such swampy land into cultivation.

POTATOES

Potatoes are important in several highland areas, for they do well above 2,000 metres where few other staple crops are successful, are more suitable than wheat for peasant production and are generally popular as a food. They are grown primarily for subsistence, but some are sold as there is a growing market for potatoes in the towns.

About 60,000 hectares are planted annually in Kenya. Only maize and beans occupy more land in Kiambu District, where much land is high and cool, where the dense population requires a high-yielding crop, and where any surplus can be sold in the neighbouring Nairobi market. Potatoes are also widely grown in Nyeri and Meru Districts, but they are less important in Murang'a, Kirinyaga and Embu, where fewer people live at high altitudes. On small farms above 2,200 metres west of the rift valley potatoes occupy an area second only to maize, and in some places contribute more to food supplies. Much land suitable for potatoes is occupied by large mixed farms, but few are grown on these: potatoes are suited to high-density peasant farming where much labour is applied to little land, but wheat brings a higher return when production is mechanized.

Recorded sales in Kenya average 10,000 tons a year, half from Meru District, but substantial unrecorded sales must also take place. About 4,000 tons a year are exported to Uganda, and the Kenya market is substantially larger.

Potatoes were brought to Tanzania by the Germans, and have become a staple food crop in the Mporoto mountains and neighbouring highland areas in the south. However, maize is still generally more popular as food there, while production of such a low value crop for sale is greatly discouraged by distance from markets. Commercial production is greater in the more accessible Arusha and Kilimanjaro Districts.

In Uganda potatoes occupy only 5,000 hectares, mainly in high country in Kigezi District. Few can be sold there, and although co-operative societies have organized sales to Kampala they meet severe competition there from Elgeyo District of Kenya.

GROUNDNUTS

In East Africa groundnuts are primarily a subsistence crop, valuable in diets otherwise overdependent on starchy foods; but some are also sold, as food for the towns, as raw material for the oil milling industry and for export overseas. They are not indigenous to the region, but are well suited to the environmental conditions in many areas, and are generally popular as a foodstuff. They have been accepted less readily than some other crops introduced from America mainly because their cultivation and especially harvesting, is very laborious.

About 250,000 hectares are under groundnuts in East Africa, two-thirds in Uganda, where the figure has increased from 10,000 in 1920 to 60,000 in 1935 and 160,000 today. There is no obvious explanation of the dominance of Uganda, although vigorous government encouragement there has certainly contributed. Official disapproval of maize cultivation in Uganda may have led to the supplementation of millet by groundnuts instead of its replacement by maize as elsewhere. The smaller importance of pulses in Uganda than in Kenya provided a greater incentive to introduce groundnuts into both crop rotations and diets. The annual production of unshelled nuts in Uganda is about 150,000 tons, of which 20,000 tons are sometimes marketed, bringing £½ million to the growers: but as subsistence consumption is fairly consistent variations in the harvest cause great fluctuations in sales.

The distribution of groundnut cultivation within Uganda is discussed fully by McMaster.[5] They are grown in most districts, but are concentrated in the east, where they occupy about 30,000 hectares both in Teso and in Busoga, and are grown on more than half the farms in each case. Climate and soils are satisfactory over most of the country, but the light soils and ample rainfall of the east are particularly favourable. In Buganda heavier soils make cultivation more laborious, and in the north groundnuts must compete with other crops during the single wet season. They fit well beside millet and cotton in the agricultural system of the east, and contribute to soil fertility in this well settled area, where land cannot be rested for long periods.

Busoga District contributes most to groundnut sales, which provide the second source of income for peasant farmers there, although far behind cotton. This is related to the concentration of oil milling there: the mills depend mainly on cotton seed, but buy groundnuts when this is scarce. The location of Busoga in relation to urban markets and to the overseas export route also favours sales there. In Teso there is less need to sell groundnuts as cattle sales supplement cotton income, and most are consumed by the farmers.

Whereas groundnut cultivation has expanded rapidly in Uganda, less are grown in Tanzania today than 30 years ago, for the failure of the post war Groundnut Scheme discouraged both farmers and agricultural officers. Annual production is probably about 40,000 tons, mainly from the centre of the country, in Dodoma, Singida and Tabora Regions, where low rainfall and poor light soils limit the range of possible crops. Groundnuts are also produced in Shinyanga and Mwanza Regions, south of Lake Victoria, and in Mtwara and Ruvuma Regions, in the south, but in these areas other crops are much more important. More of the crop is grown for cash than in Uganda, and recorded sales average 10,000 tons a year, chiefly from the centre, where there are no well-established cash crops. There is little commercial demand for groundnuts within Tanzania, and most of those sold are exported.

In Kenya groundnuts are important only in South Nyanza, which lacks other cash crops. Production is largely for sale and 3,000 tons leave the district annually . Some are also grown in the lakeshore zone of Siaya District, but elsewhere farmers consider that both food and cash can be obtained more easily in other ways.

Less than 10 per cent. of East African groundnut production is exported, but this trade brings £1 million a year, three-quarters to Tanzania. There are large overseas markets for the crop, and the present surplus is easily sold even in competition with Nigeria and Senegal. The East African governments have plans to exploit these markets: in Uganda it is claimed that exports of 100,000 tons a year, 15 times the present figure, are quite feasible,[6] and Tanzania envisaged an increase in sales from 16,000 tons in 1962 to 90,000 tons in 1970,[7] though the farmers had other ideas and no increase in fact materialized. Improved marketing facilities in the countryside could assist such development, but unless prices rise sharply or yields can be greatly improved, it is doubtful whether sufficient farmers will consider the return for effort worthwhile for achievement of these targets even within the next decade.

SESAME

Sesame, generally known in this region as 'simsim', is probably indigenous to eastern Africa, and was once more widely grown than now. It is a source of oil, and therefore faces competition from groundnuts, which have superseded it in some places. Its labour requirements are equally high and yields per hectare are lower, rarely exceeding 250 kg. Sesame is very sensitive to rainfall fluctuations, and is liable to insect attack when stored. Thus although it provides a tasty and nutritious food, it is now important in only a few areas. About 200,000 hectares are probably planted each year, entirely on peasant farms, and annual production is estimated at 40,000 tons, of which a quarter is sold.

Production is greatest in northern Uganda, where sesame occupies about 30,000 hectares in both Lango and Acholi. The boundary of the main producing area is sharp, for less than 30,000 hectares are planted elsewhere in Uganda. Over 15 per cent. of the cultivated land in Acholi is under sesame, but nowhere in the east, south or west of Uganda does it occupy 5 per cent. of the cropped land. The main rains in Lango and Acholi are very reliable, and the long dry season is less serious for sesame than for most crops as it ripens in four months. Traditions are stronger in northern Uganda than in much of East Africa, many crops which have become important elsewhere having hardly penetrated the area. Little sesame enters local trade there, for there are no obvious markets.

Sesame also contributes to food supplies in Mtwara and Ruvuma Regions of south-east Tanzania, although it is less important than sorghum, maize and rice. It also forms the second cash crop there, although far behind cashew nuts, sales averaging 6,000 tons a year. This area, like northern Uganda, has a rainfall of about 1,000 mm. concentrated in a single wet season, and is rather isolated from change in traditional farming systems. Mtwara Region, however, lies by the coast, and this encourages production for export. A little sesame is grown further north, in Coast and Morogoro Regions, but in the rest of Tanzania it is rarely found. The crop was once important in both Coast and Nyanza Provinces of Kenya, but it now occupies only 5,000 hectares near the coast and even less in Nyanza.

Sesame exports fluctuate greatly, but in 1969 Tanzania sold 7,000 tons for £½ million, while Uganda exported almost 4,000 tons. Much more could be sold overseas, but in most districts cash can be obtained more easily in other ways. Thus farmers in northern Uganda do better to plant more cotton, rather than grow more sesame than they want for themselves.

COCONUTS

A distinctive feature of the East African coast is an abundance of coconut palms, grown for both food and cash. The palm yields nuts 5 to 7 years after planting, and then continues to yield for 80 years, although passing its peak after about 25 years. Some trees produce 100 nuts annually, but 10 to 20 nuts is more common. These are harvested four times a year and, when separated from the husks and dried, the kernels are either used for cooking or sold as copra. Some copra is exported but most is used within East Africa for soap manufacture. Coir fibre from the kernels is also used locally, for ropes and matting. The palm may also be tapped for toddy, a good tree yielding five litres a day, but this reduces the crop of nuts. The leaves, used for thatching, increase the value of the coconut palm to the people of the coast yet further.

Coconut cultivation requires little effort, although yields are poor in the many plantations which are grossly neglected. It is much easier than growing annual crops such as cotton, and coconuts are therefore grown wherever they will thrive. They are produced in both small plots and large plantations, by Africans, Arabs and Asians. A coastal location suits the tree best: inland it bears fewer nuts. It tolerates very poor sandy soils, but needs rainfall of over 1,000 mm. and does better with much more. Rainfall therefore severely limits its extension inland, and even along the coast.

Coconuts are grown much more extensively in Tanzania than in Kenya, mainly because of low rainfall on the Kenya coast north of Malindi. On Zanzibar island 5 million trees occupy 40,000 hectares, over half the total cultivated area, for rainfall exceeds 1,500 mm. yet the prevalent sandy soils will support few other crops. Many Arabs established plantations in the 19th century, but most of the production is now from peasant holdings. Roughly half the nuts are consumed by the growers, and half are grown for sale to the mainland or overseas, mainly as copra. Fewer coconuts are grown in Pemba, where soils fertile enough for the more profitable clove tree are more extensive and production is only one-quarter that of Zanzibar. Shipments of copra from the two islands amount to about 10,000 tons annually, worth £½ million, Western Europe taking most. Whole nuts, coconut oil and coir together bring a further £¼ million; and although cloves are the islands' most important export, coconut products provide most of the remainder of their export earnings.

Coconuts probably occupy rather less land in Tanganyika than in Zanzibar and Pemba. Half the trees are in Coast Region, with a concentration on Mafia island, which also has 1,500 mm. of rain but poor sandy soils. Many are also grown north of Dar es Salaam, where several oil mills and soap works provide a local market. Coconuts are an important foodstuff in Kilwa District, although marketing difficulties limit sales there, but further south rainfall is too low for good yields. It is higher in Tanga Region, where 4,000 tons of copra are sold each year and processed in small factories in Tanga.

In Kenya there are probably 10,000 hectares of coconuts in Kilifi District and 8,000 hectares in Kwale District, both in the wet southern part of the coastlands. Around Malindi few coconuts are produced, and around Lamu even fewer. Only 3,000 hectares are on commercial estates, 70,000 peasant growers being responsible for the remainder. Copra sales in Kenya rarely exceed 2,000 tons, having declined as more and more trees are tapped for toddy, and Kenya soap works must import most of their copra from Tanzania. It seems that coconuts are grown for subsistence rather than cash to a greater extent in Kenya than in Tanzania.

SUGAR

Sugar cane has long been grown in East Africa on peasant farms for chewing raw and for beer brewing, but today there is also a substantial commercial production of milled sugar. Sugar consumption per head is only 12 kg. a year, one-fifth of that in western Europe, but it is higher than in most parts of Africa, and the local market absorbs the whole production of over 350,000 tons a year, worth more than £16 million.

Unlike most crops grown for local consumption, sugar is produced mainly on plantations. Peasant farmers can grow cane without difficulty, but it can be milled into white sugar only on a large scale. For economic operation a mill must have a large and regular supply of cane, which must be processed within 48 hours of harvesting. The cane must be grown close to the factory, since it is too bulky to be transported far, and some estates have their own light railway systems. The crop benefits from irrigation, and most large producers have invested in costly equipment to undertake this. All these factors favour estate production and, except where sugar is used for local beer brewing, it is grown for cash by peasant farmers only around the fringes of the estates. Eight large plantations, each with one central factory, account for most of the production. Several adjacent small estates swell the cane supply to these factories, but more produce a crude form of sugar, known as jaggery, in their own small mills.

One advantage over many sugar producing countries which East Africa enjoys is the even climatic regime, which allows planting and harvesting to be spread throughout the year and the factories to remain in continuous operation. Nevertheless production costs are higher than in some other countries, and protection from imports has contributed to the development of the industry, producers being paid about 50 per cent. more than normal world market prices. The sugar industry employs over 40,000 people, for it is not highly mechanized, and the two Uganda estates are the largest private employers in East Africa. Yet labour supplies are not a major problem, for people travel long distances to seek work on the plantations.

Power supplies also present no difficulties, for they can be provided by burning waste materials from the cane. The large capital requirements may formerly have hindered expansion somewhat, but this is not the case today.

Sugar consumption is greatest in Kenya; yet Uganda has dominated the East African sugar industry ever since planting began in 1921. By 1945 it was producing over 50,000 tons a year, five times as much as Kenya and Tanzania combined. There has since been rapid expansion in both these countries, and the 1969 Uganda production of 140,000 tons represented only 40 per cent. of the East African total.

Within Uganda production is largely confined to two 7,000-hectare plantations, one at Kakira, near Jinja, and one centred on Lugazi, between Jinja and Kampala. The wide sweeps of cane extending from hilltop to valley floor afford a sharp contrast with the intricate pattern of peasant farms on the surrounding land. Sugar cane is botanically similar to the elephant grass which dominates the vegetation of the country bordering Lake Victoria, and the physical environment there is very satisfactory. For good yields temperatures should average at least 20°C., and rainfall of over 1,000 mm. should be spread over nine or more months. At Jinja mean monthly temperatures range only from 21° to 22°, and mean annual rainfall is 1,200 mm. with some in every month. Irrigation is not essential in these conditions, but it is employed on both estates to increase yields. At Kakira water is available from Lake Victoria, while at Lugazi it is pumped from swamps, which can then be used for cultivation. The soils on both estates are deep and fertile.

Both Kakira and Lugazi are well placed in relation to markets, for Buganda and Busoga account for 70 per cent. of the Uganda consumption of sugar, and that surplus to Uganda requirements is easily railed to markets in Kenya. Sugar cultivation near Lake Victoria is limited mainly by shortage of land. Even when the estates were first established land could not easily be alienated, and their exact location depended on availability of land on abandoned coffee estates. Some land near Kakira is unoccupied because of sleeping sickness carried by tsetse flies which would be eliminated by clearing the ground for sugar, but the local government will not approve this since it would allow more land into non-African hands. The only large area available near the lake is in southern Masaka, and a third estate has been established there, although soil and rainfall conditions and accessibility are poorer than around Lugazi and Kakira. Sugar production at Kinyala in Bunyoro is also planned, although that area also suffers from poorer physical conditions and greater distance from markets than the existing producing area. In addition, peasant farmers near the estates are now growing cane, although their contribution is still small. [8]

Kenya has more land under sugar than Uganda, but production in 1969 was only about 115,000 tons, for less effort has been made to increase yields. Until 1963 Kenya had only two important plantations, although there was unused land suitable for sugar and its occupation by non-Africans had not been discouraged, and although the market is larger than in Uganda or in Tanzania. The larger occupies 6,000 hectares at Miwani, east of Kisumu, and is adjoined by several small estates some of which supply the Miwani factory and contribute to its annual production of 40,000 tons. The second large estate lies near the coast 130 km. south of Mombasa, but this produces only 10,000 tons of sugar a year from its 5,000 hectares of cane. A third estate was established in 1966 at Muhoroni, not far from Miwani, by the Lugazi company, which invested in Kenya mainly because if could not obtain further suitable land in Uganda. A fourth followed at Chemelil, close by, in 1968 as a result of the joint enterprise of the Kenya government and a German firm.

The location of estates within Kenya is related to climatic conditions, which are most satisfactory in Nyanza and near the coast. Nyanza is nearer to the main Kenya markets, but this is immaterial to the producers since all sugar is now sold to the government at a standard price. Within Nyanza the estates lie in a belt of country between Luo and Nandi territory which was unoccupied when alien settlement took place. Many of the peasant farmers in neighbouring areas have land to spare and have no well-established cash crop other than maize, and they are now supplying increasing quantities of cane to the estate mills.

Sugar production began later in Tanzania than in Uganda or Kenya, but is now expanding rapidly. The first estate, established in the 1930s 25 km. south of Moshi, still produced under 1,000 tons of sugar in 1952; but 12 years later 6,000 hectares of cane yielded 34,000 tons. The first harvest was taken from a second estate, in West Lake Region, in 1959, but production there was still under 5,000 tons in 1968. A much larger enterprise is the Kilombero Sugar Company, which has a concession of 10,000 hectares in Morogoro Region, and began planting in 1960. Production had reached 30,000 tons by 1968 and the estate will soon provide most of the Tanzania crop.

The distribution of sugar growing in Tanzania appears rather anomalous. The estate near Moshi, with an annual rainfall of only 420 mm. and alkaline soils, is heavily dependent on irrigation and fertilizers even for moderate yields. That in West Lake receives much more rain, but the soils are unsatisfactory as some are sandy and others require costly drainage, while the estate is remote from markets. Conditions in the Kilombero valley are more promising, for rainfall exceeds 1,200 mm. and the soils are quite satisfactory. Development was formerly hindered by periodic flooding and by inaccessibility; but the rivers have now been partially controlled, and a new rail extension almost reaches the estate. The lack of earlier settlement in fact assisted the establishment of a large plantation.

As production and consumption patterns within East Africa have until now differed considerably, there has been much inter-country trade in sugar. Since the Kilombero development Tanzania has approached self-sufficiency, but in 1970 Kenya still had to import sugar both from Uganda and from overseas. During the 1960s Uganda sent to Kenya an average of 25,000 tons a year, worth £1¼ million, and sugar was the leading export from Uganda to a neighbouring country. When Kenya reaches self-sufficiency Uganda is likely to have a surplus, but transport costs from Uganda make prospects for overseas exports poor. Indeed, if East Africa as a whole has a surplus, it might be most economic to export that grown by the Kenya coast, even though production costs there are relatively high.[9]

TOBACCO

Tobacco has been grown in East Africa for centuries, but until the 1920s little was produced, and this was for the farmers' own consumption. Subsequently cigarette manufacture was

F

established, and commercial tobacco production developed to supply the factories. The crop still occupies less than 20,000 hectares, but it brings more than £2 million to the growers, mainly peasant farmers. Tobacco is not very demanding on rainfall, will grow in poor soils, and is well suited to peasant production. As an annual crop with a short growing season it fits well into rotations with food crops, and often brings the growers over £400 per hectare. The scale of production is limited mainly by size of markets. Overseas markets have not been found until recently, and planting had to be restricted to avoid the production of more tobacco than the local market could absorb.

The main areas of cultivation are in Uganda and Tanzania, which produced 4,500 and 7,300 tons of cured leaf respectively in 1968. Within each country production is highly localized, largely because no spread from the places where it was first established has been encouraged. Physical conditions are satisfactory for tobacco over much of Uganda, yet West Nile, Acholi and Bunyoro account for 90 per cent. of the crop. The reason is indicated by the official statement that it was 'accepted policy to encourage the growing of toabcco in areas where other cash crops were difficult to grow'.[10] The West Nile uplands still have more need of tobacco as a cash crop than Lango, where many farmers would like to grow it. The direct influence of physical conditions is mainly on the type of tobacco grown, flue-cured varieties doing best on the light soils of West Nile and fire-cured varieties on the heavy clay-loams of Bunyoro.

In Tanzania fire-cured tobacco is grown mainly in Songea District in the south, which has no other cash crop, and where much government assistance has been given since 1930. Production there reached 3,000 tons in 1967. A little is grown in the north-west, notably in Kibondo and Kasulu Districts, mainly for sale locally and in Burundi as coil tobacco. European farmers developed flue-cured tobacco cultivation around Iringa during the war, when import restrictions increased prices and tobacco became the most profitable crop in that area of poor soils and moderate rainfall. Production there fell in the 1960s partly because of the departure of some of these farmers; and although some Iringa peasant farmers are taking up the crop the leading area of cultivation is now

Tabora Region, where a cash crop was required for tenants on land once cleared for groundnuts and now owned by the National Agricultural and Food Corporation.[11]

Kenya produces only 200 to 300 tons of tobacco a year. The crop is grown mainly in Kitui and Embu, but even in these districts it is of minor importance. Although no parts of Kenya are outstandingly suitable for tobacco, its small contribution to East African production must be attributed mainly to lack of encouragement by the Department of Agriculture.

One notable feature of the distribution of tobacco cultivation is the lack of any relationship to that of cigarette factories. Markets have apparently no influence on the location of production, for most of the tobacco is moved at least 300 km. across Uganda or Tanzania. Much is moved further, for consumption is greatest in Kenya, and tobacco is one of the main components of inter-territorial trade. The product is of sufficiently high value to bear the transport costs involved without difficulty.

Rapid expansion of tobacco cultivation, and its extension to new areas, will be possible only if overseas exports can be developed. Despite much effort in this direction exports were very slight until 1966, for tobacco of the quality then produced did not find ready markets. More recently, however, the quality has improved, while sanctions against Rhodesia since UDI have eased marketing conditions. By 1969 overseas sales reached 6,500 tons, worth £2½ million, two-thirds from Tanzania and one-third from Uganda, and there are plans for much further expansion. Thus the 1969–74 Tanzania Development Plan aims at an annual 25 per cent. increase in production of flue-cured tobacco, a higher rate than for any other crop, and this must depend on overseas exports.

REFERENCES

1 G. P. Murdock, 'Staple Subsistence Crops of Africa', *Geographical Review*, Vol. 50, No. 4, 1960, p. 525. A comprehensive study of the spread of maize cultivation is M. P. Miracle, *Maize in Tropical Africa*, Wisconsin U.P., Madison, 1966.

2 D. N. McMaster, *A Subsistence Crop Geography of Uganda*, Geographical Publications, Bude, 1962, p. 62.

3 *East Africa Royal Commission 1953–1955 Report*, H.M.S.O, London., 1955, p. 323.

4 Kenya, *Development Plan 1970–1974*, Nairobi, 1969, p. 237–238.

5   D. N. McMaster, *op. cit.*, pp. 77–80.
6   International Bank, *The Economic Development of Uganda*, Entebbe, 1961, p. 145.
7   Tanganyika, *Five-year Development Plan, 1964–1969*, Dar es Salaam, 1964, p. 20.
8   A useful case study is J. Smith, 'Production of Sugar Cane by Out-growers in East Mengo', *East African Geographical Review*, No. 8, 1970, pp. 47–54.
9   This is one of the main conclusions of a thorough economic survey: C. R. Frank, *The Sugar Industry in East Africa*, East African Publishing House, Nairobi, 1966.
10 Uganda Protectorate, *Report of the Tobacco Advisory Committee*, Entebbe, 1936, p. 11. On the present pattern of production in one area of Uganda see M. K. Mackenzie, 'The Geography of Tobacco Production in West Nile', *East African Geographical Review*, No. 8, 1970, pp. 31–37.
11 W. Scheffler, 'Tobacco Schemes in Central Region', in H. Ruthenberg, (ed.) *Smallholder Farming and Smallholder Development in Tanzania*, Weltforum Verlag, Munchen, 1968.

CHAPTER 5

Export Crops

COFFEE

Coffee is the most important and most widely grown cash crop in East Africa, playing a major role in the economy of all three countries. None is as heavily dependent on coffee exports as are some other producing countries, but they bring £60 to £70 million a year to East Africa, twice the income obtained from any other commodity, and one-third of the value of all exports from the region. Coffee is now the leading export of all three countries, although rivalled by cotton in Tanzania; and the prosperity of many parts of the region depends on the fortunes of the crop.

The world coffee economy is dominated by Brazil, which produces more than 1 million tons annually, and Colombia is second in importance. East African production used to be small in comparison, but the region as a whole is now the leading area of coffee cultivation outside Latin America, for its annual production of 300,000 tons exceeds that in both Angola and Ivory Coast.

Coffee was known in East Africa before the arrival of the Europeans, but commercial cultivation dates from about 1900. Planting expanded rapidly in the 1920s, especially on European farms in Kenya and on African farms in Uganda. A period of stagnation followed, but since 1950 the industry has again expanded rapidly, production trebling during the subsequent decade. This has taken place almost entirely on African farms, first in Uganda and Tanzania, and more recently in Kenya. World market conditions discouraged new planting after 1960, but production continued to expand until the late-1960s as young trees came into bearing.

Two varieties of the coffee bush, *robusta* and *arabica*, are cultivated in East Africa. *Robusta*, which occupies two-thirds of the area planted, is a hardy variety indigenous to the region.

It competes with the low grades of the Brazilian crop and is much affected by world price fluctuations. *Arabica* often gives lower yields, but is comparable in quality with the Colombia crop and commands higher prices.

There are probably about 700,000 coffee growers, a few owning large estates but the majority having less than a hectare under the crop. Some of the coffee is hulled by the farmers or by growers' co-operative societies, but most is sent to a curing works for final processing. In Uganda there are many small works, but Kenya and Tanzania have large works at Nairobi and Moshi which handle most of the crop. Most of the clean coffee is bought by statutory marketing boards, and sold by auction in Kampala, Nairobi or Moshi. Consumption within East Africa is very small, and over 95 per cent. is exported. The United States, Britain and West Germany are the most important customers, but East African coffee is sold to more than 50 other countries.

The importance of East Africa as a coffee producer is partly related to the physical requirements of the crop. It can be grown successfully only in or near the tropics, but does not thrive in the hot low-lying parts of this zone. The plateaux and highlands of East Africa provide very suitable temperature conditions, while extensive areas are sufficiently well watered and have satisfactory soils. *Arabica* coffee requires at least 800 mm. of rain well distributed over the year. It cannot survive frost but is very liable to disease if temperatures often exceed 25°C. Its requirements are best satisfied in tropical highlands above 1,500 metres, of which East Africa has a substantial share. As yields are closely related to soil fertility the volcanic soils in the East African highlands are an additional advantage. *Robusta* coffee thrives at lower altitudes than *arabica*, and is well suited to those parts of the plateau at about 1,200 metres which have over 1,000 mm. of rain with no marked dry season.

The suitability of coffee for peasant farming encourages its cultivation in East Africa. Little advantage is gained from large scale production, and the produce of many farms is easily brought together for processing. Sun-dried berries are only twice as bulky as clean coffee and suffer little from handling or delays between harvest and processing. Although knowledge and skill are needed for maximum yields, a farmer with little of either can obtain a worthwhile income from his trees. The four-year delay between planting and the first harvest limits the attraction of coffee for peasant farmers, but once established the tree produces for over 30 years even with little attention, and this has encouraged many to invest in the crop. A hectare of mature coffee demands much less effort during the year than a hectare of cotton, and brings a higher income even when prices are low. For farmers with no mechanical equipment, who cannot work more than 2 or 3 hectares, these are vital considerations.

The establishment of coffee in East Africa was based on the large market in Europe, which was not adequately supplied by Latin American producers. World production has recently risen more rapidly than consumption, however, and it is difficult to dispose of the whole supply. The price of *robusta* coffee in 1963 was only one-third of that prevailing in 1953, and this fall has greatly discouraged planting. More significant, however, is the International Coffee Agreement, designed to control production, by which exports to 'traditional' markets are limited to annual quotas. This has kept prices from falling too low, but it has forced the East African governments to forbid new planting in most areas. In the absence of this restriction the planting of Kenya *arabica* at least would continue, for this is of such quality that it is still in good demand.

The distribution of coffee cultivation is indicated on Map 7. In Kenya every plot of coffee must be licensed and reliable data are available, but for Uganda all figures are estimates liable to considerable error, while in Tanzania no estimation of area is undertaken and guesses based on production figures have been made.

The Distribution of Robusta Coffee

Robusta cultivation is largely confined to the zone just north and west of Lake Victoria, lying mainly within Uganda. The greatest concentration is in the areas within 50 km. of Kampala and Masaka towns. Coffee occupies 25 per cent. of all culti-vated land in Buganda, and more than 85 per cent. of all farmers there grow the crop. Much of Buganda has a suitable physical environment, while near Lake Victoria physical conditions are excellent. Temperatures are generally between 20° and 26°C., and most places within 50 km. of the lake receive a reliable and well-distributed rainfall of 1,000 to 1,400 mm. Drought is rare, and the only climatic problem is the difficulty of drying the crop at some periods. The soils are deeper and more fertile than those over most of the East African plateau, so that, although little manure or fertiliser is applied, good yields are obtained.

Several social factors have favoured coffee growing in Buganda, including the tradition of cultivating the perennial banana, and therefore of maintaining land in continuous use. Many Baganda own land individually, and some own much more than they need for their food, and can easily spare part of it for coffee. They may then have more land in cultivation than they can work themselves, but migrants from Rwanda have provided labour. The earlier establishment of cotton growing had implanted a desire for cash, so that the response to high coffee prices in the late 1920s, and again in the early 1950s, was very rapid. Income from cotton supplied the farmers' basic needs until the coffee began to bear, and enabled them to pay their labourers. Government encouragement also contributed, though possibly less than Baganda interest and initiative.

Away from the lake both westwards and northwards physical conditions deteriorate, and the amount of land under coffee falls off sharply. Little is grown where rainfall drops below 1,000 mm., except in southern Masaka, where the soil is so retentive of moisture that 900 mm. is adequate. In general, soils also become poorer away from the lake, and in both Mengo and Masaka coffee has been pushed inland almost to its ecological limit.

Mubende forms a salient of coffee-growing country, but there more land is under cotton. Even where this tongue of land suitable for coffee widens again in Bunyoro and Toro the crop is far less important than in Mengo and Masaka. A more distinct dry season, poorer soils, sparser population, isolation and less attention from the Department of Agriculture have all contributed to this. The traditional agricultural system is not based on a perennial crop: few farmers can afford to employ labourers and most want a quick return if they are planting a cash crop. In Bunyoro coffee planting may have also been discouraged by the failure of several estates there during the Depression. Rather more coffee is grown in Ankole, where no alternative cash crop is well established, but most of the district is high enough for *arabica* which is now replacing *robusta*.

Until recently there was a sharp break in coffee cultivation at the Nile, although climate and soils do not change so sharply there, and although social conditions in Busoga are almost as favourable as in Buganda. Even now the area planted in Busoga is small. The failure of trials made in unsuitable parts of the district led to a belief that Busoga was not coffee country. In addition, the government feared overdependence on coffee, and therefore concentrated attention on cotton there. There was also a lack of popular interest until after marketing problems made it impossible to offer encouragement. Further east and north the dry season is too severe for coffee, while soils are also poorer than in Buganda. The crop has been tried in Bukedi, and also over the Kenya border, but without much success.

The main extension of the Buganda coffee zone is southwards across the Tanzania border. In an area extending 80 km. along the lakeshore, but only 20 km. inland, coffee is as important as in Masaka. It declines more sharply inland than to the south since mean annual rainfall drops from 2,000 mm. at Bukoba to 1,000 mm. only 15 km. to the west. Even within this narrow belt coffee is limited to the relatively small pockets of land with fertile soils, and little new planting was taking place even before marketing problems arose, since most of the suitable land has been taken up. As in Buganda, the banana is the staple food crop, and coffee growing spread rapidly in the 1920s when the government encouraged it. Remoteness has not seriously hindered production, for lake steamers move the crop from Bukoba to Kisumu. Little *robusta* coffee is grown elsewhere in Tanzania, as few areas have suitable climatic conditions.

The Distribution of Arabica Coffee

Map 7 shows that there is little overlap between *robusta* and *arabica* cultivation. The temperature requirements of *arabica* are satisfied only in country lying between 1,300 and 2,300 metres, for at lower levels the plant generally succumbs to rust disease. Whereas most areas with temperatures suitable for

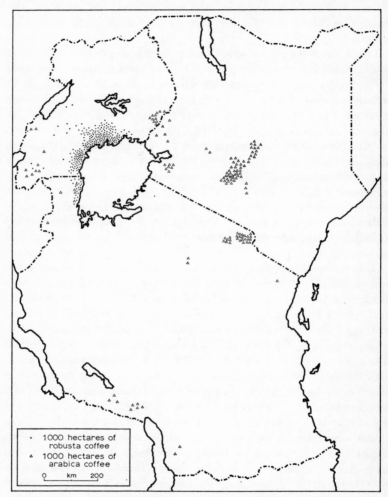

Figure 7. EAST AFRICA: Coffee Cultivation, 1969

robusta coffee have a rainfall too low for the crop, many of the higher areas suitable for *arabica* have sufficient rain, and cultivation of this variety is more widely dispersed. All three countries contribute to the East African *arabica* crop, production in 1969 amounting to 54,000 tons in Kenya, 40,000 tons in Tanzania and 15,000 tons in Uganda.

Kenya, the leading producer, has the largest area of land suitable for the crop. The relationship is not simple, however, for much of the production comes from country not very well suited to coffee, while other places with more satisfactory physical conditions grow little. The crop was originally confined to European farms, and these still account for 40 per cent. of the production: but the land most suitable for coffee is in areas of African settlement, where its cultivation has only recently been allowed to develop.

The importance of Kenya as a coffee producer reflects in part the existence of European settlers with the means to establish estates, who were given every encouragement to grow the crop.[1] They have been provided with good transport and marketing facilities, and have had an adequate supply of labour from neighbouring areas of dense settlement. The area planted rose to a peak of 40,000 hectares in 1936, and although it has since fallen yields have improved so much that estate production is now higher than ever before. Nevertheless, European settlement may have resulted in less coffee production in Kenya than might otherwise have been, through the hindering of African production. This was nowhere permitted before 1935, and as late as 1954 Africans were still forbidden to plant coffee in some districts and given little encouragement elsewhere. Following a rapid change in government policies the area planted on African farms rose from 2,000 hectares in 1953, to 50,000 in 1966: this surely suggests that far more would now be grown on peasant farms if official encouragement had been given earlier. Whatever its effects on total production, this aspect of government policy has certainly affected the distribution of coffee cultivation in Kenya.

One advantage of the delay in establishing coffee cultivation by peasant farmers is that they now benefit from fifty years of experience and research. They have first-class strains and practise such good husbandry that both yields and quality are generally higher than on the estates. Hulling by co-operatives under strict supervision also contributes to the high quality. The crop fetches a price 30 per cent. higher than that of *arabica* coffee from Tanzania and Uganda, and as yields average 1,500 kg. per hectare, compared with 400 kg. in those countries, the Kenya farmers are obtaining much higher incomes from this source. Unfortunately this development has come when exports are limited by quotas, and further planting has again had to be prohibited. Production, of course, continued to rise as young trees began to bear, until an outbreak of disease caused a

TABLE 4

COFFEE AND TEA CULTIVATION IN KENYA, 1962–69

	Thousand hectares		Thousand tons	
	1962	1969	1962	1969
COFFEE				
Large Farms	30	31	19	22
Small Farms	21	50	8	31
Total	51	81	27	53
TEA				
Large Farms	17	22	16	31
Small Farms	1	13	0·3	5
Total	18	35	16·3	36

The figures for area planted include much immature coffee and tea in most cases.

check in 1967, and small farms now provide more than half the Kenya crop (Table 4).

The greatest concentration of coffee growing in Kenya is just north of Nairobi, where there are numerous small estates, some owned by people working in the city, for whom coffee is a secondary source of income. Between Nairobi and Thika many larger estates are found on land with fertile volcanic soil, but with mean annual rainfall of only 750 mm., where producers have had either to accept low yields or to install costly irrigation equipment. This area took the lead in coffee growing fifty years ago, when accessibility to Nairobi was a major consideration, and when a railway was built from Nairobi to Thika through a zone of unoccupied land: and its present importance is clearly a legacy from the past.

Rainfall is greater in the higher African-settled country to the north-west, and coffee growing has now developed there. Kiambu, Murang'a and Nyeri Districts all have much land well suited to coffee, but population pressure is such that many farmers have no land to spare for the crop. Partly for this reason, more coffee is grown on small farms in Meru District, where 12,000 hectares have been planted on the slopes of Mount Kenya between 1,300 and 2,300 metres. The low price obtainable for maize in this relatively remote district also encourages cultivation of coffee, which can bear transport costs more easily. Throughout the zone from Meru to Nyeri the local distribution of the crop is affected by poor soils at high altitudes and inadequate rainfall on lower land as well as by temperatures.

Kisii, in western Kenya, was the first district in which African farmers grew coffee, but local interest seems weaker than in central Kenya, and production is small. Much less coffee is also grown on European farms west of the rift valley than on those to the east, only the Solai and Kitale areas being of any importance. A more seasonal rainfall regime and settlement after the main period of coffee planting are perhaps contributory factors.

Tanzania has much land suitable for *arabica* coffee in the southern highlands, and a little such land in the north, but only in the north have the opportunities been effectively exploited. The high, well-distributed rainfall and volcanic soils on the southern and eastern slopes of Mount Kilimanjaro are excellent for coffee, and some 50,000 Chagga farmers with about ½ hectare each there produce half the country's *arabica* crop. Traditional dependence on the banana assisted the adoption of coffee, and where land is scarce the two crops are often interplanted. Accessibility, vigorous government assistance and a strong co-operative movement have all favoured coffee cultivation, and it now occupies most of the land that can be spared from food crops. Peasant production also takes place in a similar, but smaller, zone around Mount Meru; and European estates around Arusha make an important contribution to the northern Tanzania crop.

The area suitable for *arabica* coffee in the southern highlands is far more extensive, but several factors are less favourable there. A dry season is much more marked than in the north, and only a little land has fertile volcanic soils, so that yields are generally very low. Most people in the southern highlands grow only annual crops, and few are interested in investing in a perennial cash crop. Only in Rungwe District are physical conditions and traditional agricultural practice comparable to those on Kilimanjaro. There coffee cultivation has been hindered mainly by isolation, resulting in a low level of both agricultural extension work and commercial activity. Even so, coffee is the chief source of cash income there, and also in Mbozi and Mbinga Districts.

The pattern of *arabica* coffee production in Uganda is remarkably similar to that in Tanzania. The main area of cultivation is on the slopes of Mount Elgon, in Bugisu and Sebei Districts, where the zone between 1,500 and 2,500 metres has rainfall of over 1,200 mm. spread over 10 months of the year. As on Kilimanjaro volcanic soils and dense population favour continuous use of the land, and the banana is the staple food crop, while Bugisu too benefits from accessibility to export routes. Government assisted the industry by providing free seedlings and establishing numerous markets and, as among the Chagga, a tradition of co-operative activity has been important. Mbale, the marketing and processing centre at the foot of Elgon, is very comparable to Moshi at the foot of Kilimanjaro. Here little land is available for an expansion of area, although there is ample scope for improvement in quality and, if the extra production can be sold, in yields.

Western Uganda, like the southern highlands of Tanzania, has more land on which *arabica* coffee would grow, but produces much less. Much unoccupied land in the west has adequate rainfall and fair, though not volcanic, soils: but this area suffered in the past as much as southern Tanzania from inaccessibility, from little commercial activity and from relative neglect by government. Attempts were made to establish coffee in the 1930s, but attack by the *antestia* bug brought failure. This problem has been overcome, and some *arabica* coffee is now grown in Toro, Ankole and Kigezi; but just as planting has begun to spread, marketing problems have prevented the government from giving encouragement.

It is clear that restrictions on coffee exports from East Africa have not only curbed expansion of production, but also led to freezing of its distribution when this was showing signs of considerable change. In this context the advantage of an early start for Buganda, Bugisu, Kilimanjaro and the Kenya estates is clear. In Brazil the distribution of production is changing despite the restrictions: and if East Africa cannot sell more coffee it would benefit if *robusta* production in Buganda were to fall and *arabica* production in central Kenya were to rise, as the latter brings a much higher income. But in the absence of a better source of income for farmers in Buganda such change is unlikely.[2]

COTTON

Cotton generally ranks second among East African exports, earning about £25 million a year. The leading producer is Uganda, where cotton occupies more land than any other crop. It is grown by almost two-thirds of the country's farmers, and was for many years the mainstay of the cash economy. Production is only a little smaller in Tanzania, where cotton cultivation has expanded rapidly since 1950; and only in Kenya is the crop of small importance.

Cotton is an annual plant with a growing season of five or six months, which bears numerous bolls containing seeds attatched to a soft lint. It is grown for the lint, but the seeds provide a useful by-product. In East Africa it is produced entirely on small farms, usually in plots of under $\frac{1}{2}$ hectare as a farmer and his family with no mechanical equipment and no hired labour can rarely handle more than this. Cotton is often the first crop on newly opened land, where food crops will be grown later. Preparing the land, planting and weeding are all laborious, but harvesting is even more so. Much cotton is damaged through lying too long in the field, and often some remains unpicked. This is one reason why yields are under 500 kg. of seed cotton per hectare, compared with over 1,000 kg. in Egypt. Another reason is the planting of much cotton too late to benefit fully from seasonal rainfall, because the farmers are preoccupied with food crops or just do not get round to it earlier.

The cotton is taken, normally as a headload or by cycle, to a buying centre, where the farmer sells it at a price fixed by the government. The lint and seed are separated in some 170 ginneries scattered through the cotton-growing areas. Asian firms long dominated the ginning industry, but many works are now owned by co-operative societies, which are handling an increasing share of the crop. Both lint and seed are bought by marketing boards which then supply the lint to exporting firms and the seed to the local oil milling industry. The world cotton market is not really one, but several, according to length of staple. Although it cannot match cotton from Egypt and Sudan, East African cotton is of fairly long staple, normally around 28 mm., and markets for it are found without difficulty, notably in Asian countries. The local textile industry absorbed only 7 per cent. of the 1964 lint production, but the figure is now well above 10 per cent.

East Africa accounts for only 1 per cent. of world cotton production and 3 per cent. of world exports: but within Africa only Egypt and Sudan are greater producers than either Uganda or Tanzania. The physical environment is suitable for cotton in many parts of the region, although nowhere ideal. Temperatures should average at least 18°C. throughout the growing season, and most districts below 1,300 metres satisfy this requirement. But the crop does best where they exceed 24° with days of unbroken sunshine for ripening, conditions which are not found where rainfall is adequate. At least 500 mm. is needed during the growing season, unless irrigation is to be used, and most agricultural areas of East Africa receive this, although the timing of the rainfall is often erratic. Cotton is in fact grown less because physical conditions are especially suitable for it than because over large areas they are not satisfactory for any more profitable cash crop.

Cotton is an appropriate crop for East African peasant farmers in that the savings resulting from large scale operation and from mechanization are small. Cotton suffers little from delays between picking and ginning, and its weight is not greatly reduced in processing. It can be incorporated into the agricultural system in most places without difficulty, sometimes providing an occupation for the men while the women take care of the food crops. The governments provided the original stimulus for cotton growing, and in some places strong pressure was applied through the local chiefs. The role of government continues, though now in the form of advice, financial assistance and controlled marketing. The policy of announcing a minimum price before the planting season, for example, may encourage production. The return for effort in growing cotton is poor when yields are so low, and only unpaid family labour for harvesting and sorting makes it really worthwhile: one reason for the importance of cotton in East Africa is undoubtedly the lack of other sources of income for many people.

The Distribution of Cotton Production

Uganda has always provided the largest share of East African cotton production, although its dominance was far greater thirty years ago than today (Table 5). Coffee and

TABLE 5

COTTON PRODUCTION IN EAST AFRICA, 1906–1970
Figures in thousand bales (185 kg.) of lint

	Uganda	of which				Tanzania		Kenya	
		Buganda	East	North	West		Lake Area		Nyanza & West
SEASON									
1905/6	1								
1915/6	22	6	14	2	—				
1925/6	180	58	93	25	4	22	9	2	1
1935/6	316	141	135	33	7	59	39	16	12
1945/6	227	127	72	20	8	41	35	5	4
1955/6	364	120	170	60	14	122	109	16	12
1965/6	420	58	215	126	21	369	342	20	12
1969/70	464	45	223	160	36	393	384	23	12

The data are drawn primarily from the annual reports of the Department of Agriculture of each country, Lake area of Tanzania includes the present Mara, Mwanza, Shinyanga, Tabora and West Lake Regions.

cotton together form the present mainstays of Uganda's commercial economy, but it was upon cotton that its development was based. The opening of the railway from the coast to Lake Victoria in 1902 and the existence of a market for cotton were both vital for its establishment in Uganda, and their coincidence in time was of particular significance. The administration was seeking a source of revenue just when Britain was seeking new sources of cotton. The considerable influence of the chiefs assisted the adoption of the crop, but there was also much popular interest in it.[3]

Cotton is far more widespread within Uganda than coffee, for physical conditions are suitable for it over most of the country. Its importance is greatest in the south-east, where it occupies over one-third of the cultivated land in Busoga and Bukedi in pure or mixed stands. The rainfall there is sufficiently high and well-distributed to permit cotton and a food crop to be grown on the same plot within a year, and soils are sufficiently fertile to require only a short resting period. The relatively dense population was enthusiastic from the start, and there has been vigorous government encouragement for sixty years. The area was accessible earlier than many other parts of Uganda, and by 1920 numerous ginneries provided outlets for the crop. The desire for cash is now strong, and for most people cotton is the only major source, so that some is planted on almost every farm. During the cotton picking season the whole atmosphere of this area is changed: there is more traffic on the roads, and the weekly turnover of many shops is five times higher than during the rest of the year.

Northwards, across Teso, Lango and Acholi Districts, the amount of land planted with cotton steadily declines, for physical conditions deteriorate and population becomes sparser. The rainfall is increasingly concentrated into a single wet season, and cotton must compete with food crops for land and especially for labour. Throughout these districts soils are poor, and more land is required for food crops than in the south. Ox-ploughing enables more land to be cultivated per head in Teso than elsewhere, often more than can be weeded or harvested properly so that yields are among the lowest in Uganda.

In the past inaccessibility led to inadequate marketing facilities and low prices to the growers in the north, but growers everywhere now receive a standard price, and this aspect of government policy has assisted an expansion of cotton cultivation in northern districts. West Nile District has shared in this recent expansion, for the low-lying east provides very suitable conditions for cotton. This remote district still suffers from the late development of the crop, and many men migrate to work in southern Uganda in preference to cultivating a cash crop, but cotton production there has risen fourfold since the early 1950s.

Buganda was the first part of Uganda to grow cotton, yet the crop is now less important there than in the east and north. Physical conditions are in some respects even more suitable, but they also favour coffee which brings a higher income and has largely replaced cotton. Some cotton is still grown even in the high rainfall zone near Lake Victoria, partly by immigrants unable to wait four years for a return from their labours: but it is now important mainly in the zone away from the lake that is marginal for coffee. Indeed, within Buganda there has been an 'expanding frontier', with coffee pushing cotton northwards into drier and more sparsely settled country. In Mubende cotton is still an important crop, but population there is so sparse that production is small. The greatest decline of cotton growing has been in Masaka where the zone between the wet lakeshore and the very dry country inland is narrow.

Cotton has never been of great importance in western Uganda. In Bunyoro the proportion of cultivated land under cotton, and the area planted per head, are as high as in the north; and production is small because of sparse population. Both rainfall and soil conditions there are very satisfactory, and Bunyoro is the district offering the best opportunities for future expansion. Much of Toro, Ankole and Kigezi is too cool for cotton, but the Bakonjo migrate seasonally from their mountain homes to grow the crop on the rift valley floor in Toro. Rainfall is low, but streams from the Ruwenzori are used for the only major attempt at irrigated production in Uganda.

In Tanzania cotton cultivation made slow progress until the 1950s, but between 1953 and 1963 production increased six-fold (Table 5). It has continued to rise since, though more slowly, and is now almost as great as in Uganda. Yet the crop is much less widely distributed in Tanzania, for 95 per cent. is grown in the area south and east of Lake Victoria. Climatic conditions there are very satisfactory, for the rainfall regime allows both cotton and a grain crop to be grown within the year, and there is a hot sunny period for ripening. The latter has prevented replacement of cotton by coffee, and other sources of income are few. Cattle occupy much of the land and the interest of the Wasukuma, and this might seem to be at the expense of cotton: but the desire to buy more cattle is in fact a major stimulus for cotton cultivation. A large and strong co-operative union, representing over 200,000 farmers, has assisted the expansion of cotton growing. Whereas most farmers showed little interest in cotton in the 1920s, when it was developing rapidly in Uganda, they now show more enthusiasm than anywhere else in East Africa.[4]

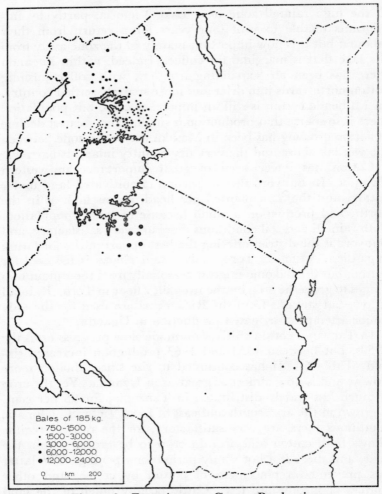

Figure 8. EAST AFRICA: Cotton Production

The circles represent the annual average cotton lint production of
ginneries in the late 1960s. Production rather than planting
figures have been used as these are liable to a much smaller margin
of error, and as little cotton moves very far before being ginned.

The oldest-established areas of production are in Mwanza,
Kwimba and Shinyanga Districts, but cotton is now grown
everywhere within 100 km. of the lake from Geita to the Kenya

border. A spread of settlement into formerly empty parts of Geita and Maswa Districts has assisted this extension of cotton cultivation. As plenty of land is available, many of these farmers have larger plots than is customary elsewhere. The government has encouraged this movement by such means as the provision of water supplies, in order to relieve overcrowding in Sukumaland. There is scope for further resettlement and for cotton growing further west in Biharamulo and to the south-west in Kahama District. Eastwards cotton cultivation is restricted much more by inadequate rainfall, for the Serengeti Plains in eastern Maswa and Musoma do not receive 500 mm. in any six-month period.

Several other parts of Tanzania appear to have physical conditions suitable for cotton. In the 1920s the main cotton growing areas lay near the coast, and a little is still grown there. Unfortunately the bollworm, favoured by high temperature and humidity there, is a serious problem. It wiped out cotton in the far south, and the crop has not been re-introduced as it might provide a bridge by which bollworm could spread from Mozambique to northern Tanzania. A uniform price to growers for the whole country eliminates the advantage of production near the ports: and alternative cash crops, and employment opportunities on sisal estates and elsewhere, have reduced the incentive to grow cotton in Tanga, Morogoro and Coast Regions.

Cotton production in Kenya fluctuates sharply, but never exceeds 25,000 bales. Nyanza and Western Provinces generally provide about three-quarters of the total, and Coast Province one quarter. In the west the main concentration is near the Uganda border, although some cotton is grown in the lakeshore areas of Siaya and South Nyanza. In Coast Province Malindi stands out, but a little is produced around Lamu, Kwale and Taveta.

Much of Kenya is either too dry or too cool for cotton, but far more could be planted in the present producing areas, and the 1966–70 Development Plan anticipated a ninefold expansion by 1970. Fearn attributes the small importance of cotton in Nyanza compared with that in Uganda to less government interest in peasant cash crops, the absence of influential chiefs, trials of the crop in unsuitable places, a weaker desire to acquire cash at first and subsequently greater opportunities for obtaining it in other ways.[5] The last is now probably the main consideration limiting cotton growing in Kenya as a whole. Price support policies result in maize bringing a much higher return per hectare than cotton, while even more may be earned by urban employment, much more of which is available in Kenya than in Uganda or Tanzania.

The Ginning Industry

Map 8 indicates the very dispersed nature of the ginning industry. Most ginneries are very small, but they are focal points in the economic life of many rural areas. Lint and seed can be handled more easily than seed cotton, which cannot be baled without damaging the lint; and this provides an incentive for local ginning. However, the excessive dispersal of the industry, especially in Uganda, is partly a legacy of historical conditions. The first Uganda ginneries were in Kampala, Entebbe and Jinja, but the industry soon spread up country, and 165 were in operation by 1925. Numerous ginning firms, competing for the crop, located works as close as possible to the source of supply to avoid being intercepted by others. Dispersal was also assisted by dependence on labour rather than costly plant. Many ginneries were set up for under £1,000, so that the financial risk was small; and the seasonal demand for labour has probably been met more easily at numerous locations within the well populated countryside than it would have been in the towns. There is now less competition, the advantages of larger units are greater, less labour is employed, and transport of seed cotton is easier, but the old distribution pattern remains. The number of ginneries in Uganda has fallen to 130, but many of these work only at half capacity.

The legacy of past conditions is shown particularly by the distribution of ginneries between regions, for there are three times as many in Buganda as in Northern Region, where production is now greater. Although the Buganda works are small, all operate far below capacity since the crop there has declined. Where cotton cultivation spread after the period of fierce competition, ginneries are fewer, larger, and working almost to capacity. The pattern of ginneries thus corresponds more closely to that of cotton cultivation 40 years ago than to that of today.

In the Lake Victoria zone of Tanzania, where the main development of cotton growing is quite recent, and where most processing is undertaken by co-operative societies, there are fewer ginneries, and most are kept busy throughout the season. In eastern Tanzania and in Kenya, however, there are many works suffering from high costs because of their small size and even smaller intake of cotton. All are over 30 years old, and many inefficient, but they cannot be modernized unless they are assured of more cotton to gin.

SISAL

Sisal was once the most valuable export of Tanzania and second only to coffee in Kenya. The sisal plant belongs to the genus *Agave*, and is grown for the fibre obtained from the leaves.[6] Almost all the crop is exported as baled fibre, used chiefly for the manufacture of rope and twine. Sisal competes in the same markets as henequen and abaca (manila), but is much more important than either, contributing 70 per cent. of the world supply of hard fibres. The plant was brought to East Africa from Mexico, yet Tanzania and Kenya together account for half the world production, and thus for one-third of the supply of all hard fibres. The only other important sisal producers are Brazil, Angola and Mozambique.

Commercial production in East Africa began in the early years of this century, and then expanded continuously, except during the First World War and the Depression. By 1950 production had reached 150,000 tons a year, and in 1964 it was 297,000 tons, worth almost £30 million. The area planted was then 350,000 hectares, of which 70 per cent. was in Tanzania and 30 per cent. in Kenya. Since 1965, however, competition from synthetic products has caused prices to slump; and although production had dropped only slightly by 1969, to 250,000 tons, the value of exports had fallen by then to only £12 million. Some further contraction is now anticipated, especially in Kenya which is much less dependent on the crop than Tanzania.

In contrast to coffee and cotton, sisal is grown almost entirely on large plantations. There were once over 250

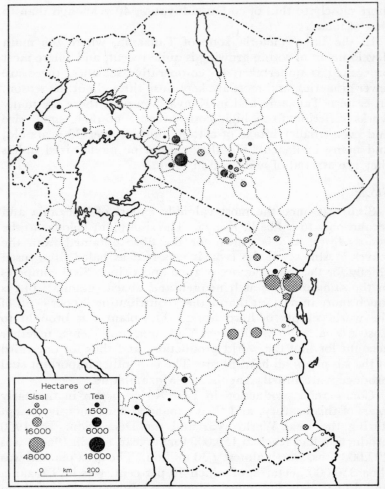

Figure 9. EAST AFRICA: Sisal and Tea Cultivation, 1969
The symbols represent planting in the administrative unit outlined,
but are placed over the most important areas of production.

estates, mostly between 2,000 and 4,000 hectares, owned either
by companies or by individuals of many nationalities; but the
slight contraction of the industry has involved the elimination
of many of the smaller estates, while in Tanzania the government has taken over a majority interest in most of the largest.

In some areas African farmers have planted sisal hedges, cutting when prices are high, but the crop is unsuited to peasant production. As the fibre represents only 4 per cent. of the weight of the leaf, processing must take place very near the point of production. 2,000 hectares of sisal is generally considered the minimum that can keep an efficient plant running at full capacity, and only if this area is under one management can a constant flow into the factory be assured. As sisal is a perennial, yielding for ten years with little attention, production costs are low: but the annual return per hectare is much lower than from most crops, and sisal is not worth while for farmers with only 2 or 3 hectares.

The dominance of East Africa in world sisal production is not easily explained, but certain favourable factors may be distinguished. Sisal was introduced just as European settlement was beginning and suitable crops were being sought. It needs high temperatures, but tolerates a wide range of rainfall and soil conditions and is well suited to the extensive areas of Tanzania and Kenya where low and unreliable rainfall and poor soils prevent the cultivation of other cash crops. In fact, sisal will grow where conditions are marginal for any cultivation and where the land was therefore unoccupied at the time of European settlement. Sisal production requires much unskilled labour, for no method of mechanizing the arduous task of harvesting has yet been found; but labour has easily been recruited, especially in Tanzania where other opportunities of earning cash are limited, and initially the very low cost of labour gave East Africa an advantage.

The distribution of sisal production is shown on Map 9, which suggests that accessibility to the coast has had a great effect on the broad pattern. Much is grown within 200 km. of the coast, and most of the remainder is produced near to a railway. Transport costs are more significant than for coffee or cotton since sisal is of lower value for a given weight, averaging £50 a ton compared with £250 for cotton. Unlike most peasant farmers, the sisal planter chooses among a wide range of locations and, as his profit margin is small but his production is large, there is a strong incentive to choose a site near the coast or near rail facilities.

The direct influence of the physical environment is smaller

than for most cash crops, for sisal could be grown in most parts of East Africa. It has, however, favoured the dominance of Tanzania rather than Kenya, for Tanzania has far more land which will support sisal but will not support other cash crops. Much of Kenya is too dry even for sisal, and parts are too cool, while over much of the remaining area climate and soils are suitable for more profitable crops.

Physical conditions have also affected the distribution of sisal cultivation within the parts of each country accessible to ocean ports. Over half the Tanzania estates are concentrated in Tanga Region, where sisal occupies extensive blocks of country beside the railway and road from Tanga to Korogwe. No other plantation crop is really suitable for the country around Korogwe, which lies below 300 metres and has only moderate rainfall and a very distinct dry season. Yet the abundant sunshine, high temperatures, and fairly fertile soils give very good yields of sisal. The combination of proximity to the coast and good local communications greatly assisted the early development of the industry there, and is still of great benefit to it. The exact location of estates, there as elsewhere, has been guided to a large extent by the availability of unoccupied land.

Rainfall decreases sharply further inland, but sisal estates extend far along the railway at the foot of the Usambara and Pare mountains, where numerous streams cross a zone of deep and well-drained soils before debouching onto the clay plains. Much water is required for processing the crop, and supplies are very satisfactory in this mountain-foot zone. There are other scattered estates in Kilimanjaro, and Arusha Districts, where the railway taps country marginal for coffee.

A further quarter of the Tanzania estates are clustered around the central railway line. There are few estates for the first 150 km. inland, in complete contrast to Tanga Region, partly because most land with fair soils and water supplies was already occupied. Most lie around Morogoro and Kilosa, where mountains rising sharply from the plateau offer many suitable sites. Westwards from Kilosa increasing transport costs discouraged the establishment of sisal estates. In the south a railway extended inland only for a short period after the main phase of sisal planting, and the crop is concentrated near the coast, and especially around Lindi Creek, which provided opportunities for cheap water transport. The isolation of the south from the main centres of commercial activity in Tanzania has certainly contributed to the small amount of sisal planting there.

In Kenya most of the land beside the railway within 500 km. of the coast is unsuitable for any form of agriculture, for it has a rainfall under 500 mm., and supports only poor scrub vegetation. Nevertheless nearly one-third of the sisal area in Kenya is in Coast Province. There are some estates on the coastal fringe north of Mombasa; but more land is under sisal around Voi, 150 km. inland, where the Taita hills give rise to slightly higher rainfall than in the surrounding country and also provide water supplies, but where Europeans found the land unoccupied.

A further third of the Kenya area is around Thika, where the soil is fertile but rainfall is inadequate for coffee. Some is on land originally planted with coffee which failed. Proximity to Nairobi and a local branch railway running through empty country between areas of Kikuyu and Masai settlement encouraged the choice of this area for plantations. Sisal is also grown in the dry country of the rift valley, especially around Rongai, but there is very little in the surrounding highlands, for sisal does less well there and other crops bring better returns.

The sharp fall in world prices in the late 1960s was particularly serious because local markets for sisal products are very limited. A little is used for the sacks in which other products such as coffee are exported, but jute is better for this purpose. As long as synthetics do not completely capture the market, there is clearly scope for exporting rope and twine rather than raw sisal, as happens with henequen in Mexico, and a start has now been made in this direction, exports of sisal products earning more than £1½ million in 1969. Meanwhile much effort is being put into seeking alternative uses for sisal, and in the mid-1970s a factory is to be built in Tanzania to use 30,000 tons a year for the manufacture of paper pulp, mainly for export.

TEA

Tea occupies much less land in East Africa than coffee, cotton and sisal, but cultivation is expanding more rapidly than that of any other crop. Production rose from 9,000 tons in 1950 to 32,000 tons in 1964 and 62,000 tons in 1969, and exports of tea are now worth over £17 million a year. East Africa provides only 5 per cent. of total world production, but it is the leading tea growing area outside Asia.

Tea is a perennial plant which yields after 4 years and should remain productive for over 50 years, so that all planting increases the total area. Cultivation is mainly on estates of 400 hectares or more, most owned by large British companies. The long-term nature of the crop, the costs of establishing it, specialised techniques of cultivation, and the need for processing within a short time of picking all favour plantation rather than peasant production. An efficient processing factory requires an annual intake of 1,000 tons, obtainable from 200 hectares, and should be supplied from the immediate vicinity as the green leaf is very easily damaged.

Tea cultivation has been extended to small farms, however (Table 4), and the crop is very popular since, in contrast to sisal, it brings a high income per hectare. It takes place under close supervision either around an estate or in a highly concentrated area with efficient movement of leaf to a central factory.

Only a small part of East Africa provides a suitable physical environment for tea. All areas under 1,000 metres are too hot, while the crop cannot stand the long dry season characteristic of much of the region. An annual rainfall of 1,300 mm. is adequate only if it is both reliable and well distributed. Tea will grow on many soils, but does best on those which are acid and which normally remain damp but never waterlogged. Not even all the physically suitable land is available, for much is either needed for food crops or scheduled as Forest Reserve.

Much more tea could be grown in East Africa, however, and the present small amount may be attributed partly to shortage of capital. About £½ million is needed to establish a 400-hectare estate, and current expansion is involving very heavy investment. It has been encouraged by the government's wish to diversify the economy in each country, and by favourable market prospects. One-eighth of the production is sold locally, and the remainder is exported, mainly to Britain. The International Tea Agreement hindered development in the 1930s but the market could now absorb greatly increased

East African production. Prices rose sharply around 1953 for tea as for coffee, but tea prices have suffered no serious subsequent fall.

Although the area of tea in East Africa is only one-eighth that of sisal, it is more widely distributed (Map 9). The crop occupies 36,000 hectares in Kenya, 15,000 in Uganda and 2,000 in Tanzania. Tea growing developed in Kenya mainly between 1925 and 1935, but renewed planting since 1950 has taken tea to second place among Kenya's exports. A combination of suitable physical conditions and a firmly established tradition of large-scale agriculture there has contributed to the dominance of Kenya. The industry has always received much government assistance, whereas in Tanzania and especially Uganda the attitude towards it was for many years somewhat ambivalent; and many British firms considered investment in Kenya less risky than investment in Tanzania and Uganda.[7]

Kericho District accounts for almost half the Kenya tea area, and as most was planted there long ago it provides well over half the production. Around Kericho town most of the land is under tea, presenting a very distinctive landscape. Standing at 2,200 metres Kericho is cool, yet never suffers frost, while the mean annual rainfall of 1,800 mm. is reliable and evenly spaced over the year. The soils are acid, and the rolling surface ensures good drainage. There was land available in this area, which formed a marchland between the Kipsigis and Kisii peoples, and labour has been recruited without difficulty from among the Luo of Nyanza Province. Kericho is only 30 km. from a railway and is linked to it by an excellent road. Indeed, almost all factors affecting tea production are as favourable in this area as anywhere in East Africa.

The second tea-growing area is in the Nandi hills, where physical conditions are similar to those around Kericho except that rainfall is about 400 mm. lower, and where much good land is unoccupied. Annual production is only 6,000 tons, however, compared with 16,000 tons around Kericho. The Sotik and Limuru areas each produce 2,000 tons a year. The former is an outlier of the Kericho area, but the latter lies across the rift valley, far to the east. Limuru receives only 1,300 mm. of rain a year and experiences a marked dry season: this was the first district to grow tea, and the estates there are a legacy

from the time when proximity to Nairobi was of grea
importance.

The development of tea cultivation on small farms ha
brought changes in the distribution of the crop on both loca
and national scales. There has been some dispersal in Keriche
and Nandi Districts, the former having over 2,000 hectare
under tea on peasant holdings by 1969, but many of these are
close to, and dependent on, the estates. Meanwhile tea ha
been established for the first time in Kisii District, and there
more than 2,000 hectares have been planted without any
estate nucleus.

Most land suitable for tea in central Kenya has dense
African settlement, and the crop has become important there
only since the government has begun to assist peasant tea
cultivation. The first planting was in Nyeri District where a
factory was opened in 1957. Six years later 3,000 farmers there
each had about ¼ hectare under tea. The crop has spread into
Murang'a and Kiambu Districts, mainly in the zone above
2,000 metres. Below this both climate and soils are more suited
to coffee. By 1969 almost 6,000 hectares had been planted on
17,000 small farms in Central Province: and although much o
this was still immature enough tea was plucked to enable the
many new factories to turn out 4,000 tons. The tea-growing
zone, like the rather lower coffee-growing zone, extends also
round the east of Mount Kenya into Embu and Meru Districts

Although plantation agriculture has not generally been
encouraged in Uganda, tea is the third export crop there. I
has been produced on European and Asian estates since the
1920s, but investment by the Uganda Development Corporation has contributed much to recent expansion. Until 1961
the whole production came from three groups of estates
two in Buganda and one in Toro, but it has since extended to
Ankole, Kigezi and Bunyoro Districts, and also to peasan
farms around the estates.

The first estates were established in Buganda, but temperatures there are rather high and rainfall only just adequate
In much of Toro the climate is cooler and wetter, and soils are
also more acid. The main factor favouring Buganda was
accessibility, for until 1930 transport costs discouraged planting
in the west. Improvement of the road to Toro then assisted

some development, but the district was still considered too remote by many European planters. Now that most planting is being undertaken by a public enterprise this factor no longer operates. Indeed, planting in the west rather than in Buganda fits the government policy of providing income for the poorer parts of the country.

Tea is of sufficient value to bear present transport costs from western Uganda without difficulty, and Bunyoro, Toro and Ankole Districts all have more suitable unoccupied land than Buganda. Kigezi has less empty land, and it is there that peasant production is developing most rapidly, although even there a small estate provides a nucleus.[8]

In Tanzania tea was a very minor crop until recently, but production trebled between 1954 and 1963, and is now little smaller than that in Uganda. The crop was first established in the Usambara mountains, in the north-east, and this is still a leading area of production. It is very accessible, and the land was previously unoccupied; but the amount of land sufficiently cool and wet for tea is very limited and, as in Uganda, a second area is of increasing importance. The southern highlands now have more land under tea, although much is immature. Most estates lie on the 2,000-metre plateau in Mufindi District or in the mountainous country around Tukuyu, but since 1957 tea has also been established in Njombe. Much of the southern highlands has soils and temperatures suitable for tea, and receives over 1,300 mm. of rain, but is unsatisfactory because of a 4-month dry season. Tukuyu, however, has a mean annual rainfall of over 2,500 mm., and the other producing areas have over 1,500 mm., with a shorter dry season. Although conditions are not ideal, there is more unoccupied potential tea land in southern Tanzania than anywhere else in East Africa. Inaccessibility probably discouraged investment there in the past, but tea is a suitable crop for the area in that it can bear high transport costs. In this area too some of the planting is taking place on small farms, and the lack of other cash crops increases the incentive for this. In Tanzania as a whole the area on small farms is to rise from 2,000 hectares in 1969 to 13,000 in 1974.

Tea offers one of the best prospects for agricultural development in East Africa, and especially for some of the poorer parts of the region. Production will certainly continue to expand as immature tea begins to yield, and much more is likely to be planted in all three countries

PYRETHRUM

Pyrethrum is a perennial herbaceous plant, with daisy-like flowers from which a substance useful in insecticide manufacture is obtained. The pyrethrins contained in the flower heads are toxic to many insects but not to man or animals, and therefore pyrethrum insecticides are particularly useful in food storage and for household sprays. They are less useful for plant sprays, since pyrethrins decompose quickly in the open air.

The demand for pyrethrum is at present small, and world production is less than 20,000 tons a year; but in East Africa, which provides well over half the total, the crop is of considerable importance. It was introduced in 1927 and developed very slowly, but since 1950 it has become the chief cash crop of several highland areas. It now ranks third among Kenya's export crops, bringing the country about £3 million a year, and exports from Tanzania are worth a further £1 million.

Production was once confined to European farms, but today over 80 per cent. of the crop comes from African farms. Pyrethrum is very popular among farmers with little land, for it normally brings £150 to £200 per hectare. It also gives quick returns, yielding less than a year after planting and continuing to flower for about four years. Production is strictly controlled to ensure that it does not outstrip the very limited demand. The market could easily be swamped, and the crop has been established on small farms by granting quotas to co-operative societies which re-allocate them among their members.

The flowers are dried on the farm or at a co-operative centre, and sold to the Pyrethrum Boards. At first most was exported as dried flower, but now there are three processing factories in Kenya and one in Tanzania, and concentrated extract is exported. This is of such small bulk that much is despatched by air. The United States takes about 35 per cent. and Britain about 25 per cent. but some is sent to over 50 countries.

Pyrethrum could be grown in many countries, but the only other important producers are Congo, Ecuador and Japan. The dominance of East Africa owes much to the Kenya and

Tanganyika Pyrethrum Boards, which assisted the farmers and publicised the product overseas. Physical conditions are more favourable in tropical highlands than in temperate countries mainly in that harvesting may continue all through the year. One advantage enjoyed by certain highland areas in East Africa is availability of labour, including unpaid family labour on peasant farms. Pyrethrum is more demanding on labour than on land, for the flowers should be gathered every two or three weeks, and no mechanical methods have been developed.

The distribution of the crop within East Africa is largely related to its physical requirements. It needs temperatures falling below 15°C. at times to stimulate flowering, and survives frost: it is therefore nowhere successful below 1,500 metres, and it does best above 2,000 metres. There is far more land over 2,000 metres in Kenya than elsewhere, and much of this has soils suitable for cultivation as well as ample rainfall. Within the Kenya highlands pyrethrum cultivation is spread very widely, for the licenses have been distributed as evenly as possible among potential growers.

In 1964 the crop was still more important in European than in African farming areas, but this has changed rapidly. The change has not always affected the location of production, for the leading area of production is still the Kinangop plateau, on which Europeans grew pyrethrum before resettlement took place. The other major areas of production on small farms are around Limuru and in the Kisii highlands. Pyrethrum is now grown on large farms mainly around Molo, Meroroni, Ol Joro Orok and Kipkabus, all among the highest cultivated areas where the choice of crops is limited.

In Tanzania a little pyrethrum has been grown in both the north and southern highlands for some years, but the crop has expanded rapidly since 1959 mainly in the latter area. The slopes of Mount Kilimanjaro and Mount Meru, above the coffee zone, are very suitable, but little more land is available there unless the Forest Reserve is reduced. The southern highlands have both spare land and many peasant farmers with no cash crop. In the Mporotos government encouragement around 1959 brought a rapid response, and pyrethrum is also grown around Njombe and in the Kipengere mountains.

Pyrethrum extract is produced at factories in Nairobi,

H

Nakuru and Arusha. The Nairobi plant was set up in 1945 to process pyrethrum which was being sent to Britain while shipping was scarce and then sent on as extract to the Far East. Since Kenya benefits substantially from local processing the Pyrethrum Board established another factory in the centre of the producing area. The private firm operating the Nairobi plant decided to handle the Tanzania crop locally, choosing a site close to the nearer, but not larger, of the two producing areas there.

Pyrethrum provides a very useful source of income for East Africa, but markets govern the size of the industry. These could be lost entirely if synthetic pyrethrum now produced in Japan were improved, but more probably they will expand as the use of insecticide increases, permitting further development of the crop in East Africa.

CASHEW NUTS

Cashew nuts provide the chief source of income in some coastal areas, notably in southern Tanzania. Production was very small until about 1947, but it has since risen steadily to 120,000 tons a year, and exports now bring £7 million a year to Tanzania and £1 million to Kenya. World production is small, and although it is dominated by India, the only other country that rivals Tanzania is Mozambique.

The cashew tree is indigenous to Brazil but has been grown in East Africa for several hundred years, having been brought by the Portuguese. It bears in the third year after planting. and yields for twenty years even with little attention. Harvesting is easy, for the nuts are collected from the ground, often by the children, after they have fallen. The tree is very resistant to drought, and will grow where annual rainfall is only 600 mm., although higher rainfall brings greater yields; and it can be grown in very poor soils where few other crops thrive. It does, however, require high temperatures, and this confines it to the coastal lowlands. The main disadvantage of the crop is a low return per hectare, but land is not generally scarce near the East African coast.

Cashew nuts are produced almost entirely by peasant farmers, and most are shipped unshelled to India. That country will always take the East African crop, but prices fluctuate greatly

according to the local supply there, and this may have discouraged higher production. There is a firmer market for
shelled nuts, especially in the United States, and local shelling
would greatly increase the value of the crop; but the first
shelling factories to be established were not very successful.
The process cannot easily be mechanised, and the corrosive
properties of the shell demand skilled labour. A great expansion
of local processing is now planned, however, in Ujamaa villages
in the case of Tanzania.

Mtwara Region of Tanzania produces two-thirds of the total
East African crop, and the remainder is evenly divided between
the rest of the Tanzania coastlands and those of Kenya. The
concentration of cashew cultivation in the far south is related
both to the proximity of Mozambique, whence it has spread,
and to the presence there of a fairly dense population with no
other well-established cash crop. The Department of Agriculture has encouraged cashew planting more strongly there
than elsewhere, and people with few alternative sources of
income have responded. Newala is the leading area of production, but Lindi, Mtwara and Masasi Districts all make substantial contributions. Although the Southern Province
Railway had no effect on the distribution of the crop, local
accessibility is important. Distance from a major port,
inadequate roads, and lack of traders all hinder production
north of Lindi. Lower temperatures where the land rises,
sparse population and lack of marketing facilities combine to
limit the extension of cashew cultivation inland.

Further north the population is generally concentrated into
a narrower zone by the sea, where the more profitable coconut
can be grown. Around Dar es Salaam, and in Coast Province of
Kenya cashew nuts are grown on numerous small farms, but
they are usually subsidiary to some other source of income.
Cashew nuts are most suitable for the zone between the well-
watered and relatively prosperous coastal fringe and the
sparsely settled country inland: and this zone is much narrower
in Kenya and in Tanga Region than in southern Tanzania.

CLOVES

Cloves are another very minor item in world trade which is
nevertheless important to East Africa. The region accounts for

half the total world production and over two-thirds of all exports, although the entire crop comes from Zanzibar and Pemba. These islands are very heavily dependent on cloves, which contribute over two-thirds of their combined exports. They normally earn between £2 million and £3½ million a year, but prices fluctuate sharply and in 1969 cloves brought in £7½ million.

The cloves of commerce are the dried unopened buds of a tree, of which there are probably about 4 million on Zanzibar and Pemba islands. Most are grown in pure stands, but some are interplanted with coconuts on small farms. Yields fluctuate greatly, partly in response to the weather, and annual production varies between 5,000 and 20,000 tons. The whole crop is exported, though a little is first processed into oil, and large stocks must be maintained to ensure supplies. The main customer is Indonesia, where the cloves are used for a type of cigarette, and most of the remainder is sold to India and through Singapore.

The importance of Zanzibar and Pemba in world clove production is largely a matter of historical accident. The tree is indigenous to the Moluccas, and was probably brought to Zanzibar via Mauritius in 1818. Its cultivation was strongly encouraged by the Sultan, and it was very readily adopted by immigrant Omani Arabs, who required a source of cash even at that date. The crop is particularly suitable for these small, densely populated islands as it is far more demanding on labour than on land. Until 1897 the plantations relied on slave labour: today a seasonal flow of labourers from the mainland supplements the local supply. The long trading tradition of Zanzibar has helped it to sell its cloves, especially to the Orient.

The physical requirements of the clove tree prevent its extension to the mainland, for it needs constant high temperatures and rainfall of at least 1,500 mm. The rainfall is only just adequate on Zanzibar island, and in fact about 80 per cent. of the 30,000 hectares under cloves are on Pemba island, which receives 500 mm. more rain and has more land with fertile soils. The area on Zanzibar was higher before a hurricane hit the island in 1872, destroying most of the trees. The crop is there confined to the area with deep soils in the west, whereas it is grown in all parts of Pemba except the extreme east and north-west, where the soils are too thin and infertile. Despite the concentration of production on Pemba island, all the cloves pass through Zanzibar town on account of its dominant position in the trade of both islands and its port.

Until 1963 the clove industry appeared remarkably static and because of its importance to Zanzibar and Pemba this led to a stagnant economy. It was also a weak economy in view of both its dependence on one crop and the limited world demand for that crop. Cloves provided not only most of the islands' exports, but also over one-third of government revenue; and in contrast to the rest of East Africa, much of the export earnings were used to buy food. The union of Zanzibar with Tanganyika has reduced the problem, though it has not solved it. Political revolution in 1964 brought perhaps more significant changes. The Arabs, who owned the majority of the plantations, have been dispossessed, and ownership of the clove trees has been spread much more widely among the population. It is not yet possible to assess the effect of this upon production.

WATTLE

The bark of the wattle tree is the chief source of tannin, widely used in leather production. As with cashew nuts there is only one major producer and a few minor ones, among which Kenya and Tanzania are prominent. South Africa provides most of the world's supply, but East Africa produces 80,000 tons of bark annually. Exports of concentrated extract bring £1 million a year to Kenya and £½ million to Tanzania, having remained almost static throughout the 1960s.

The wattle tree is indigenous to Australia, which was the chief producer until labour costs there became prohibitive. It does well in the cool East African highlands, and much was planted in African-settled areas in the 1940s, and on European farms during the following decade. The tree grows very quickly, and is cut down after about 8 years, the bark being stripped off and the wood commonly used for fuel. The local demand for tannin is very small, and most of the wattle bark is exported as a concentrated extract. India and Pakistan are now the chief customers, but boycotts of South Africa and the approaching exhaustion of South American quebracho, the main competitor with wattle, may provide wider markets in future. On the other hand a synthetic substitute may be developed, while the leather industry itself is threatened by alternative products.

Temperature requirements confine wattle to land above 1,700 metres in East Africa. There is more of such land in Kenya than elsewhere, and it is there that wattle planting has received most official encouragement. It was formerly considered the most suitable cash crop for the Kikuyu areas, and was the only one allowed there. It was popular even in overcrowded areas partly because much-needed fuel is a by-product. The area on small farms has fallen as a result of the Emergency, the consolidation of holdings and the development of coffee growing, but over 40,000 hectares are still under wattle. Two-thirds is found below the Aberdare Forest in Kiambu District but there is also some in Nyeri and Murang'a and in the Kisii highlands, often on steeply sloping land unsuitable for other crops. On large farms in Kenya wattle occupies 18,000 hectares, of which 85 per cent. is on the Uasin Gishu plateau. Temperatures there are ideal, while the range of possible crops is limited by a rainfall that is unusually low for such altitudes. Wattle is grown there mainly by large companies rather than by individual farmers.

The smaller Tanzania production is largely in the hands of one company, which planted 13,000 hectares between 1950 and 1955 near Njombe in the southern highlands. Land was available there for estate development which is too high and too remote for sisal, but which suffers a dry season too severe for tea or coffee. The rest of the Tanzania production comes from small patches, mainly on peasant farms, in parts of the Usambara mountains which receive under 1,000 mm. of rain a year, and are unsuitable for crops such as tea.

The only part of Uganda with physical conditions suitable for wattle is Kigezi, where some used to be grown. But in such a remote and overcrowded district wattle cultivation is only worth while if prices are exceptionally high.

CASTOR SEED

Castor trees grow wild in many parts of East Africa, and oil from their seeds has long been used for oiling the skin. Today castor seeds provide a useful export, for their oil is in demand for the manufacture of lubricants, paint, linoleum and cosmetics. The trees are still usually semi-wild, preserved rather than planted, and not cared for. Castor grown as a crop in large stands suffers greatly from pests, and is rarely a success. Castor is of particular value because it thrives where no other cash crop does, requiring only 500 to 600 mm. of rain a year and growing in almost any soil. In places marginal for cultivation trees are carefully preserved, and sometimes even planted around plots of millet or cassava.

Production fluctuates greatly according to market prices and the income obtained from other crops. In some years seeds are collected from as many trees as possible, while in other years little interest is shown. Exports from East Africa in recent years have averaged about 20,000 tons, worth £¾ million, and a little is also used in the local paint industry.

Tanzania generally provides about 70 per cent. of the production, Kenya 20 per cent. and Uganda 10 per cent. This distribution clearly reflects physical conditions in the agricultural areas of each country. In much of central Tanzania rainfall is so low and soils are so poor that farmers can obtain cash only by selling castor seed, cattle or any surplus of food crops. Dodoma Region, most of which has a rainfall of under 600 mm. is the main area of production, but many districts make some contribution. Most farmers in Kenya and Uganda live in a more favourable environment, but in Kitui District of Kenya agricultural settlement extends into country receiving little over 500 mm. of rain a year, and castor seed is important there.

OTHER EXPORT CROPS

Many crops are grown in East Africa for export on a smaller scale than those discussed above. Pineapples bring £½ million a year to farmers in Kenya, and exports of tinned pineapples are worth almost £1 million a year. Sunflower, chillies and kapok are among the other minor crops which there is not space to examine here.

REFERENCES

1 M. F. Hill, *Planters Progress*, Coffee Board of Kenya, Nairobi, 1956, is an account of the development of coffee in Kenya.
2 Valuable studies of coffee in Kenya, Tanzania and Uganda are provided in J. W. F. Rowe, *The World's Coffee*, H.M.S.O., London, 1963.

3 C. C. Wrigley, *Crops and Wealth in Uganda*, E.A.I.S.R., Kampala, 1959, Ch. 2.
4 J. C. De Wilde, *Experiences with Agricultural Development in Tropical Africa*, Volume II, Johns Hopkins Press, Baltimore, 1967, Ch. 6; and D. Von Rotenhan, 'Cotton Farming in Sukumaland', in H. Ruthenberg (ed.), *Smallholder Farming and Smallholder Development in Tanzania*, Weltforum Verlag, Munchen, 1968.
5 H. Fearn, *An African Economy*, Oxford U.P., London, 1961, pp. 67–78.
6 A full account of the sisal plant and its cultivation is available in G. W. Lock, *Sisal*, Longmans, London, 1969. C. W. Guillebaud, *An Economic Survey of the Sisal Industry of Tanganyika*, Nisbet, Welwyn, 1966, is a useful study, although it contains almost nothing geographical.
7 M. W. McWilliam, 'The Kenya Tea Industry', *East African Economics Review*, Vol. 6, No. 1, 1959, pp. 32–48, is very useful.
8 An exhaustive study is Commonwealth Development Corporation, *Uganda Tea Survey*, London, 1964.

CHAPTER 6

Livestock

Livestock are very important to the people of East Africa, and there are some 20 million cattle and 24 million sheep and goats in the region.[1] Their significance is partly social rather than economic, and animals are often kept primarily as a symbol of wealth and prestige, and for the payment of bride-price. Nevertheless they provide meat and milk within the subsistence economy, and now also contribute increasingly to cash incomes. They are much more important than in the Congolands or West Africa: the ratio of 75 cattle per 100 people in East Africa compares with 18 in Nigeria and 7 in Congo.

The cattle are mainly of the Zebu type, thought to be of Asiatic origin and brought to Africa by the Arabs about 1,000 years ago. There are also some Sanga cattle, probably of Ethiopian origin, while others are a cross between the two. In addition some breeds have been brought from Europe during this century, and in certain areas these exotics thrive with good husbandry. The only other important animals are sheep and goats, of which goats are the more numerous and the more widespread, forming an element in rural life almost everywhere. Most of the sheep differ little in appearance from the goats, and both are often kept together: but exotic woolled sheep are a distinctive feature of certain areas. Pigs are of small importance, but poultry is widespread and some hens are to be seen around most homes.

In some ways livestock epitomise the variety so characteristic of East Africa. There are herds and flocks which form the basis of life for nomadic pastoralists; stock kept as an adjunct to peasant agriculture; large ranches; and small herds of dairy cattle. In some areas animals are regarded largely as a social asset: elsewhere they are kept entirely for commercial motives.

And in parts of the region there are few livestock at all, even where the land is well settled.

In much of East Africa the importance of livestock reflects limited opportunities for cultivation. As the 1953–55 Royal Commission stressed,[2] the rainfall over at least one-third of the region is too low and too unreliable to permit any alternative to a pastoral economy. Over half of Kenya falls into this category, while both Tanzania and Uganda have some land of this nature. Further extensive tracts, especially in Tanzania, are marginal for cultivation and much more suited to pastoralism. However the density of stock in the dry areas is low, for conditions are not very satisfactory even for grazing, and far more animals are kept in the better-endowed country where cultivation does take place. Indeed, the majority are owned by cultivators rather than pastoralists, although the combination of activities does not constitute true 'mixed farming' since the animals are rarely integrated into the farming system.

Thus, although much of East Africa is physically suited only to livestock rearing, the importance of this activity is not related to physical conditions to the same extent as in Chad or Mali. It is related more to social attitudes,[3] especially among tribes which have a pastoral tradition but which now depend mainly upon cultivation. Where cattle are sought as a measure of wealth, and even a medium of exchange, numbers are all-important and matter much more than quality. In addition however, meat and milk are appreciated throughout the region, and as local self-sufficiency is the general rule, most people want their own stock to provide these. Animals demand little effort from the farmer, provided that he is satisfied with poor yields, and there is normally sufficient spare land for grazing.

CATTLE

High-density Areas

Cattle are fairly evenly distributed between the countries of East Africa, but Map 10 shows sharp contrasts in density within each country. The heaviest concentrations are in Nyanza Province of Kenya, Eastern Region of Uganda and Mwanza Region of Tanzania. In Nyanza there are about 100 cattle per square km., and in Kisii District the density exceeds

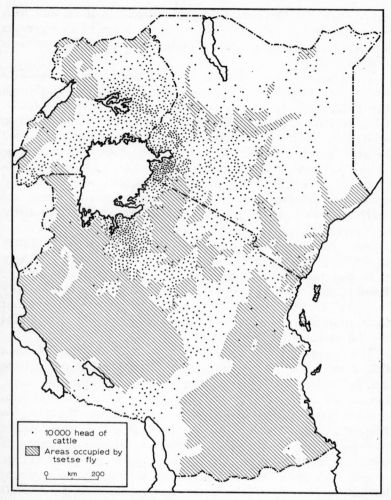

Figure 10. EAST AFRICA: Distribution of Cattle, and Areas occupied by Tsetse Fly.

120. There is an average of five or six head per holding, although most animals are grazed communally rather than on the farm. They are rarely used for ploughing, and few are exported from the region, for even more than elsewhere the motive for keeping cattle is social rather than economic. Nevertheless

they provide the farmers with some meat and milk, and with some cash from local sales. The dense cattle population permits a higher level of meat consumption in Nyanza than in most parts of East Africa.

The importance of cattle in Nyanza would seem related to the pastoral traditions of the Luo and Kipsigis people, although the Kisii, with no such tradition, keep just as many cattle. Climate and soil permit a higher density than in most of Kenya, while land pressure is less severe than in some other favoured areas, notably in Central Province, where little land can be spared for grazing. In Nandi District, where a pastoral people have only recently taken to cultivation, but where physical conditions are excellent, cattle are even more important and most farmers have large herds. The average holding there occupies 6 hectares, of which 5 hectares are under grass.

Some cattle are kept throughout the densely settled country of the highlands even though grazing is scarce, and it is there that the most encouraging development is taking place. Exotic cattle have been introduced on peasant farms, notably in Nyeri District, where by concentrating on quality rather than quantity farmers have begun to obtain a substantial regular income from milk sales.

The zone with a dense cattle population extends from Nyanza into eastern Uganda, where there are 60 cattle per square km. in Teso District. Cultivation is the main occupation there, but cattle contribute to the subsistence economy and also provide cash income since many are sold for shipment to Buganda. Most farmers also use their cattle for ploughing, in contrast to those elsewhere. The importance of cattle is related to a strong pastoral tradition among the Iteso. These people have good reason to retain an attachment to animals, for soils in Teso are as poor as any in Uganda while the rainfall permits only a small range of crops. The government has also given special attention to cattle in Teso, which has twice as many Veterinary Assistants as any other district.

Cattle are important in the neighbouring agricultural areas of Lango and Bukedi, both of which have a small surplus; and although they are imported regularly into Busoga and Buganda, this mainly reflects a relatively high meat consumption there, for these areas also have considerable numbers. There is a further concentration in western Ankole, and this is another minor exporting area.[4]

In Tanzania, Sukumaland, between Mwanza and Shinyanga, has the greatest concentration of cattle: in Maswa and Shinyanga Districts alone there are almost 3 million, or over 100 per sq. km. Strangely enough the Wasukuma have no long pastoral tradition, but they have taken to cattle-keeping enthusiastically and their land is now severely overstocked. Dry conditions limit the range of alternative activities there, and favour rapid increase of stock by keeping the area free of many diseases. Regular sales are small, for cattle are regarded as security against drought, when they can be either sold or eaten, and except in times of drought numbers rise steadily. The local distribution of cattle closely matches that of population, and is discussed by Malcolm.[5]

The zone in which cattle are very numerous extends southeastwards across Singida and Dodoma Regions. There population is sparser and the poor land will support fewer animals; but their importance in the economy is greater than in Sukumaland, for they provide the chief source of cash. As no cash crop will grow well, the farmers must sell some cattle, albeit reluctantly.

The Pastoralist Areas

Map 11, showing the ratio of cattle to population, indicates a very different pattern from Map 10, and reflects more closely the importance of cattle in the local economy. This is greatest in the semi-arid zone extending from central Tanzania, through Masai country, east and north of Mount Kenya, and into northeast Uganda. The climate there is unsuitable for cultivation, but the vegetation provides grazing for livestock, though not for the high densities found in Nyanza or Sukumaland.

The importance of cattle in this zone is related to the character of the people as well as the land, for most are members of pastoral Nilo-Hamitic tribes. Many despise cultivation, and even where it would be practicable little is undertaken. Just as most cultivators keep some livestock, so most pastoral groups till some land; but for the Masai, the Galla, the Turkana and the Karamojong livestock provide most of the diet and the only source of cash.

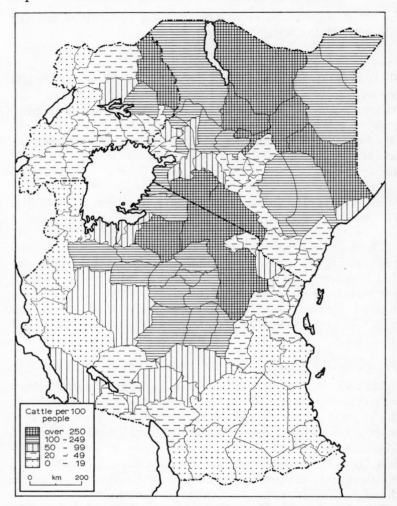

Figure 11. EAST AFRICA: Numbers of Cattle per head of Population

This map, indicating the importance of cattle in the local economy, presents a quite different picture to that in Map 10.

Rainfall in this zone varies from 800 mm. in parts of Karamoja to 150 mm. near Lake Rudolf, and there is a corresponding range of vegetation from acacia savanna to semi-desert scrub.

This greatly affects the carrying capacity of the land, which is very low in northern Kenya. There cattle are restricted to land near mountains or seasonal streams, whereas in Karamoja herds roam over wide stretches of country for much of the year. Parts of Masai country have little rain, yet have a true grassland vegetation which supports 15 cattle per head of the population, compared with less than 5 where the vegetation is thicket and scrub. Masailand benefits from a better spread of rain over the year than elsewhere, for the carrying capacity of grazing land is always governed by dry-season conditions. Everywhere the seasonal regime demands periodic movement, and some nomadism is found; but transhumance is more common, as in Karamoja where stock are driven westwards as grazing deteriorates. [6]

There are marked variations in the degree of dependence upon cattle. The Masai and the Turkana both concern themselves almost exclusively with livestock; but whereas these are mainly cattle in Masai country, goats and sheep are equally important to the Turkana. The life of the Jie and Kara-mojong is dominated by cattle, but they also practise some cultivation, and sorghum porridge forms part of their diet. While most Suk shun cultivation, they often buy grain to vary their diet; but livestock provide the whole food supply of many Turkana, milk being of particular importance. Meat cannot be a staple food since the herds would quickly be reduced if it were, but blood is drawn from the animals instead.

The extent to which cattle are exploited commercially also differs between tribes. Some cash is needed everywhere, and therefore some sales take place, but the extent of marketing varies according to the attention that governments have given to each area. Sales are probably best developed in Karamoja, where cash income per head is higher than in agricultural Kigezi. In Kenya far more sales take place in accessible districts, such as Samburu, than in remote areas near the Ethiopia and Somalia borders.

Cattle on Large Farms

The large farm areas do not have a high density of cattle, and account for a very small proportion of the total number in

East Africa. They merit special attention, however, in view of the distinctive nature and high productivity of stock rearing there. The number of cattle on the large farms in Kenya reached a peak of 980,000 in 1960, fell steadily to 710,000 in 1965, and recovered slightly to 770,000 by 1968. Most of these animals are exotics or an exotic/local cross, and a clear distinction can be made between the 60 per cent. which are beef cattle and the 40 per cent. which are dairy cattle. Both types are widely distributed over the mixed farms of Trans-Nzoia, Uasin Gishu and Nakuru Districts, but beef cattle are also kept on large ranches in Laikipia District, which is both drier and less accessible than most parts of the highlands.

In neither Tanzania nor Uganda are physical conditions as suitable as in Kenya for high-grade stock, but opportunities for large-scale cattle rearing exist in both countries. There are 90,000 cattle on large farms in Tanzania, mainly beef animals kept on National Agricultural and Food Corporation ranches in the east and centre. The area of ranchland was increased in the late 1960s, when falling sisal prices led some estates to turn much of their land over to beef cattle; and during the 1970s the government aims to increase productivity in some of the pastoral areas by bringing many cattle owners together in ranching associations. In Uganda ranching has begun as the method of using the grazing potential of areas reclaimed from the tsetse fly, first in Bunyoro and later in Ankole, and is now to be extended to other areas such as Acholi. There, too, both government-owned ranches and co-operative associations are represented.

Areas with Few Cattle

Areas where cattle are largely absent vary greatly in character, from the forests of western Uganda to the arid wastes of the Kenya-Somalia border. Yet, apart from the zone where water supply is too limited, all extensive tracts with no cattle have one feature in common, namely infestation by tstese fly. Map 10 illustrates the close correlation between the distribution of cattle and that of tsetse flies, which have kept cattle out of large stretches of country by spreading the disease trypanosomiasis. Other diseases take heavier annual toll on cattle, but none has a comparable influence on their distribution.[7]

GOATS AND SHEEP

Goats and sheep are commonly regarded as an economic asset to a greater extent than cattle, and the annual take-off is much higher. They therefore make a large contribution to East African meat supplies, although generally within the subsistence economy, Milking is not common, but is now spreading in some areas such as Kikuyu country. These animals are certainly as important in East Africa as anywhere else in Africa even including such countries as Ethiopia and Chad.

The largest number of goats and sheep found is in Kenya, where there are between 6 and 7 million of each. They are very widely distributed, and are important to both cultivators and pastoralists. Sheep are particularly numerous in high districts such as Kericho and Elgeyo, where there are about 10 per holding, but they are also interspersed among the goats elsewhere. Goats are of great value in northern Kenya, where the grazing is often too poor for cattle, for they will browse off the scrubby bushes which are much more abundant than grass. There are probably 800,000 small stock, 10 per head of the population, kept on a truly nomadic basis in the Turkana area, west of Lake Rudolf.

About 450,000 Merino and Corriedale sheep are kept on the large farms in the highlands, primarily for their wool. They are more localized than cattle kept on such farms, for two-thirds are concentrated in cool country above 2,000 metres in the Molo, Naivasha and Nanyuki districts. They do very well there, and probably bring their owners more cash income than the remaining 13 million sheep and goats in the country.

Small stock are widely distributed in northern and central Tanzania, but there are very few in the east and south. Goats are sometimes found where cattle are absent, as they are affected rather less by tsetse fly, but in outline the pattern is similar to that of cattle. Most groups which keep cattle have a comparable number of goats and sheep, upon which they largely depend for meat. The distribution matches that of population more closely than does the distribution of cattle, for whereas many farmers own no cattle, most manage to keep one or two goats.

I

This applies also to Uganda, where the heaviest concentration of goats and sheep is in densely-populated Kigezi and western Ankole where land for grazing is very limited and many people cannot afford cattle. In Uganda too they have a rather more widespread distribution than cattle because of their ability to survive in areas lightly occupied by tsetse fly. Thus they are found in parts of Toro and Bunyoro where cattle are absent, but where there is a substantial agricultural population.

OTHER LIVESTOCK

In parts of northern Kenya cattle are replaced by camels which survive the arid conditions far better, and which can browse off the scrub vegetation. No census of camels has ever been taken, but Gulliver estimated that there were 80,000 in Turkana country in 1950. Their position in the economy is similar to that of cattle, for they provide milk, blood, hides and occasionally meat. They are milked several times a day, and give a higher yield than most East African cattle.

Donkeys are also found in northern Kenya, and some are kept by the Masai and by agricultural tribes in Tanzania and Kenya. They are rarely regarded as a source of meat, but are reared mainly for carrying loads. There is scope for their use in this way by far more people in East Africa, but the animal is unfamiliar to most tribes. By the time that outsiders could encourage their use, the bicycle had become the beast of burden in most parts of the region.

Pigs are more widespread than either camels or donkeys, but the total number kept is even smaller, amounting to only 100,000 compared with $3\frac{1}{2}$ million in all tropical Africa. In 1958 there were 70,000 on European farms in Kenya, but by 1964 the number had fallen by half, mainly through displacement of farmers from the Kinangop plateau which had been the leading area of pig rearing. Some are kept by African farmers notably in Nyeri District, but they are not found very profitable. Tanzania and Uganda each have about 20,000 pigs, in the former case widely scattered, in the latter heavily concentrated in Buganda.

Poultry are more important than pigs, and chickens contribute to local meat supplies in most agricultural areas. The egg yield is very low, but even this is not fully exploited, for many tribes show little interest in eggs as food. There is, however, a small commercial market for eggs, which is supplied mainly by a few specialist producers in each country. There is scope for increased sales of eggs and chickens for meat, although marketing problems are very great, but there is also a case for expanding this sector of subsistence activity. 'Why is there a single family in our rural areas which does not keep decent chickens?', asks President Nyerere in an introduction to the Tanzania 1969–74 Development Plan.[8]

MEAT

Most meat produced in East Africa is consumed either by the owner of the animal concerned or by his neighbours. Little information is available on meat production within the subsistence economy, or on sales to local butchers; but hide and skin sales suggest that 2 million cattle and 6 million goats and sheep are slaughtered annually in rural areas. Meat consumption is low everywhere, but there are sharp differences between Nyanza or Sukumaland where livestock are abundant, and eastern or southern Tanzania where meat is extremely scarce.

Contrasts within East Africa in the availability of meat give rise to an important trade in slaughter stock in certain areas. One of the largest regular movements is that from Teso to Busoga and Buganda, which normally involves 60,000 cattle and 20,000 goats each year. Most of these are railed from Soroti, but northern Buganda and Busoga are supplied by boat across Lake Kyoga. Most of the meat is consumed in rural areas even though many cattle and goats are reared within Buganda and Busoga: the ratio of animals to people there is lower than in Teso, and an equally important reason for the trade is that many more people there can afford to buy meat. There is a similar, but smaller, trade between Lango and Buganda. The small movement of cattle from western Ankole to Masaka must depend primarily on difference in income, for Masaka has only slightly fewer cattle per head of the population than Ankole. Some of the many goats in southwest Uganda are also bought by butchers in Buganda.

Another form of trade in Uganda is a large-scale supply from Karamoja to Kampala and Jinja.[9] The problems involved in establishing cattle markets in remote Karamoja have led the government to organize the marketing of surplus stock there, at the same time providing meat supplies for the main towns. By ensuring that animals are railed direct to the Kampala and Jinja abbatoirs it has reduced the risk of spreading diseases, which are less well controlled in Karamoja than elsewhere.

In Tanzania, Dodoma and Singida Regions are the main areas with surplus cattle and provide half the 60,000 head moved annually between regions, most being sent to the east. Many cattle are also sent from Arusha to Tanga Region, where a dense population has very limited local meat supplies. The small surplus available from the dense cattle population of Sukumaland is normally sent mainly to Bukoba, although in some years some are shipped to Uganda. The trade operates through 150 primary markets in the heavily-stocked parts of Tanzania, and fewer large re-sale markets in the consuming districts. Traditionally the animals were walked long distances over regular routes, but an increasing proportion are now moved by rail.

This form of trade no longer accounts for most long-distance cattle movements in Tanzania, for larger numbers are now supplied to the Dar es Salaam meat canning industry. This handles 100,000 head a year, having been established in 1960 with the government as majority shareholder with the aim of obtaining the maximum economic return from the country's surplus cattle. The Dar es Salaam site seems anomalous, lying far from all cattle rearing areas and making the factory heavily dependent on rail transport; but it was favoured by the intention of exporting much of the tinned meat produced. This intention has been fulfilled, and meat exports to Britain now bring £2 million a year to Tanzania.

In Kenya the pattern of trade in slaughter stock is more complicated. Almost half the recorded sales take place in Nyanza and Western Provinces, but these are normally for local meat supplies only. Long-distance trade is handled partly by a government organization which buys 40,000 cattle a year, 40 per cent. from Samburu District. Other northern districts provide almost as many, while others are obtained from the Masai in the south. Many of these animals, together with rather more supplied by private traders, are supplied to the Kenya Meat Commission, which has a large factory at Athi

River, near Nairobi, and a smaller plant at Mombasa. The K.M.C. takes a further 100,000 head of cattle annually from large-scale farms, the Nakuru, Laikipia and Nanyuki areas each providing about 20,000. This represents an annual off-take of 12 per cent. of all cattle on such farms, far higher than the figure for most small-farm areas.

Half the meat handled by K.M.C. is canned, a third is sold within East Africa, and the remainder is exported in frozen form. As most of the canned meat is also exported, meat is an important source of foreign exchange for Kenya, earning £2½ million in 1969. Meat worth a further £350,000 was sent to Tanzania and Uganda, most being chilled beef.

In Kenya, as in Tanzania and Uganda, goats and sheep provide meat mainly for local consumption, but a substantial number are shipped out of the north each year, while sheep from large highland farms provide some mutton for the towns. A much higher proportion of the pigs are sent away for meat production, mainly to one factory north-west of Nairobi, which meets most of East Africa's small requirements of sausages and bacon.

MILK

Milk is an element in the diet of most East Africans, although average consumption per head is very low. As cattle are so widespread some milk is available in most places, but the quantity is limited by the low yield of most cows. Apart from the small affluent class, large amounts are consumed only by the nomadic pastoralists who can depend on milk as a staple food on account of the size of their herds.

The total volume of milk produced annually in East Africa is probably between 1,000 and 1,500 million litres, of which no more than 400 million litres are sold. Many cultivators as well as pastoralists supply their own needs, while few can afford to buy milk regularly. Subsistence production is probably relatively evenly distributed among the three countries, but the total is certainly greatest in Kenya, for it is there that the main concentration of production for sale is found. Although the high grade dairy cattle of the highlands account for only 6 or 7 per cent. of all cows in Kenya, they provide a substantial share of the total milk production.[10]

Within both Tanzania and Uganda the distribution of milk production must coincide more closely with that of cattle, although there are now increasing numbers of exotic dairy cattle in certain areas such as Kilimanjaro District and Buganda, and there is no doubt some variation in the yields from Zebu cows.

As the distribution of cattle differs from that of population some areas, such as eastern Tanzania, are very short of milk, while elsewhere, as in eastern Uganda, it is relatively plentiful. There are great opportunities for trade between the better-supplied and the more poorly-supplied areas, but many problems hinder this. Elaborate marketing arrangements are necessary for moving milk from innumerable scattered farms to consumers far away; and the dispersed nature of most rural settlement makes it very difficult to supply consumers other than in the towns. These problems are aggravated by the tropical climate and the high cost of refrigeration facilities. Some milk is moved between rural areas, as from Arusha District to the slopes of Kilimanjaro, but commercial milk production is largely confined to the supply of urban markets.

Kenya has not only the largest number of high-yielding dairy cattle, but also the largest urban markets, and the value of milk sales there is estimated at £6 million a year. Most used to come from the large farms, but now almost half comes from small farms, notably in the Kikuyu areas which have urban markets close at hand. At present production exceeds demand in Kenya, and much milk is sent to Uganda, amounting in some years to 12 million litres worth £1 million. The trade is extremely efficient, with supplies arriving daily by rail from Eldoret, although it can effectively supply only the larger towns of Buganda and the east. These exports are expected to decline in the 1970s, however, for a dairy industry is developing in Uganda. Exotic cattle were bought from departing European farmers in Kenya during the 1960s, and these have already been successfully established on farms in the vicinity of Kampala.

The main towns of Tanzania lie too far from the dairying areas of Kenya to receive supplies from there, and are seriously short of milk. The International Bank mission estimated that urban consumption was only $\frac{1}{10}$ pint per person per day around 1960.[11] Dairying has been established on a small scale in the Arusha, Moshi and Dar es Salaam areas, and the present development plan accords a high priority to its expansion, but until government efforts to show cattle owners how to increase yields find a better response, and until improved methods of marketing any surplus are devised, Tanzania is likely to continue importing from overseas tinned and dried milk worth £1 million a year.

Kenya produces more milk than can be marketed in fresh form, and much is manufactured into butter and ghee, of which production exceeds 5,000 tons a year. This is far more than the Kenya market can absorb, and Tanzania and Uganda each take 700 tons annually, worth £¼ million, while a similar quantity is exported overseas. This trade is possible since butter is both less bulky and less perishable than milk, but it needs efficient organization linking the milk producers with the factories. Several of these are scattered over the highlands, supplied mainly from large farms within fifty miles of each. They also produce some cheese, but its value is small compared with that of butter and ghee.

No factory butter is produced in Tanzania or Uganda, but in both, as in parts of Kenya, some cattle owners who have surplus milk produce ghee for sale. The leading area of such ghee production is Mara Region of Tanzania, where co-operative marketing brings £100,000 a year to the local farmers, partly from sales to Kenya and Uganda. Elsewhere trade takes place only on a local scale.

HIDES AND SKINS

Hides and skins are normally regarded as by-products of livestock rearing, but in East Africa they are the products which are exploited commercially to the fullest extent. Even where animals are kept primarily for social reasons, their hides are generally sold when they die. Hides and skins were often traditionally used for clothing and for many household purposes, and many are still so used within the subsistence economy. Most, however, are now marketed, and in some areas they are the leading source of cash. They are normally bought by local traders, often Arab or Somali, who then supply them to a few large exporting firms. The local market is very small, but there is a firm demand overseas, notably in Italy, Spain and Britain.

Exports of hides are worth £3 million a year to East Africa, and goat and sheep skins bring a further £2 million. These earnings are fairly evenly divided among the three countries, for hides and skins generally bring £1¾ million to Kenya and to Tanzania and £1¼ million to Uganda. This pattern might be expected for the by-products from a very widespread activity, commodities on which no country can specialize. Within each country, however, the importance of these products varies greatly. The distribution of production shows a relationship to that of livestock, but it matches far more closely that of meat consumption.

Thus Buganda provides one-third of the hides sold in Uganda although it has only one-fifth of the country's cattle, and Teso is not outstanding in hides production as so many of its cattle are sold to butchers elsewhere. The production of skins reflects more closely the distribution of goats since there is less long-distance movement of these. Ankole and Kigezi are therefore particularly important, providing 30 per cent. of the Uganda supply of skins. Karamoja contributes substantially to the production of both hides and skins, but little to exports, as most are there used by the local population.

In Kenya and Tanzania the meat packing factories are important sources of hides and skins, although the rural areas provide most of the supply. Production is very widespread in Tanzania, even districts with few cattle such as Bukoba making some contribution since they import stock for slaughter. In Kenya hides sales are important both to the cattle-owning farmers of Nyanza and to the nomadic Masai; but few are sold in the northern pastoral areas, sales of cattle on the hoof being much more important there. The north does, however, provide many of the more valuable skins from sheep and goats slaughtered locally.

WOOL

Most East African sheep are covered in hair rather than wool, and cannot be clipped, and wool production is confined almost entirely to the highlands of Kenya. Most takes place on large European farms, but African farmers in the same area are now providing an increasing share. The tropical climate of the region as a whole is not only unsuitable for woolled sheep but also limits the demand for wool for local use. The industry has had to depend on overseas markets, and only in the most favoured parts of the region can wool be produced efficiently enough to compete successfully in world markets. The three districts of Nakuru, Nyandarua and Laikipia provide three-quarters of the total clip of about 1½ million kg., which earns £½ million a year. The 1964–70 Kenya Development Plan aimed at a trebling of production but this was not achieved and emphasis has now shifted away from wool production, since sheep are proving less satisfactory than cattle in most resettlement schemes, and since market prospects for wool are poorer than those for beef.

REFERENCES

1 A thorough study of future prospects as well as the present situation is FAO, *East African Livestock Survey*, 3 Volumes, Rome, 1967.
2 *East Africa Royal Commission 1953–1955 Report*, H.M.S.O., London, 1955, pp. 254–255 etc.
3 The social motives for cattle keeping in one area are examined in depth in P. Rigby, *Cattle and Kinship among the Gogo*, Cornell U.P., Ithaca, 1969.
4 For a fuller account see P. R. Baker, 'The Distribution of Cattle in Uganda', *East African Geographical Review*, No. 6, 1968, pp. 63–73.
5 D. W. Malcolm, *Sukumaland*, Oxford U.P., London, 1953.
6 P. H. Gulliver, *The Family Herds*, Routledge & Kegan Paul, London, 1955, gives an excellent account of two pastoral economies. Another useful discussion of pastoralism is S. H. Ominde, 'The Semi-arid and Arid Lands of Kenya', in S. H. Ominde (ed.), *Studies in East African Geography and Development*, Heinemann, London, 1971.
7 See B. J. Turner and P. R. Baker, 'Tsetse Control and Livestock Development: A Case Study from Uganda', *Geography*, Vol. 53, No. 3, 1968, pp. 249–259.
8 Tanzania, *Second Five-Year Plan, 1969–1974*, Dar es Salaam, 1969, p. xv.
9 P. R. Baker, 'Problems of the Cattle Trade in Karamoja', in H. Berger (ed.), *Ostafrikanische Studien*, Friedrich-Alexander-Universitat, Nurnberg, 1968.
10 M. F. Hill, *Cream Country*, Kenya Co-operative Creameries, Nairobi, 1957, is a history of dairying in Kenya.
11 International Bank, *The Economic Development of Tanganyika*, Dar es Salaam, 1960, p. 98. The whole of Ch. 7, Livestock Development, is very useful.

CHAPTER 7

Fisheries

The most elementary forms of economic activity, hunting and gathering, have little place in life in East Africa today. As in the more developed parts of the world, only a specialized form of each is now important, these being fishing and forestry. East Africa has a coastline of 1,300 km., and lakes occupy 110,000 square km. of the interior. Both coastal and inland waters provide great opportunities for fishing, and the people of the region have taken advantage of this. About 80,000 people earn their living mainly by fishing, while another 10,000 or more are occupied as fishmongers. Fish is a foodstuff of considerable importance, providing the main source of protein in some areas.

The annual catch in East Africa is estimated at 300,000 tons, with a landed value of £13 million. Tanzania accounts for almost half the total and Uganda for most of the remainder; and fishing plays an important role in the economy of both countries. While some is undertaken for subsistence most of the catch is sold. There is some long-distance trade within the region, but fish is of little importance in its external trade.

MARINE FISHERIES

A broad distinction may be made between marine and freshwater fisheries. The former are little developed, and account for only about 12 per cent. of the total catch (Table 6). Landings of 38,000 tons on the East African coast in 1968 compare poorly with those of 290,000 tons on the coast of Angola, which is not much longer. The difference is related partly to more limited fish resources off Kenya and Tanzania than off Angola, where the cool Benguela current provides an excellent habitat, but there are sufficient fish near the East African coast to support a larger industry than now exists. Although the continental shelf is very narrow, pelagic fish such as tuna and bonito are abundant in the off-shore waters, while there is also scope for a large sardine fishery. Even the smaller potential of the inshore waters has not yet been fully exploited, and the intensity of the fishing effort is less than in other zones of similar potential, such as much of the West African coast.

One factor hindering development has been the slender capital resources of most of the fishermen. While many coast-dwellers engage in fishing, most have only one small canoe, and each man's catch is very small. Few boats have even an outboard motor, and they cannot venture far from the landings. A large scale fishing industry, tapping deep waters, would probably require foreign investment, as in Ghana or Senegal, and little interest in this has been shown. Japanese concerns are operating in many parts of the Indian Ocean, but none of their catch is landed in East Africa.

The small local market has also discouraged expansion of marine fishing. Fish is a popular food throughout the coastlands, but the population is generally neither dense nor affluent, and local consumption is not high enough to support a large fishery. Dried or frozen fish can be sent across the belt of sparsely populated country to places further inland, although some of these are adequately supplied by production from the lakes. Many people up-country would buy more fish if it were available cheaply, but exploitation of widely scattered markets in the interior would require great improvement in the organization of trade. Opportunities for overseas exports are limited, for there is currently overproduction of fish such as sardines, and any country easily accessible by sea from Kenya or Tanzania has its own coastline and will import fish only at very low prices.

The Distribution of Marine Fisheries

Fishing is very unevenly spread along the coast, and the distribution is not easily explained. About 9,000 fishermen from Zanzibar and Pemba, operating from 3,000 canoes, provide one-third the total catch, although for many fishing is only a part-time activity. Their catch is worth £½ million a year, and it contributes much more than meat to the islands' food supplies. Limited agricultural opportunities and a dense population to be fed, especially on Zanzibar island, have encouraged the growth of the industry, but the local market is now satisfied. A 22 per cent. import duty long hindered the export of fish to the mainland, and full implementation of the union with Tanganyika may now assist the industry by providing wider markets. Overseas markets have as yet been found only for the crayfish gathered in small numbers around the shores.

Along the Tanganyika coast much less interest is shown in fishing, and the annual catch is only about 15,000 tons. The availability of alternative occupations contributes to this, especially around Dar es Salaam and Tanga, where the potential demand is greatest. Elsewhere the problems of marketing are very great and could be overcome only with a substantial injection of capital. Little of the catch now moves far from the landings, and the distribution of fishing along the coast closely matches that of population.

Under 7,000 tons of marine fish is landed annually in Kenya. The greatest interest is shown around Malindi and Lamu, but the local markets, especially around Lamu, are very small. The price of fish rises southwards, one species generally fetching 70 cents per kg. in Lamu, 1/20 in Malindi and 1/60 in Mombasa. Around Mombasa, however, there are many other sources of income, while the problems of moving fish there from Lamu hinder any large-scale trade.

FRESHWATER FISHERIES

The lakes are the main source of fish in East Africa, and although further expansion is possible their potential is tapped much more fully than that of the sea. The catch from the lakes has expanded steadily in recent years, and now exceeds 240,000 tons a year, obtained entirely by small-scale African enterprise. There are about 70,000 fishermen, who receive about £11 million for their catch. Small canoes form the normal craft, although many now have outboard motors, especially in Uganda; and most of the fish are taken by gill nets, an increasing number of which are made of nylon. In some areas the fishermen and their families consume much of the catch, but generally most is marketed. Some is sold fresh, but more is smoked, salted or sun-dried at the lakeshore, and bought by itinerant fishmongers who distribute it throughout the neighbouring countryside.

In contrast to the ocean, the lake waters are largely within easy reach of the shore, and may be tapped by fishermen setting out daily in small canoes. This favours intensive exploitation, especially of the smaller lakes. Fish are abundant in most of the lake waters, and only rarely have limited resources restricted fishing activity. The dense population of many areas around the lakes provides large local markets, and most of the fish are consumed within 100 km. of the landings.

The Distribution of Freshwater Fishing: Lake Victoria

Table 6 shows that Lake Victoria contributes the greatest share of the freshwater catch. It is much the largest of the lakes, and contains many species of economic value. The population around parts of its shores is both dense and relatively prosperous, and the fishermen have no difficulty in disposing of their catch. Yet it ranks low among East African lakes in yield per square km., mainly because much more of this lake than of any other lies beyond a day's journey from a landfall. No fishermen have the capital to use large boats with refrigeration facilities, which would be necessary for extension of the range. Instead more and more people tap the inshore waters, until the catch per man in some parts falls so low as to be hardly worth the effort.[1]

Tanzania has the longest shoreline along Lake Victoria, the greatest number of canoes and the largest catch. A recent extension of the fishing grounds has been assisted by the use of offshore islands where fish are landed, smoked, and stored until a load is ready for the mainland. The most important species are *Tilapia* and *Haplochromis*, but the deep-water *Bagrus* has acquired importance as outboard motors have been introduced. Fishing effort is remarkably evenly distributed along the Tanzania shore. The incentive to fish, in terms of resources, marketing opportunities and alternative sources of income, seems to be similar everywhere. The dense population of Sukumaland could offer a larger market for the Mwanza shore, but this has not yet been extensively tapped. The clearest contrasts are in the species taken. Musoma and

Nyamirembe are the most important landings for *Tilapia*; Mwanza and Ukerewe Island account for most of the *Haplo-chromis*; and most *Bagrus* is landed around Bukoba, where deep water lies closest to the shore.

The catch on the much shorter Uganda shore is only a little smaller, for fishing there is much encouraged by the great

TABLE 6

EAST AFRICAN FISH PRODUCTION, 1969

(Figures in thousand tons)

Lake	Tanzania	Uganda	Kenya
Victoria	54	41	17
Tanganyika	41	—	—
Kyoga	—	33	—
Rukwa	15	—	—
Albert	—	14	—
Edward/George	—	12	—
Other lakes and rivers	13	10	8
Freshwater total	123	110	25
Marine fisheries	27	—	7
TOTAL	150	110	32
TOTAL IN 1963	83	68	19
TOTAL IN 1953	58	24	18

There is no comprehensive recording of fish landings. The figures above are estimates based on information supplied by the Fisheries Department of each country, and are liable to a considerable margin of error.

concentration of population and prosperity in the zone around the lake. A great expansion of fishing coincided with the coffee boom between 1953 and 1956; but the subsequent slackening of growth cannot be attributed to marketing problems, for all fish landed are quickly snapped up, and few are carried more than 50 km. inland. Fishing takes place from about 200 landings, of which the largest is at Jinja, where over 1,500 tons are landed annually. Further west there is a concentration around the Entebbe peninsula, while other important landings are at Bukakata, on the western shore, and at Mjanji, near the Kenya border. Accessibility to markets has greatly influenced the distribution of fishing. Jinja itself is an important market, while the Entebbe peninsula and Bukakata are within 40 km. of Kampala and Masaka respectively. From each landing fresh fish can be taken by van to the town and the densely populated area around. Mjanji is less well placed, but is the nearest point on the lake to the towns of Tororo and Mbale. The waters off the mouth of the Kagera River, possibly the richest in the lake, are very lightly fished, since that area is remote from centres of population and is poorly served by roads. The south Busoga shore, where sleeping sickness has prevented settlement, has no landings at all. As long as fish must be landed on the day that they are caught, the waters off the Kagera and the Busoga shore cannot easily be exploited by boats working from landings elsewhere, and thus they remain under-fished.

The catch in Kenya waters fluctuates greatly: only 4,300 tons was landed in 1961, but almost 11,000 the following year. Kenya's share of the lake is very small, but fishing is a traditional occupation of the Luo living around the shore. Fish is very popular among this group, as indicated by the large expenditure on it by migrant Luo in Nairobi and Kampala: and large markets exist in densely-populated central Kenya, which has few alternative sources of supply. The fishing effort has therefore been more intensive in Kenya waters than elsewhere. This fishery is distinctive in that dhows are widely used, and that some are Asian-owned, although all the fishermen are Africans. Much fishing from canoes also takes place, while considerable use is still made of baskets and traps by the shore and along the rivers. The Nzoia River is intensively fished in its lower reaches, yielding over 1,000 tons in many years. There are over 100 landings around the Kavirondo Gulf, of which those near Kisumu are much the most important. The gulf has yielded 100 tons per square km. in good years, compared with 5 tons for all the Uganda waters; but stocks of fish have been greatly reduced, and this is one area where resources now limit production.[2]

Lake Kyoga

Lake Kyoga was the last of the major lakes to be heavily exploited. In 1953 the catch was only 3,000 tons, but it was 13,000 tons by 1963 and 33,000 tons by 1969. More than half consists of *Protopterus*, most of which are caught in shallow water with baskets or lines by the Bakenyi, a very small group living along the eastern shores. The other tribes living around the lake show little interest in fishing, and the development of net fishing from canoes had to await an influx of immigrants from Kenya, Tanzania and Sudan. It was greatly assisted by the clearance of crocodiles which formerly consumed large quantities of fish, damaged nets and even threatened the fishermen.

The very irregular outline of Lake Kyoga encourages more intensive fishing there than on Lake Victoria, for all parts lie within easy reach of the shore. Production is now limited mainly by marketing problems. Many landings on long peninsulas lie far from a road, and the local governments have been slow to build roads to serve minority and immigrant groups. The market east of the lake is reduced by the reluctance of many people there to accept *Protopterus*. The market elsewhere is very scattered, for there are no large towns around the lake; and is very seasonal, for cash is plentiful only when the cotton has been harvested. In view of these problems the extent of commercial fishing is remarkable. From the southern shores 10,000 tons a year are moved by bicycle to assembly markets on the nearest roads, and then distributed through northern Mengo and Busoga. From the northern shores fish are taken by cycle, van and bus to all parts of Lango and Teso, and some are sent to Acholi.

Lake Albert

The Uganda waters of Lake Albert are more intensively fished than those of Lake Victoria, but less so than those of Lake Kyoga. There is much untapped potential even in the inshore waters, while the middle of the lake has hardly been touched. About 1,000 canoes operate from the Uganda shore, mainly from landings around Butiaba and Panyimur, in the north. Further south several factors have discouraged fishing. A steep escarpment has hindered the building of roads to the southern shores, while most Banyoro and Batoro appear unwilling to include fish in their diet. In addition, tsetse infestation has restricted settlement near parts of the shore, some land being officially closed until the 1950s.

Marketing is certainly the greatest problem facing the Lake

Albert fishery. Until 1960 half the catch was sold in Congo, but since then the Congolese have had no currency acceptable in Uganda and this trade has almost disappeared. The main species caught are different from those in Lake Victoria and find little demand in Buganda. Fortunately sales in West Nile and Acholi have increased greatly, although markets there are widely scattered, while the antipathy to fish in Bunyoro is slowly breaking down. To the south, the establishment of a freezing plant at Fort Portal has provided a small outlet for Nile Perch. The opening of the railway to Pakwach improves the prospect of sales elsewhere in Uganda, but little advantage has yet been taken of this.

Lakes George and Edward

South of Lake Albert the rift valley floor is occupied by two smaller lakes which are much more intensively fished than those already considered. Lake George covers only 250 square km. and is mostly under 4 metres deep, but its fish population is extremely large. Two favourable factors are a rich growth of algae fertilized by hundreds of tons of hippo manure a day, and the complete absence of crocodiles. Commercial fishing under close government control began in 1950, and 150 canoes now take about 6,000 tons of fish a year. The catch from the more extensive Uganda waters of Lake Edward is similar in size, about 130 canoes operating from the large settlement of Lake Katwe and 100 others from smaller landings. Most have outboard motors, and this helps to make the catch per man higher than on most lakes.

As on Lake Albert the main problem today is that of marketing. The local demand is very small, and until 1960 Congo provided the main outlet, much of the catch being sold to Greek traders who took it by road as far as Kisangani, 700 km. away. The main species taken, *Tilapia*, is familiar and popular in Buganda, and much is now despatched in smoked form to Masaka and Kampala. *Tilapia* is also suitable for processing into frozen fillets, which find markets among those who can afford them throughout Uganda and Kenya. The government established a freezing plant beside Lake George to provide a market for the fishermen there, and private firms have subsequently established others at Lake Katwe, and

K

beside the Kazinga Channel which links lakes Edward and George.

Lake Tanganyika

Lake Tanganyika is much deeper than most East African lakes, and the fisheries are quite different from those elsewhere. The main species taken is the *Dagaa*, a small pelagic fish found in vast numbers, which rises to the surface only at night, is attracted to the boats by bright lights and is scooped out of the water with nets. The lake is poor in other useful species, but the *Dagaa* fishery could be greatly expanded. In Tanzania waters few fishermen venture far from the shore, for the canoes cannot withstand the storms which develop very suddenly. Nearly all the commercial catch of 30,000 tons is taken in a small area around Kigoma and Ujiji, where the railway assists despatch of dried fish to a remarkably wide area of Tanzania. Some fishing is undertaken all along the coast, but mostly on a very small scale, chiefly for subsistence. The density of population in the lakeshore zone is too low to support a large fishery, and most of the lakeside settlements have no inland communications There is a small export to Zambia from the south of the lake, and this might be expanded since that country's fish resources are very small.

Other Lakes

Lake Rukwa, in south-western Tanzania is extremely shallow, but has large stocks of *Tilapia* and other species. Fishing is hampered by great fluctuations in lake level. In 1949 three-quarters of the lake completely dried out and stocks fell drastically, but they have since recovered. The market once provided by the Lupa goldfields has disappeared, and that elsewhere in south-western Tanzania is kept small by the low income level there, yet the catch rose sharply in the 1960s.

For a distance of 300 km. the shore of Lake Malawi lies within Tanzania, and fishermen go out from settlements all along this shore. Most are providing mainly for the needs of their families and neighbours, for accessibility to markets elsewhere is extremely poor. But in this area where cattle are almost entirely absent fish consumption is high, and the annual catch probably exceeds 6,000 tons.

Lake Rudolf, one of the largest East African lakes, is very well stocked with fish, but the extremely sparse population of the surrounding area and its remoteness from potential markets have hindered exploitation of these resources. There are few other prospects for development in this area, and so the government has plans for encouraging 2,000 of the local pastoral people to become fishermen, in the hope of increasing production from the present 3,000 tons to 15,000 tons a year. Sales of this quantity, however, will become possible only when a new 400 km. road to Kitale is built.

Among other minor fishing areas are lakes Kachira, Kijanebola and Nakivali in southern Uganda, and Lake Baringo in Kenya. In all three countries the development of fish ponds has attracted much attention from government, but their present importance is sometimes exaggerated. They contribute a very small share of the total catch, although they are valuable in making fish available in areas far from either lakes or the sea, and could become of importance in the future.[3]

Fishing, then, is a very widespread activity in East Africa, and is expanding faster than any other sector of the rural economy, for the total catch doubled between 1958 and 1968. Even so, the potential of both seas and lakes is far from fully exploited, while there is still much scope for raising the protein content of most people's diet, and therefore a further increase in fishing activity is a feature of the development plans of all three countries. There are also opportunities for larger scale fishing operations if the necessary capital and enterprise can be found: but an even greater need may be for an infusion of these into the marketing of fish.

REFERENCES

1 D. J. Garrod, 'The History of the Fishing Industry of Lake Victoria', *East African Agriculture and Forestry Journal*, Vol. 27, No. 2, 1961, pp. 95–99.

2 H. Fearn, *An African Economy*, Oxford U.P., London, 1961, devotes much attention to fishing in Nyanza.

3 C. F. Hickling, *Tropical Inland Fisheries*, Longmans, London, 1961, provides a fuller discussion of some aspects of inland fisheries in East Africa, and is very useful for comparison with other regions.

CHAPTER 8

Forestry

Clearing for cultivation has greatly reduced the area of forest in East Africa, but that which remains is now carefully preserved. About 10 per cent. of the land surface of the region is scheduled as Forest Reserve, but much is in fact open woodland, and only 1½ per cent. of the land carries true high forest (Map 3). The direct economic value of the forests is for timber, building poles and fuel, but they also regulate run-off of rainfall, thereby reducing soil erosion and ensuring a steady water supply for land at lower altitudes. Some forest areas are protected to provide timber in the future; others to control water, with no prospect of cutting.[1]

TIMBER

Almost 1 million cubic metres of timber is produced annually in East Africa, valued at over £6 million. This yields about 300,000 cubic metres of sawn wood, which satisfies most local needs, and allows exports of about 40,000 cubic metres, worth over £¾ million. Natural hardwood forests provide most of the timber, but new softwood plantations make a contribution, and their importance is steadily increasing. The trees are felled by private sawmilling concerns which are licensed to work in particular sections of Forest Reserve, and the logs are sawn either in the forest itself or in a near-by town. There are about 200 sawmills in East Africa, most of which are small Asian-owned concerns; but a few large European and Asian enterprises, some owning several mills, control much of the trade. The numerous African handsawyers make only a small contribution to the total production but their participation in the industry does help to spread its profits more widely. The companies employ over 20,000 people, however, providing a valuable source of income in several otherwise poor areas: and additional employment is provided by the government Forest Departments.

The extent of forest would permit increased timber production, but as local markets are already satisfied this could only be for export. The nature of the forest does not favour large scale production for export, since large stands of species in demand overseas are rare. Most of the forests contain many intermixed species, most of little commercial value. It is not possible to cut only the useful trees, for this would result in the eventual colonization of the whole forest area by useless species. Costs of production therefore tend to be high, and few East African sawmillers can compete in world markets. A further discouraging factor is the location of most forests far inland, which makes transport costs high. The situation contrasts sharply with that in West Africa, where forests lie mainly close to the coast, and where both Ghana and Ivory Coast earn over £15 million a year from timber exports.[2]

The fact that timber is costly to transport provides a strong incentive to satisfy domestic requirements locally, and all the East African governments have encouraged the development of the sawmilling industry. Its size is limited mainly by that of the local market, which is very small in relation to the population of the region. For many uses timber must compete with other materials, ranging from dried mud and cowdung in construction to steel and aluminium in furniture. Private domestic use, chiefly for doors and for furniture, probably accounts for two-thirds of consumption, and government and industrial use for the remainder.

Timber production is widely spread over East Africa, as are areas of Forest Reserve. The relationship between the two patterns is far from exact, however, for only in western Tanzania does the woodland provide much timber. Even some true forests are not at present exploited, whereas others are worked intensively. The pattern of sawmilling is different again, since logs are often moved out of the forests before being sawn. Proximity to markets has a great effect on where timber felling takes place, and affects the location of milling even more.

The annual cut in Uganda is about 200,000 cubic metres, while that in Kenya and in Tanzania exceeds 300,000 cubic metres. Kenya, with its higher income, and Tanzania, with its larger population, both have larger home markets than Uganda, while both are better placed for exports overseas. Both also have a larger area of high forest, about 9,500 square km. compared with 7,000 in Uganda.

Areas of forest in Kenya are largely confined to the well-watered highlands, which also provide the main markets for timber. Production is therefore more localised there than in Tanzania or Uganda. Two-thirds of the people employed in logging and sawmilling work in Rift Valley Province, notably in the forests just west of the rift. Settlements such as Timboroa, Londiani and Elburgon are largely dependent on this industry. The forests there all lie above 2,300 metres, and consist mainly of the indigenous conifer, *podocarpus*, and recently-planted cypress. Despite the altitude, two railways and several good roads give accessibility, and dense population in adjacent areas provides ample labour.

East of the rift valley, Laikipia District has extensive tracts of Forest Reserve, but neither the composition nor the accessibility of the forests is very satisfactory. The area around Nyeri is a more important source of timber, for there are productive forests on the slopes of the Aberdare mountains, and the dense population of Central Province provides local markets. The forests extend southwards nearly to Nairobi, and there they are intensively worked to supply the city sawmills. The main species cut are again podocarpus and cypress. Although the latter occupy only a small area, they form the chief concern of the Forest Department throughout the highlands. The trees mature within 30 years, compared with over 100 years for all indigenous species, and cypress plantations have now become the main source of timber in Kenya.[3]

The Mount Elgon forests are not very fully exploited, partly because of problems of local accessibility and their distance from large markets. Fuller use is made of the forests around Kakamega and Kapsabet to supply Nyanza and Western Provinces, although more of their needs are met from the Londiani district. Small tracts of hardwood forest north and south of Mombasa supply Coast Province, and floor blocks made in Mombasa from the exceptionally hard muhuhu are exported overseas.

One interesting recent development in Kenya is a shift of

sawmilling towards the towns. Between 1957 and 1963, for instance, employment in this industry fell considerably in Kenya as a whole, yet within the seven largest towns it rose.

Tanzania has a far larger area of Forest Reserve than the other countries, but most is open woodland of little value for timber. Mninga (*Pterocarpus*) and brachystegia are cut from the woodland in Tabora Region, which lies far from alternative sources of timber, but most production is confined to small patches of true forest in the north and east of the country. Tanga Region accounts for 30 per cent. of the total, the forests of the Usambara mountains being very intensively exploited, notably for muhuhu (*Brachylaena*) and camphorwood (*Ocotea*). They are conveniently situated in relation to internal markets and to the coast for exports, and have a relatively high proportion of useful trees. Accessibility to markets also encourages exploitation of the forests of the Uluguru mountains around Morogoro, although these form a poorer timber resource.

A higher and cooler zone on Kilimanjaro provides softwood, mainly natural podocarpus but including some planted cypress. Other softwood forests exist in the southern highlands but these lie much further from large markets and some are very inaccessible. They, therefore, provide much less of Tanzania's timber cut than those on Kilimanjaro. A forest area on the Rondo plateau in Mtwara Region, containing much valuable mvule and quite close to the coast, attracted the largest sawmilling enterprise in the country: but production there ceased in 1961 when the most easily worked areas were exhausted. Some timber is still cut for export in Mtwara Region, however, notably mninga. [4]

The largest surviving blocks of the former extensive forests of Uganda are in Western Region, with numerous smaller remnants in Buganda and the east. The pattern of sawmilling shows some similarity, for the largest mills are in the west, although many small mills are situated in Buganda and Busoga. Timber felling is of greatest importance in Bunyoro District, where rainfall is sufficient to support high forest, much of which remains uncleared because of the sparse population. The trees include mvule and mahogany, which can bear the cost of transport to markets elsewhere in Uganda and even overseas. The Budongo forest is the most productive in Uganda, one mill there handling 20,000 cubic metres of timber annually. Further south the Kibale and Kalinzu forests offer a good potential, and one mill has operated in each since about 1950: but little of these forests has yet been tapped. Useful species are so interspersed with others of little value that costs of working are high, and in competitive market conditions both mills are mainly dependent on the very limited local demand. The largest Uganda forest is that on Ruwenzori, but this is maintained to protect river catchments, especially since more accessible sources of timber are available.

Most patches of forest in Busoga District are now very small, but because of their accessibility to markets and because they contain much mvule they are intensively worked, and Jinja is the main centre of the Uganda timber trade. The Mabira forest, across the Nile in Buganda, is a valuable source of timber for both Jinja and Kampala. Elsewhere in Buganda many small mills cut both from Forest Reserves and from private land: but costs are high, and the activity is encouraged only by proximity to the main Uganda markets. There is a potentially productive forest on Mount Elgon, but its exploitation is discouraged by its inaccessibility and by its value in protecting land on the lower slopes from the effects of rapid run-off of rainfall. There is no large scale timber production in northern Uganda, where most Forest Reserves consist only of poor woodland.

Overseas exports developed rapidly during the Second World War, when Britain had to seek new sources of timber: but they fell as this demand eased and as local consumption expanded, and today timber makes only a small contribution to East African exports. Tanzania provides more than half the total, partly because it has productive forests near the coast, and partly because there is a particularly strong demand in Europe for mninga which is not found elsewhere in East Africa. Kenya and Uganda both send less timber overseas, but for different reasons. There is little demand in Europe for the softwoods produced in Kenya, since large supplies are available closer at hand, and although podocarpus finds markets elsewhere the quantities involved are small. Timber export from Uganda is hindered by its inland location, and is largely confined to mvule and mahogany which are both in demand in Britain, bring double the price of Kenya softwoods, and can therefore bear higher transport costs.

Most timber produced in East Africa is supplied to small woodworking enterprises, of which over 600 are recorded in employment returns. Most are in towns, but are less concentrated into large centres than most industries, for they must be near their markets. They are one of the main forms of enterprise in the poorly-developed industrial area of many small East African towns. Timber provides the raw material for several small industries. Plywood factories at Jinja, Moshi and Tanga supply chests for East African tea exports. Pencil slats are manufactured in Kenya and blocks for parquet floors in Kenya and Tanzania: each is mainly for export to Europe, and each brings a higher income than would the export of the equivalent volume of timber.

Although East Africa is largely self-sufficient in timber, imports of wood products are large, with a value far greater than that of timber exports. One step recently taken to overcome this, and to provide a new market for local timber, is the decision to establish a large pulp and paper mill in Kenya. This has provided the main stimulus for the increased effort now being put into afforestation in areas near to the mill, such as the Turbo district.

BUILDING POLES AND FUEL

Much more wood is consumed in East Africa as building poles and fuel than as timber. They are the main economic products of the savanna woodlands gazetted as Forest Reserve, while even more wood is probably cut for poles and fuel outside the Forest Reserves, although there are no records of this. Thus, although these items are unimportant in the commercial sector of the economy, they are of more concern than timber to most of the region's population.

According to two FAO experts the annual consumption of poles in East Africa probably approaches 4 million cubic metres compared with the timber cut of 1 million cubic metres.[5] The demand is essentially for house-building, poles forming a framework upon which mud walls can be built up and the roof can be laid. No area specializes in commercial production of such poles, and few are moved long distances, for a local supply is available in most of the settled areas of the region. Where this is inadequate small patches of fast-growing eucalyptus have often been planted, especially around the towns, although these are equally important as a source of fuel. Some poles are used by the Posts and Telegraphs and by the electricity concerns, but this commercial demand is very small. The distribution of pole production is thus closely related to that of population, and is very widely spread throughout East Africa.

A specialized form of pole production takes place in the coastal mangrove forests which occupy 500 square km. in Kenya and 800 square km. in Tanzania. Their exploitation is one of the few economic activities of areas such as the Rufiji delta: but its contribution to the whole economy of each country is extremely small, especially since exports by dhow to the Persian Gulf have declined.

The consumption of wood for fuel is far greater even than that for building poles, the FAO team's estimate being of over 40 million cubic metres a year. The use of wood for fuel also falls mainly within the subsistence economy, and most is obtained from small patches of woodland and from scattered trees rather than from forests. The distribution of production, like that of pole production, is therefore closely related to that of population, although consumption varies with the climate. In most areas wood fuel is used chiefly for cooking, but in the highlands it is also needed for heating. In Kikuyu country, for example, women and children can be seen everywhere carrying huge bundles of firewood.

Fuel for domestic use is produced commercially mainly in the form of charcoal to supply the few who can afford this and who do not now rely on kerosene or electricity. The demand for charcoal in the towns has declined as alternatives have become available, but large quantities are still brought in daily by van or by bicycle from the surrounding country.

Wood fuel is still used by some industrial concerns, such as sugar factories and oil mills. Many tea factories are located far from public electricity supplies, but on the edge of a forest, and these also use wood fuel. Much is also consumed in tobacco curing and in the drying of fish, and cutting for fuel is therefore especially great in the vicinity of such forms of enterprise.

The railway was once a major consumer, but now all locomotives use oil fuel.

Less has been said about poles and fuel than about timber, partly because their production is more evenly spread over East Africa, and partly because little information is available about them. However, estimates of the Gross Domestic Product of the three countries indicate that while commercial timber production contributes about £4 million a year, predominantly subsistence production of poles and fuel can be valued at about £10 million. So it perhaps merits more attention in future, both in studies of present patterns and in national development plans.

REFERENCES

1 The aims of forestry in East Africa are set out in W. T. W. Morgan (ed.), *East Africa: Its People and Resources*, Oxford U.P., Nairobi, 1969, Ch. 17–19.
2 On the timber industries of Africa in general see F.A.O., *Timber Trends and Prospects in Africa*, Rome, 1967.
3 Details of existing as well as planned plantations in Kenya are given in Kenya, *Development Plan 1970–1974*, Nairobi, 1969, pp. 283–291.
4 An excellent survey of the Tanzania timber industry is provided in Tanganyika Forest Division, *Tanganyika's Timber Resources*, Dar es Salaam, 1962. Further information is available in A. D. Little Inc., *Tanganyika Industrial Development*, Dar es Salaam, 1961.
5 S. L, Pringle and J. E. M. Arnold, *Present Wood Consumption and Future Requirements in Uganda*, FAO, Rome, 1960; and similar reports for Kenya and Tanganyika.

CHAPTER 9

Mining

Mineral exploitation probably provides the easiest path to higher income for poor countries. East Africa is unfortunate in this respect, for mining contributes much less to its economy than to that of the continent as a whole. Minerals provide over one-third of the value of exports from Africa,[1] but well under 10 per cent. of those from East Africa. They account for only 2½ per cent. of the monetary sector of the Gross Domestic Product, and 1 per cent. of all paid employment in the region. Nevertheless, mining is more significant now than before the Second World War, when gold and soda ash were the only minerals of any importance.

The mineral resources of the region are by no means fully known, for much land has not been thoroughly prospected; and much exploratory work is now in progress. Investigations so far made have revealed a wide variety of minerals, but few deposits large enough to be of value. However, not all of these are yet exploited, for although the distribution of known minerals determines the maximum possible extent of mining, many other considerations, ranging from geological to political, also affect the pattern.[2]

DIAMONDS

Diamonds are the most valuable mineral now worked in East Africa, earning over £8 million in most years, although production is confined to one locality. Of the 780,000 carats won in 1969, over 90 per cent. was from the Williamson mine at Mwadui, in Shinyanga Region of Tanzania, and the remainder from the adjacent Alamasi mine (Map 12). Commercial production of diamonds began in 1925, but they became important only after the discovery of the Mwadui deposit in 1940. Production then developed rapidly until 1946, when it was worth almost £1 million, and after a period of great fluctuation rose again steadily between 1956 and 1961. The industry is highly successful, and operating profits now represent about two-thirds of income. It is particularly important to Tanzania since the government is part-owner of the enterprise and so gains revenue from the profits as well as from royalties and taxation.

There is little to be said about the location of the industry, for the Mwadui deposit is the only commercially workable source of diamonds known in East Africa. The diamonds are found only in kimberlite pipes, and although there are many such pipes in Shinyanga, no others have yielded a rich supply of stones. Many factors, however, had to be considered before it was decided to undertake diamond working in East Africa rather than elsewhere. The physical nature of the Mwadui deposit is very satisfactory, for the pipe reaches the surface over an area about 2,000 metres in diameter, and the diamondiferous gravel may be worked opencast. The suitability of many of the diamonds for gemstones enhances their value, and the reserves were adequate to justify the large investment required. The diamond content of the gravels is not high, and over 3 million tons a year must be worked to produce 800,000 carats, but this handicap is reduced by processing at the mine.

As diamonds are of exceptionally high value for their weight, they present no transport problems, but the location of the mine close to the main road and railway between Tabora and Mwanza assists the movement of supplies, while the accessibility of the area probably contributed to the discovery of the deposit. In relation to the value of production labour requirements are not large, and only 2,600 people are employed in the industry. As the mine lies near to well-populated country where other employment opportunities are scarce, these numbers have been easy to obtain.

The low labour requirements indicate that the mine is capital-intensive rather than labour-intensive. The fixed assets of Mwadui are valued at about £12 million, and the industry benefited greatly from availability of private capital for its establishment. Today the Williamson concern is owned jointly by the De Beers Corporation and the Tanzania Government, which acquired half the shares in 1958. Marketing is controlled by De Beers through the Diamond Corporation, which places the whole production on the London diamond market. Despite the possibility of synthetic diamonds, and of increased output from the main producers, South Africa and Congo, market prospects are good, especially as Tanzania has a quota which would allow increased exports. The main constraint is now geological, for the highest grade material is rapidly being worked out, and may not sustain mining beyond the 1970s. Finds elsewhere in Tanzania have proved disappointing, and there are no apparent prospects in Kenya or Uganda.

COPPER

Copper ranks second in value among East African minerals, the production being worth £5 to £6 million in most years. All is exported overseas, and although the industry is minute compared with that in Zambia it provides the third source of foreign exchange for Uganda.

The whole production is now obtained from one mine at Kilembe, in a narrow valley among the lower eastern slopes of the Ruwenzori mountains. The existence of copper there was proved in 1906, and the deposit was fully investigated twenty years later; but no more was done until 1946, when exploration was resumed by a Canadian concern. Mining began in 1956, and ore output now exceeds one million tons a year. The ore is extracted from both surface and underground workings on each side of the valley, and is treated in a crushing and flotation plant on the site, where a 26 per cent. concentrate is produced. This is railed 425 km. to a smelter at Jinja, from where blister copper is sent on to Mombasa for export. These exports amounted to 15,000 to 18,000 tons a year throughout the 1960s.

Copper mining involved no choice of location within Uganda, for no other workable deposit is known, but the entrepreneurs could have invested in copper elsewhere. The physical nature of the Kilembe deposit encouraged its exploitation, for although the ore occurs in highly folded rocks it is in tabular masses averaging 6 metres in thickness, and it contains about 2·2 per cent. copper, which compares favourably with many worked deposits. The indicated ore reserves in 1953 exceeded 11 million tons, and it seemed likely that more would be found.

Little more has been found, however, and development might not have taken place if the limited extent of the deposit had been known.

Since the Ruwenzori are snow-capped, the mine has ample water supplies; and it has been possible to develop hydro-electricity in the neighbouring Mobuku valley. The terrain prevented rail facilities reaching Kilembe, but the concentrate is easily moved the 13 km. to railhead by pipeline. The building of a railway from Kampala was a prerequisite for development, for a 320-km. road haul to the former railhead there was not considered economically feasible. The people who live near the mine have shown little interest in working there, but labour has been readily available from overcrowded Kigezi, which supplies over half the 4,000 employees.

Jinja was selected as the site for the smelter only after much discussion. Its most obvious advantage is the Owen Falls power supply, for the smelter operates at a temperature of 1,200°C. and consumes 50 million kwh. a year. Taking electricity from Jinja to a plant at Kilembe would have cost £2½ million for power lines, a sum then not readily available. A site near Kilembe seemed to offer a saving in transport costs by moving blister copper rather than bulky concentrates, but in fact the railway administration could not have provided any transport facilities without the guarantee of bulk concentrate traffic. Jinja was further favoured by the hope that the smelter would handle copper from Kenya, although this has not happened. The sulphur content of the concentrate might also have been used at Jinja as a raw material for other industries, although it is now driven off in a form which does not permit economic recovery.

The industry represents an investment of £8 million, provided mainly by Canadian private enterprise, and it is fortunate for Uganda that it was considered an attractive country for investment at a time of high copper prices. The project has proved disappointing for the entrepreneurs because of both the failure to find large new ore deposits, and unsatisfactory world market conditions. No copper was produced until prices passed their peak, and soon after mining began the price fell to £160 a ton, compared with production costs of £230. By 1961, however, prices had stabilized around £230 while costs had fallen to £185; and by 1970 prices had risen substantially. One attraction of the Kilembe deposit was the 0·18 per cent. cobalt content of the ore, but cobalt concentrates have merely been stockpiled at the railhead, for the market has been flooded since 1956, and prices do not justify its shipment for export.

The profits obtained by Kilembe Mines Ltd. have been very small, and the Uganda Government has received no royalties from the industry, but it contributes £2½ million a year to the economy in wages and local purchases. Even this may not continue beyond 1976, however, for unless some addition to the present reserves of 6 million tons of ore is found, there will soon be no copper mining in Uganda.

Mining has already ceased in Kenya, where a small deposit in South Nyanza was worked from 1961 to 1966. Provision of capital by the Colonial Development Corporation, abundant local labour and a potential power supply at Gogo Falls all assisted the establishment of this mine; but the amount of workable ore proved to be very small.

SODA ASH AND SALT

The most valuable mineral worked in Kenya is soda ash, of which production generally exceeds 100,000 tons a year, worth over £1 million. All is obtained from one deposit, which has been worked continuously since 1914, and which consists of a precipitate containing 97·7 per cent. sodium carbonate. It lies on the edge of Lake Magadi, 100 km. south-west of Nairobi in arid and very sparsely populated country. The deposit is continuously replenished by saline springs, and therefore, unlike most minerals, is not a wasting asset. Despite the isolation of Magadi labour is obtained without difficulty, a diesel generator supplies the necessary power, and a branch railway provides adequate transport facilities. Since 1924, when I.C.I. took over the enterprise, ample financial resources have been available.[3] Other soda ash deposits exist, but none is so rich as Lake Magadi, and the enterprise there is so well established that any other could not easily break its monopoly.

Soda ash production is limited mainly by the size of the market. The local demand is very limited, for its main uses are in the glass, fertilizer and paper industries. South Africa formerly took almost half the production but, since political considerations have closed this outlet, the company has had difficulty in disposing of the production. It is sold in numerous countries, from Argentina to Thailand, but the demand is limited and ever since 1962 production has been below full capacity.

Lake Magadi also provides most of Kenya's annual production of 30,000 tons of common salt. The remainder comes from a small coastal evaporation works north of Malindi. The pattern of salt production in Tanzania is similar, an inland source at Uvinza providing two-thirds, and various coastal works one third, of the annual production of 35,000 tons. In Uganda only one small deposit is worked, yielding 8,000 tons a year, and most requirements are met by imports from Aden. There is an export trade from Uvinza to Congo and Burundi, and Tanzania plans to expand this greatly in the 1970s, but there is little scope for overseas exports. The coastal works suffer from the high humidities prevailing most of the year, which make solar evaporation of sea water less efficient than in Aden; and the other works lie too far inland.

PHOSPHATES

Phosphates are possibly of greater potential value than any mineral already considered, for East Africa is particularly well endowed with phosphates, which are of increasing importance in fertilizer production. The largest deposit was found in 1950 near Tororo in Uganda, while a second was discovered in 1956 near Lake Manyara in Tanzania. The former consists of 200 million tons of material derived from a carbonatite plug, containing about 13 per cent. apatite (P_2O_5), together with magnetite and pyrochlore, both of potential value. This is the largest phosphate deposit in the Commonwealth, and it is believed that none of the world's major producers can match the 42 per cent. concentrates easily produced at Tororo. The Lake Manyara deposit is smaller, only 10 million tons having been proved as yet, but this too is of very high grade. Other deposits are known, but are all smaller or of lower grade.

Physical conditions for mining both major deposits are excellent: each forms a single deep mass, and there is little overburden to remove. Power is available at Tororo from

L

Owen Falls, and could be made so at Lake Manyara from the new station at Nyumba ya Mungu. Private capital has shown interest in the possibilities of large scale working of phosphates. Yet the Tanzania deposit remains untouched, and that in Uganda is worked only on a small scale. The main problem lies in moving the phosphates to potential markets. World supplies do not match demand and offers are frequently made, but the cost of moving this bulk commodity to a port is too high to permit a reasonable profit. Exports of 400,000 tons a year, once envisaged for Tororo, would require £3 million expenditure on expanded rail and port facilities, and therefore no special reduced rate could be offered for the 1,100-km. haul to Mombasa. Lake Manyara is nearer to the coast, but is 110 km. from a railhead; and the costs of a rail extension through country unlikely to provide any other freight would be prohibitive. Prospects would have been better at Tororo if markets had existed for the associated minerals, but the demand for pyrochlore is unreliable, while the price obtainable for magnetite does not justify its export.

There is some demand for fertilizers within East Africa, and apatite working began at Tororo in 1963 to supply a small factory producing superphosphate. Only about 150,000 tons of phosphate rock have been mined each year as yet, but operations are likely to expand as the local demand for fertilizers rises. If overseas markets for these could be found, mining at Tororo might become of great importance.

GOLD, TIN, WOLFRAM AND BERYL

Gold is much more widely distributed in East Africa than either diamonds or copper, and it was once the chief mineral export of the region; but it has never been of as much value as these are now, and in the late 1960s its importance dwindled. Thirty years earlier mining had been widespread, and exports were worth over £1½ million a year; but subsequently the industry became concentrated into a few units, mainly in northern Tanzania, and eventually even these closed down as costs rose above the fixed price of gold. Certain small operations have been revived recently, but in 1969 gold sales were worth less than £½ million, half from Tanzania and half from Kenya.

Tin mining is important in Rwanda, and tin bearing rocks extend across its border into Tanzania and Uganda. Production reached a peak around 1938, but declined in the 1950s, and revived only slightly in the 1960s. Wolfram, the ore of tungsten metal, and beryl, which has been used in the field of nuclear energy, have both been worked in south-west Uganda, but in each case former high hopes have been dashed as the small scattered deposits have proved costly to work and as world market conditions have fluctuated sharply.

MINERALS NOT YET WORKED: COAL AND IRON

The minerals which have played the greatest part in world economic development are both found in East Africa, but neither is yet worked. This cannot be explained by the nature of the deposits: the coal is of fair quality, and one field contains at least 300 million tons in undisturbed seams over 1 metre thick; and the iron ore includes some large deposits of high grade, those in Kigezi having 30 million tons of ore containing over 90 per cent. Fe_2O_3. The main factors hindering development of these resources have been the lack of local markets and the cost of transport to the coast for overseas export. The magnetite iron ore now obtained as a by-product from phosphate working at Tororo offers the best prospect for export, but although the mine is rail-served the lowest possible freight charge to Mombasa equals the f.o.b. price offered by prospective Japanese buyers. Southern Tanzania has both iron and coal deposits nearer the coast, but export prospects were not sufficiently certain to warrant extension of the former Southern Province Railway towards them. Iron ore mining for export may become practicable if a branch from the Tanzania-Zambia rail link is built, although transport costs would still be considerable.

For countries seeking opportunities for industrialization coal and iron mining for local consumption is, of course, more attractive than exploitation for export, but as yet this is only an idea in East Africa, for internal markets cannot support a modern iron and steel industry. For the future the basis for such an industry exists in southern Tanzania, where the large Ruhuhu coalfield lies only 55 km. from a deposit of at least 44 million tons of ore containing 49 per cent. iron at Liganga.

The iron deposits of Uganda and Kenya lie much closer to the main potential markets for steel, but in the absence of coal these must await improved techniques for smelting iron ore with electricity. In the short term it is unfortunate that coal and iron have not been found together nearer the main foci of economic activity in East Africa. In the long term the development of these resources in southern Tanzania may assist a wider disperal of industry, and benefit an area that is otherwise likely to fall ever further behind the rest of East Africa.

CONCLUSIONS

The role of mining in the East African economy is clearly very limited at present. It provides some useful sources of export income, but little employment, and only a very slight stimulus to industrial development. Its impact on the economic geography of the region is particularly feeble, for the two main enterprises form tiny, largely self-contained enclaves, which have little effect on the districts within which they lie. Furthermore, the general tenor of the 1960s has been one of stagnation, and even in some cases decline, in the mining industry, and the prospects for the 1970s for the main minerals now worked are not bright, as the best of the known resources are worked out.

Certain features of the geography of East Africa contributing to the small extent of mining development may be distinguished. Physical factors hindering prospecting are the thick layer of lateritic material covering the rocks in many areas and the dense vegetation of parts of the region. The sparse population reduces the chances of accidental discoveries. More important perhaps are the youthfulness and the small resources of the Geological Survey Department in each country, and the absence of many other enterprises able to undertake exploration work.

Neither labour nor power supplies present great problems, except that small mines dependent on large amounts of labour are no longer economically viable. Transport costs have hindered the exploitation of some large deposits of low value minerals, and contributed to the present concentration on minerals of high value: but it is not certain that more mining would be taking place if all mineralized areas had better transport facilities. The International Bank suggested that 'venture capital is the single element most vitally needed to explore and develop Tanganyika's mining potential'.[4] No doubt with more capital more prospecting could be done, but wherever a mineral deposit has shown a prospect of worthwhile returns foreign capital has been forthcoming. Some has even been provided for exploration, for the Colonial Development Corporation spent £1 million investigating Tanzania's coal deposits, and Shell-BP have spent large sums drilling, as yet unsuccessfully, for oil along the Kenya coast.

Although this is rarely conceded, the main reason for the small importance of mining may be the limited extent of mineral resources. The maps included in official reports on the geology and minerals of each country suggest at first glance great resources; but although a great variety of minerals has been found, they are in fact too widely scattered, and the number of deposits large enough to be of commercial value is small. The maps may indeed be interpreted as indicating the substantial amount of prospecting that has been undertaken with limited success. Some of the larger known but unworked deposits will be exploited in the future, and new resources may be found. In the long term East Africa may benefit from the replacement of export-oriented mining of diamonds and copper by the mining of phosphates, iron and coal for local industrial use. But the region certainly cannot depend on mineral development as a basis for future prosperity.

REFERENCES

1 R. C. Howard-Goldsmith, 'The Role of Minerals in African Development' in G. Wolstenholme (ed.), *Man and Africa*, Churchill, London, 1965, p. 282. Note also the standard work on the continent's mineral endowment: N. De Kun, *The Mineral Resources of Africa*, Elsevier, Amsterdam, 1965.

2 Full accounts of the mineral resources of East Africa and their exploitation are provided in: W. Pulfrey, *The Geology and Mineral Resources of Kenya*, Nairobi, 1960; J. W. Barnes (ed.), *The Mineral Resources of Uganda*, Entebbe, 1961; J. F. Harris, *Summary of the Geology of Tanganyika*, Part IV. Economic Geology, Dar es Salaam, 1961.

3 M. F. Hill, *Magadi*, Kynoch Press, Birmingham, 1964, is a history of the soda ash industry.

4 International Bank, *The Economic Development of Tanganyika*, Dar es Salaam, 1960, p. 151. The International Bank report on each country discuss mining, but that on Tanganyika is particularly useful. For a more recent assessment see Tanzania, *Second Five-Year Plan*, Dar es Salaam, 1969, Ch. 5.

CHAPTER 10

Manufacturing

Manufacturing industry has as yet made only a little progress in East Africa, but its importance is increasing steadily, and hopes for future prosperity rest to a large extent on its further expansion.[1] Too often, indeed, industrialization is seen as the panacea for the poverty of the region, and all the current development plans stress that increased agricultural production is at least equally important at present. Tanzania's Arusha Declaration goes so far as to say 'we have put too much emphasis on industries',[2] though noting their importance for long-term development.

Any examination of manufacturing faces severe problems of definition. Thus the figures published by the three East African countries for its contribution to employment and Gross Domestic Product are not strictly comparable, as the size of enterprise and range of activities included differ from one to another. Various forms of agricultural processing, for example, are sometimes included and sometimes omitted. In this discussion all forms of primary processing are normally excluded, this being defined as preparing produce in the form in which it normally enters world trade. Thus sugar milling is not considered here, as cane is never exported, but flour milling is, since trade in wheat is much greater than that in flour.

Attention is also concentrated on factory rather than on craft industry. Numerous small-scale industries such as tailoring and woodworking do of course exist, and most are of steadily increasing importance; but East Africa is not notable for traditional crafts, and they still play a much smaller role in the economy than in many other African countries. And while such activities as basket-making and pottery are discussed in the anthropologists' writings on particular peoples,[3] and have even been the subject of a few special studies,[4] little precise information is available on their distribution.

Before about 1950 there was very little factory industry in East Africa. Apart from engineering workshops, it was largely confined to flour and oil milling, baking, cigarette production, brewing, brick-making and printing. Since then many new industries have been established, generally producing goods for which there is a substantial market within the region, and which were formerly imported. Even today only about 120,000 people are employed in manufacturing out of the $1\frac{1}{2}$ million in all forms of paid employment in the region, but this figure has been rising more rapidly than in most other sectors of the economy. Manufacturing contributes about 9 per cent. of total Gross Domestic Product, which is somewhat above the average figure for tropical African countries, and this share is increasing year by year.

The range of industries now represented is comparable to that in many of the less developed countries.[5] The most important use local raw materials to produce commodities that are bulky and costly to transport, such as flour or cement; but some goods of higher value that are in great demand are also made from local materials, cigarettes and cotton textiles being examples. There are also a few industries dependent mainly on imported raw materials, such as oil refining and metal fabricating, while a start has been made on extending the degree of processing of local produce before export overseas, though this meets strong resistance from the importing countries. Also included here is a group of servicing industries, such as vehicle repair, which are particularly important in providing employment.

Most factories are very small, and are owned by local businessmen, many of whom have moved from trade into industry, but a few larger concerns, some owned by overseas companies or their local subsidiaries, account for much of the production of manufactured goods.[6] Several of the largest factories represent an investment of £2 to £5 million, but there are still no more than twenty of these.

Among the factors influencing the extent of manufacturing industry in the region the size of the local market is probably the most significant. The customs union between Kenya,

Uganda and Tanzania has given firms in each country easy access to a market of 35 million people, and the range of industries might have been smaller if this had not existed. Nevertheless, the general level of income is so low that the whole East African demand for many goods is too small to justify local manufacture. The market for cement and textiles is large enough to make local production economic, but that for motor vehicles is not. At the same time it is the expansion of the internal market for most goods that has allowed industry to develop steadily in recent years.

East Africa has enough raw materials to support much more manufacturing than takes place at present. Iron ore is locally available for a future iron and steel industry; there are deposits of phosphates large enough to supply a far larger fertilizer industry than yet exists; and only a very small proportion of the region's cotton production is used locally for textile manufacture. Cordage, shoes and soap are among the other commodities which could be produced in much larger quantities from local raw materials, if adequate markets were available.

It is doubtful whether either power or labour supplies limit industrial development in East Africa today. The capacity for electricity production has generally been greater than the demand for it, and supplies are available in most places where the establishment of new industries is likely to be considered. There is also a superabundance of labour in most urban centres at present, and unemployment is a serious problem. The lack of skilled men presents difficulties to many employers; but there are few examples of enterprise having been discouraged primarily for this reason.

Lack of capital and of local business enterprise has perhaps hindered industrial development. Capital can be obtained from overseas, but interest has to be paid on it and profits have to be great to cover this. Some foreign enterprise, as well as foreign capital, has been made available, but an overseas firm demands a prospect of higher or more certain profits than it can obtain from investment in its own country. East Africa has benefited in this respect from the presence of the Asian community, many of whom have shown great initiative in using the profits from trade to open small factories and occasionally to establish larger industrial concerns. Without the Asians there would certainly be substantially less manufacturing industry.

Government policy can greatly affect the development of manufacturing, and policy has recently been to encourage it whenever possible.[7] As shown in Chapter 18, government action has been an essential factor in the establishment of several industries. On the other hand the East African governments, unlike those of some underdeveloped countries, have not adopted a policy of industrial development at any price. There are no examples of industries which have been set up on a totally uneconomic basis, producing goods which could be imported far more cheaply.

THE DISTRIBUTION OF MANUFACTURING

Manufacturing is more fully developed in Kenya than in Tanzania and Uganda. In Kenya it employs about 60,000 people, and the estimate for value added during manufacture

TABLE 7

EMPLOYMENT IN SELECTED INDUSTRIES, 1967

	Kenya	Tanzania	Uganda
Grain milling	2180	1024	835
Textiles	3746	2579	5952
Clothing	3145	2057	803
Building materials	2036	1236	1578
Metals and machinery	6877	1792	3092
Printing and publishing	3104	1389	1020

in 1969 was £45 million. The equivalent figures for both Tanzania and Uganda are 30,000 to 35,000 people and £20 to 25 million. There is some evidence to suggest that industrial growth was more rapid in Tanzania than elsewhere in the late 1960s, but this reflected the limited extent of previous development; in absolute terms Kenya has undoubtedly maintained its lead. Not only is the total amount of industry greater in Kenya than elsewhere, but also the range of goods produced is much wider, as indicated by the figures for trade amongst the three countries. There are at least twenty products of which Kenya factories supply more than £200,000 worth annually to the other two countries: the equivalent figure for each of these is four.

The concentration of industrial development in Kenya is closely related to the existence of a larger market for most goods there than elsewhere. Many manufactured goods are quite beyond the pocket of most of the population, so that the total number of people in each country gives little indication of the size of the market. This is governed mainly by the number of people with a regular income and by the size of the income, and by these criteria Kenya provides much the most important market in East Africa.

In addition, a factory in central Kenya is better located to supply all three countries within the East African customs union than one in either Uganda or Tanzania. Distribution costs would generally be higher from a point in either of these countries than from a point in Kenya. Much manufacturing in East Africa represents replacement of imports by local production and much of the import trade of Uganda and of northern Tanzania is in the hands of Kenya firms (Chapter 13). These firms have often taken the initiative in establishing a local factory, and they have usually seen no good reason to look outside Kenya for a site.

Labour has been more abundant in Kenya than elsewhere, both the existence of a dense population with inadequate land and the restrictions placed on African production of cash crops for many years having contributed to this. Power supplies would appear to be more readily available in Uganda, but electricity from Owen Falls is now supplied to much of Kenya at low rates; and Kenya is better placed to import oil fuel.

Kenya has benefitted from the availability of more local capital than the other two countries, as a result of its larger Asian and much larger European population. It has also attracted more investment from overseas partly just because it is better known to the rest of the business world. Once Kenya had taken the lead in industrial development, this greatly assisted it in progressing further ahead, since each industry enjoys greater external economies there than in Tanzania or Uganda, and since the process of industrial linkage soon began to operate.

The distribution of manufacturing within Kenya stands out clearly on Map 12, and the most striking feature is the dominance of the city of Nairobi, without doubt the leading industrial centre of East Africa. In 1968, almost 60 per cent. of all employment and value added in manufacturing in Kenya was concentrated there, and the city had a total of almost 30,000 people working in its factories.[3] In certain individual industries the concentration is even greater, Nairobi accounting for 80

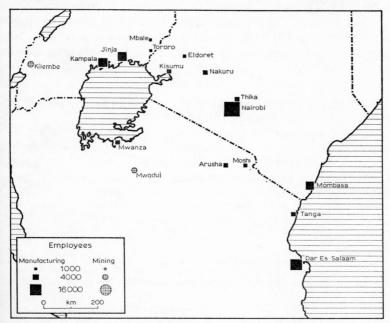

Figure 12. EAST AFRICA: Employment in Mining and Manufacturing, 1968

The centres indicated are all those with over 1,000 employees in mining or manufacturing.

per cent. of the 3,200 people employed in printing and publishing, for instance. In addition there are many manufacturing concerns in the adjacent parts of Central Province, notably in Thika, 45 km. to the north-east.

The only other important industrial centre in Kenya is Mombasa, which accounted for 14 per cent. of the employment and 18 per cent. of the value added in manufacturing in 1968. There are a few factories in Nakuru, Kisumu and Eldoret, but in none of these towns do they employ more than 2,000 people;

while elsewhere in the country there is hardly any manufacturing industry. Most factories located outside the Nairobi area and these other towns are sugar mills, sawmills and the like, which we have excluded from this discussion.

The concentration of industry in the towns, and especially in Nairobi, Thika and Mombasa, is tending to increase (Table 8). Employment in manufacturing rose much faster in these centres between 1957 and 1968 than in Kenya as a whole, and they have been chosen as the sites for most factories established

TABLE 8

DISTRIBUTION OF INDUSTRIAL EMPLOYMENT AMONG MAJOR TOWNS

Per cent. of national total in:	Kenya		Tanzania		Uganda	
	1963	1968		1968		1968
Nairobi	42	53	Dar es Salaam	45	Kampala	28
Mombasa	13	13	Arusha	5	Jinja	26
Thika	4	6	Tanga	5	Mbale	4
Nakuru	4	3	Mwanza	5	Tororo	4
Kisumu	3	2	Moshi	3		
Eldoret	3	2				

These figures are taken from official enumerations of employees and industrial censuses, which sometimes adopt a rather broad definition of manufacturing including much agricultural processing located outside the towns. For this reason they differ from those in the text.

since 1968. Several new factories have been erected in Nairobi's industrial area, while a number of existing plants have been extended. Employment in Thika has also increased sharply, especially with the establishment of new textile mills.

Elsewhere in Kenya a common trend is the closure of small factories, which find it increasingly difficult to compete with the larger enterprises in the main towns. Some expansion is taking place in Nakuru and Kisumu, but at a slower rate than in Nairobi and Mombasa, while there is no sign of new development in smaller towns, such as Kitale. Kenya is still at the stage, however, where one or two new large concerns can alter the pattern of manufacturing considerably; the prospective paper factory at Broderick Falls, for instance, will bring a significant dispersal.

Some of the factors favouring the concentration of industry in and around Nairobi can easily be distinguished, although a full explanation is probably impossible. The oldest industrial enterprise is the railway workshops. These were established at the point where the railway rose into the highlands and where an extra locomotive had to be taken on: this was also the nearest well-watered place to the mid-point of the original line from Mombasa to Kisumu. The selection of Nairobi as the administrative capital, together with its function as the railway headquarters, encouraged its growth as a commercial centre, and more recently industry has followed commerce.

The city itself provides a substantial market for many goods while there is a dense population in the country immediately to the north. Communications with the rest of Kenya and other parts of East Africa are good, while Nairobi already acts as the main distribution centre for imported goods. There is ample flat and unused land on the edge of the city, and services such as water supply and sewerage are provided. There is abundant unskilled labour close at hand, and electricity from Uganda is available. Many industrialists find it convenient to be at the financial centre of East Africa, while, now that many industries are established there, these in turn attract others.

The position of Mombasa as the second focus of industry is related to its function as the chief port of the country. Its largest factories either depend on imported raw material, examples being the oil refinery and the metal products factories, or export part of their production, like the cement plant. Much the most important servicing industry is the maintenance and repair of ships, employing over 1,000 people. The local market for manufactures is very limited, but good communications assist the despatch of goods both to the rest of Kenya and to northern Tanzania.

Manufacturing in Tanzania is also heavily concentrated in and around the capital city, Dar es Salaam providing about almost half of all industrial employment. Most industries found anywhere in Tanzania are represented there, and the city's factories are in general larger than those in other towns. Among the important older enterprises are a large flour mill, two breweries, cigarette, shoe, rayon textile and metal can factories. Even larger factories added in the late 1960s include a cement plant, an oil refinery and two cotton textile mills.

The only other town which has experienced an industrial boom in the 1960s is Arusha in the north, and the new factories established there are mostly small. Manufacturing is also represented in Tanga, Moshi and Mwanza, but until the opening of the Mwanza textile mill in 1969 most of the enterprises employed fewer than 200 people and sold their products only within the surrounding region. The situation may perhaps change in the next decade, for the 1969–74 development plan makes clear the government's intention to direct new industry away from Dar es Salaam to these provincial centres.[8] Thus only 24 per cent. of the employment provided by new industrial projects is scheduled for the capital city.

The attraction of a site in Dar es Salaam for a factory serving Tanzania is particularly strong, for as the capital and chief port of the country it combines the advantages of Nairobi and Mombasa. Manufacturers there can keep in touch with all national affairs, and are also in a good position to make overseas contracts. Accessibility to the Tanzania market as a whole is better from Dar es Salaam than from anywhere else, while raw materials and fuel from overseas are readily available.

The main attraction of Arusha is its fairly central position within the whole East African market. This is effective only in relation to movement by road or air, however, for rail connections between Arusha and most other towns are poor. To some extent the town's industries serve the northern parts of Tanzania, which are rather distant from the capital, but for this Arusha is no better placed than Moshi or Tanga.

Within Uganda manufacturing is largely confined to the south and east, and especially to the capital city, Kampala, and the second town, Jinja. Kampala accounts for over one-third of the country's 35,000 employees in this sector, while Jinja accounts for only slightly less of the employment and rather more of the value added. Mbale and Tororo, in the east, are lesser industrial centres, where factories employ 1,200 to 1,500 people, but in most other towns the figure is less than 150.

The towns differ considerably in the nature of their manufacturing. Kampala has many small light industries, attracted by the city's position as the commercial centre of Uganda. Jinja has fewer factories, but some are larger concerns, drawn there by greater availability of land, the opportunity for negotiating cheap rates for power and some government pressure. The pattern is repeated on a smaller scale by the various small factories of Mbale, the commercial centre of eastern Uganda, and the few larger plants at Tororo based on local sources of bulky raw materials.

The incentive for establishing manufacturing elsewhere in Uganda is very small. Markets are much smaller in the north and west, and communications are good enough to allow the limited needs of these areas to be supplied from the south-east. Nevertheless, as in Tanzania, it is now government policy to disperse industrial development more widely whenever possible, and three of the recent projects implemented by the Uganda Development Corporation are outside the existing industrial towns, namely the meat packing plant at Soroti, the cotton spinning mill at Lira and the cement factory near Kasese.

FOOD, DRINK AND TOBACCO

Even when concerns such as sugar factories are omitted, this forms the leading group of industries in East Africa. Within the group the most important activity is grain milling, in which over 5,000 people are employed in factories with more than five workers, and possibly a similar number in smaller mills. The largest factories are located in Nairobi, Nakuru, Eldoret, Jinja, Arusha and Dar es Salaam, and are mainly engaged in the production of wheat flour. Some of these also produce maize flour, but most of this is manufactured in smaller mills, widely scattered throughout the region. Both the supply of grain and the market for the product are less localized than for wheat, and maize-milling lends itself to small scale enterprise. Economies of scale are greater in milling wheat flour, and although the 1960s witnessed a dispersal from Kenya to Tanzania and Uganda, so that these countries now import wheat rather than flour from Kenya, this dispersal is unlikely to proceed much further.

Much of the wheat flour is used in the baking industry, which employs about 2,500 people. This is normally strongly market-oriented since the finished product is perishable and bulky, and bakeries are found in most of the larger towns of the region. Nevertheless, the largest concerns are capturing an increasing share of the limited market for bread, and over half the Kenya production, for example, is now concentrated in Nairobi.

Cotton seed provides the raw material for a large oil-milling industry, the cooking oil produced being one of the main items of expenditure of many East Africans.[9] The industry is heavily concentrated in the main areas of cotton production, Uganda and the Lake Victoria zone of Tanzania, and oil worth over £1½ million is sent annually from Uganda to Kenya. Mills were set up in many parts of Uganda during the 1940s, but there has recently been a great concentration of production into large factories in the Jinja and Kampala areas. This process has been assisted by the Lint Marketing Board's policy of paying for the transport of seed to the oil mills, for there is now no advantage in proximity to the cotton ginneries.

Brewing takes place in every village, but it is also a factory industry, and the leading breweries are among the largest manufacturing enterprises in East Africa. In value added during manufacture, beer is the most important commodity produced in the region. There are four large breweries in Kenya, of which three are in Nairobi, and one is in Mombasa. In Tanzania there are two in Dar es Salaam, and one in Arusha, and in Uganda one in Kampala and one in Jinja: but Kenya provides almost two-thirds of the total East African production of 100 million litres a year. Within the limits imposed by the need for large scale operation, the distribution of production is closely related to that of the market. The main raw materials by weight are water, which is available almost anywhere, and empty bottles, which are returned by the consumers; and the finished product is both bulky and fragile. The greatest demand for bottled beer was initially provided by the European population of Kenya and is now provided by the urban dwellers among the African population, and the breweries are well located to supply these markets.

Most tobacco cultivated in East Africa is consumed locally as cigarettes, and their production was one of the first manufacturing industries in the region. It is one of the most highly concentrated, for although the annual production is worth over £8 million, there is only one factory in each country and all three are owned by the giant British-American Tobacco Company. That in Nairobi is the oldest and largest, and employs about 700 people. The plant at Jinja dates from 1932, but that at Dar es Salaam was built only in 1961. Production was formerly more closely related to the pattern of tobacco cultivation, for this takes place mainly in Uganda and until 1955 there were two factories there. That at Kampala then ceased production, however, and expansion took place at Nairobi, which is better placed to supply the Kenya high lands which provide the largest market. Nairobi also supplied Tanzania at that time, but as the market expanded there it was an obvious step to use the tobacco grown in southern Tanzania for production at Dar es Salaam. Proximity to the market is, however, a matter of convenience rather than of transport costs for such a valuable commodity as cigarettes; and in fact a substantial trade in cigarettes continued until the Tanzania and Uganda governments persuaded the company to supply most of each country's requirements from the local factory.

TEXTILES AND CLOTHING

The manufactured goods in greatest demand among the mass of the population are textiles in various forms. Over £10 million worth of these are imported each year, but local production is now developing rapidly. The very large local production of cotton provides an added incentive for the establishment of textile manufacture, and it is felt that the export of cotton lint to Asian countries and import of cloth from these has continued for long enough. Furthermore this industry is relatively labour intensive, and offers better prospects as a source of new employment than any other in East Africa today.

The largest factory is that at Jinja, opened in 1956 and subsequently expanded until it now produces 45 million square metres of cloth annually. It represents a capital investment of £5 million, and gives employment to 4,000 people. The factory lies in the leading cotton growing district of Uganda, and the finished product can easily be distributed by rail throughout East Africa. For such a high-value commodity transport costs add very little to retail prices anywhere in the region. The selection of a location within Uganda, rather than at Mwanza

M

or Kisumu in other cotton growing areas, was encouraged by the participation of the Uganda Development Corporation in the venture. This body provided part of the original capital and now owns the whole enterprise. Jinja was a particularly attractive site since power requirements make up a large proportion of the operating costs, and it was possible to negotiate a bulk supply at a low rate. Location beside the Nile also ensures a water supply, and provides an outlet for effluent.

A second mill, with a capacity of 30 million square metres, was opened at Jinja in 1965. Once again initiative was a significant locational factor, for this is part of the Madhvani industrial empire. Three years later Uganda's third plant, smaller in scale, was established at Mbale. Neither Kenya nor Tanzania was content to replace overseas imports with imports from Uganda, however, and cotton textiles are now produced in both these countries also. In Tanzania four mills were opened between 1966 and 1969, two in Dar es Salaam, one in Arusha and one in Mwanza. Three have a capacity of about 24 million square metres and cost £3 to £4 million each to build: that at Arusha is rather smaller. Kenya already had two textile factories in the early 1960s, one at Mombasa and one at Thika, but both depended mainly on imported rayon. Its first factory using cotton was established at Kisumu, in the main growing area, in 1966.

This proliferation of textile factories has resulted in over-production of cheaper lines of cloth, and although this is probably only temporary it has caused the planned construction of further mills at Nakuru and Eldoret to be delayed. One project which is going ahead is rather different in nature, for this involves a £5 million plant at Lira in northern Uganda built with Soviet aid and designed to spin local cotton for export as yarn to the Soviet Union. If in the future such processing before export could be undertaken more extensively, this should greatly increase the value of East Africa's cotton production.

A small proportion of the output of the textile industry, together with some imported cloth, is used in about 20 clothing factories, most of them quite small concerns making underwear or shirts. The greatest concentration of such enterprises is in Nairobi, but there are others in Mombasa, Dar es Salaam,

Tanga and Kampala. This industry is protected by a tariff similar to that on textiles, and will probably expand considerably in the near future. Most of the increased local production of textiles will probably be used as at present, however, by innumerable tailors and dressmakers such as those who work their sewing machines outside many of the shops in most up-country trading centres.

Two other industries worth noting are the manufacture of shoes and the production of sacks and bags. There are many small shoemakers, but mass production of shoes also takes place, in a large factory at Limuru, near Nairobi, and a smaller one at Dar es Salaam. The former employs over 1,000 people, produces leather and rubber shoes, prepares its own leather from local hides and now produces other rubber goods such as cycle tyres. The latter, established by the same company in 1961, initially turned out canvas and plastic shoes but now produce leather shoes also. These factories satisfy most of the local market for footwear, and the size of this is the main factor governing the scale of production, though some shoes have been shipped to Somalia and Mauritius.

The limited extent to which East African sisal is used for local manufacture was noted earlier: but there is one large factory between Nairobi and Thika which uses it, together with some imported jute, to produce bags and sacks for agricultural produce. This enterprise employs 1,900 people, and turns out about 8 million bags a year for use in both Kenya and Uganda. A similar, though smaller, factory was opened at Moshi in northern Tanzania in 1968 to supply the needs of that country. Three other factories, which together consume much more of the Tanzanian sisal crop, now transform it into rope and twine before export, and as with Uganda cotton it is hoped that a much larger share of the crop will be exported in processed form in the future.

BUILDING MATERIALS

Cement production is one of the first large-scale industries to have been established in many poor countries, even though it is relatively capital-intensive and provides only a modest amount of employment. The main raw material, limestone, is very widespread, and the bulky finished product is costly to transport. It is of particular importance in that cement is required for many types of physical development, and its availability affects the growth of other types of economic activity. It is an industry in which economies of scale are great, and production is usually concentrated in a few large plants. In East Africa there are now five, which together manufacture about one million tons annually, worth over £7 million.

The first factories were built in 1953 at Tororo in Uganda and just north of Mombasa. Another was established in 1958 at Athi River, 25 km. from Nairobi and a fourth, near Dar es Salaam, came into operation in 1966. Uganda's second plant, near Kasese in the west, was opened in 1969. The Mombasa factory is much the largest, its capacity having been raised in 1968 from 400,000 to 700,000 tons. The others all had a capacity of rather less than 200,000 tons in 1970, but expansion was planned both at Dar es Salaam and in western Uganda.

The factory near Mombasa is sited on a raised coral reef, and limestone of excellent quality is available on the spot. Fuel accounts for a large proportion of all costs in the cement industry and, since this has to be imported, a coastal site is an advantage. The railway leading inland from Mombasa assists in the distribution of the product through much of Kenya, while the coastal location facilitates exports overseas. When a second factory was built in Kenya, however, there was a strong incentive to locate it near to the main market, which is provided by Nairobi. Athi River lies between the city and the nearest suitable source of limestone.

The main stimulus to the establishment of the industry in Uganda was provided by the construction of the Owen Falls Dam, for which large quantities of cement were required. It was thought that the demand for other purposes within Uganda would be sufficient to justify local production after the dam was completed, and the saving on transport costs resulting from local manufacture was even greater than in Kenya. Location at Tororo was influenced in part by the presence there of a large body of limestone; but the source in the west is in fact of superior quality. Tororo also offered proximity to the main markets, good transport facilities and the best position within Uganda for importing fuel. Development near Kasese had to await the building of the western rail extension, an expansion of the market, and the implementation of a government policy to promote industries in the poorer parts of the country.

The Dar es Salaam area is the obvious location for a factory in Tanzania, for coral limestone is locally available, fuel can easily be imported, and the city provides a major market, while being linked by rail to most other consuming areas. Conditions for cement production there are quite satisfactory, but ease of supply from Mombasa discouraged the establishment of a factory until Tanzania adopted a policy of reducing its dependence on imports from Kenya.

East Africa has been fortunate in being regarded as a suitable area for investment by the leading British cement producers, for they have provided most of the £12 million invested in the industry. Government has provided encouragement in Kenya and Tanzania, but it has provided capital only in Uganda, where the industry is owned by the Uganda Development Corporation. The limited demand for cement was until recently a major problem facing the industry, and the establishment of the factory at Dar es Salaam met some criticism on this account. An upsurge in the local building trade, however, brought a sharp increase in demand in the late 1960s, while the growth of export sales has justified the expansion at Mombasa. The high quality and low cost of the cement produced there have made this fully competitive in such markets as Mauritius, Reunion, Somalia and South Yemen, and in 1969 exports of 300,000 tons were worth £1½ million.

Asbestos-cement products have been manufactured since 1956 at a small factory at Tororo. There is a substantial market for these throughout East Africa, roofing sheets and drainage pipes being in demand for many purposes. Cement is the main raw material, and 5,000 tons a year is supplied by conveyor belt from the Tororo cement works. Asbestos has to be imported from overseas, but the volume needed is very small. Electric power is available from Owen Falls, while good transport facilities assist distribution throughout East Africa. The main factor influencing the location of the factory in Uganda was the enterprise of the Uganda Development Corporation, which has a share in the concern.

The brick and tile industry is smaller than the cement

industry but is much more widespread. The economies resulting from large-scale production are less, and most of the factories turn out less than £20,000 worth of bricks and tiles a year. The industry was one of the first to be established in East Africa. Raw material in the form of clay is abundant and government buildings, churches, schools and hospitals provided a market. The industry can be labour-intensive, in which case the capital requirements are small, and little power is needed. Brick-making was therefore well suited to East African conditions, and as the finished product is difficult to transport the industry was established wherever local demand and suitable clay were available. Bricks are still being made at missions in towns such as Mbarara and Gulu; but many such enterprises have now closed down and the industry has become less dispersed. The demand for bricks for institutional buildings has slackened, while that for houses is largely confined to the large towns. Thus in each country most of the production now comes from works close to the capital city. The decline in brick-making in other areas has, however, been partly offset by the development of cement block manufacture, which is suitable for very small scale enterprise and is highly dispersed.

CHEMICAL AND RELATED INDUSTRIES

Two of the most important new industrial enterprises are the oil refineries established at Mombasa in 1963 and at Dar es Salaam in 1966. This industry requires even more capital and provides even less employment than cement manufacture, yet it is clearly in any country's interest to import crude oil rather than refined products if processing can be undertaken on a scale large enough to be economic, and refineries have been built in many African countries in recent years. In some the market available is not really large enough, but both Kenya and Tanzania have been fortunate in finding export markets.

The Mombasa refinery is the larger of the two, representing a capital investment of £7 million, and having a throughput of 2,500 million litres in 1969. Even though it was originally intended to supply the whole of East Africa, Mombasa was the obvious location, since that port previously handled 80 per cent. of the refined petroleum imported into the region, and from there the various oil products could be distributed through the same channels as before. The only areas not formerly served by Mombasa were supplied through Dar es Salaam, which was therefore the most appropriate site for a second refinery. The main question that caused debate was whether a second plant was justified at all: certainly it was in part nationalism and big business competition respectively which led the Tanzanian government and the Italian state oil company to invest £2½ million each in the enterprise.

East Africa has not in fact suffered from over-capacity, mainly because since Rhodesia's UDI Zambia has depended upon the Dar es Salaam refinery for its oil supplies. Total exports of oil products from Tanzania in 1969 were worth over £5 million, Zambia accounting for two-thirds. Meanwhile the Mombasa refinery has made up for the loss of the Tanzania market by increased sales elsewhere. In addition to Uganda and the Indian Ocean islands, two important outlets are passing ships and aircraft.

For many years East Africa imported fertilizers worth almost £1 million from overseas, nearly half being phosphates, and this provided an obvious potential market for the large phosphate deposit at Tororo in Uganda. Fertilizer production began in 1963 and has reached 25,000 tons of single superphosphate a year. The Kenya highlands provide the main market, and sulphur has to be imported from overseas, yet production at Tororo is more economic than it would be in Kenya, since the phosphates are considerably more bulky and costly to transport than the finished product. Even this however, has a low value for its weight, and the enterprise is assisted by the low rate charged for movement of fertilizers by rail. Plans are now in hand to increase the value of the industry to Uganda by producing triple superphosphate and by using the sulphur available from the copper industry.

Meanwhile fertilizer imports have risen to £3 million a year, and soon nitrogenous fertilizers will also be produced in East Africa. Plans for such an industry at Mombasa were shelved in 1968, since the market still seemed too small to permit production at a lower cost than import; but in Tanzania the National Development Corporation is proceeding with its plans for a £4½ million plant at Tanga.

The soap industry shows a completely different pattern. There are about fifty soap factories in East Africa, but they employ fewer than 2,000 people all together. Much the largest is in Nairobi, producing several brands formerly imported and exporting soap worth over £½ million annually to Uganda and Tanzania. There are six other soap factories in Nairobi, five in Mombasa and four in Kisumu. The pattern of production in Tanzania is one of many small plants, mainly concentrated in and around Dar es Salaam, Tanga and Mwanza. In Uganda there are fifteen factories, mainly in the towns of Eastern Region. The main raw materials are various types of vegetable oil, and most of the factories are located near to supplies of these. Those on the coast use coconut oil almost exclusively, while those in the cotton growing areas, such as eastern Uganda, Mwanza and Kisumu, use cotton-seed oil and are often attached to oilmills. Only the Nairobi factories have to bring their raw materials from some distance, coconut oil from the coast and palm oil from Congo being the most important. For the cheaper types of soap, which make up most of the production, proximity to markets is an important factor in location, and the widespread demand for this commodity has contributed to the wide scatter of soap factories.

The establishment of small paint factories in Dar es Salaam and Nairobi has made East Africa 50 per cent. self-sufficient in this commodity, and has added to the range of industries in these cities. Another industry which has spread from Nairobi to the other three cities is glass manufacture. Its growth closely reflects the expansion of the brewing and soft drinks industries, for bottles form the main product. The manufacture of sheet glass, which requires much more expertise and costly equipment, has not yet begun. A group of industries which developed particularly rapidly during the 1960s produce pharmaceuticals and toilet preparations of various kinds. These are highly dependent on close links with publicity and distribution services, and are heavily concentrated in Nairobi.

Mention might be made here of two new industries, tyre and paper manufacture. Cycle tyres have been made in East Africa for some years, but construction of the first factories to produce vehicle tyres began only in 1970. One is being established in Nairobi by Firestone, the other in Arusha by

General Tires, at a cost of about £5 million each. The building of two plants simultaneously reflects some rivalry between the two companies, as well as between Kenya and Tanzania, for both concerns aim to sell throughout East Africa, choosing their location with this in view.

Paper is another commodity for which the market in East Africa is growing rapidly, and all three countries have plans for local production. After several years of discussions work has begun on a £12 million project at Broderick Falls in Kenya. This site lies close to the largest softwood plantations in East Africa, and should bring some industrial employment to an area greatly in need of it. Tanzania is less well endowed with suitable timber, but it has been seeking new outlets for its sisal crop, and this raw material is to be used for paper pulp manufacture in a £18 million factory near Tanga.

METALS AND ENGINEERING

In most advanced industrial countries the manufacture of metals and their transformation into machinery and scores of other products form the most important branches of industry. In East Africa, however, these activities are very little developed; and metals and metal products of all types are the leading imports into the region. Metals in simple processed form worth £40 million, and machinery and transport equipment worth £80 million have been imported into Kenya, Tanzania and Uganda in most recent years. Replacement of these imports by local production is hindered by the fact that very large scale production is necessary for most of these goods. For the manufacture of iron and steel from ore to be economic a market for 1 million tons of steel a year is sometimes considered to be necessary. East Africa now consumes little over 200,000 tons of steel a year, and the only practical possibility in this field has been steel rolling based on scrap.

Metal manufacture is therefore confined to the steel rolling mill at Jinja, built in 1962, and now producing 25,000 tons of steel plates and bars annually. Scrap is obtained from all parts of East Africa, Kenya supplying the largest share. Since Kenya also forms the chief market, sites there were considered for the factory. The choice of Jinja is related partly to the fact that the industry was sponsored and to some extent financed by the local Madhvani concern, partly to the support of the Uganda Development Corporation, which also has a share in the concern, and partly to the availability of power from Owen Falls. The power requirements are very great, and it was possible to negotiate a bulk supply at a very low charge. A second enterprise, opened in 1970 at Mombasa, undertakes re-rolling of imported steel billets to produce rods and wire, thereby saving Kenya some foreign exchange. For this activity a coastal location has obvious advantages, and a similar site has been selected for a plant in Tanzania, though as a contribution to decentralization it is near Tanga rather than Dar es Salaam.

Among the metal-using industries established in East Africa, one of the most important is the production of cans for meat, fruit, vegetable oil and kerosene. The Metal Box Company has invested £2 million in plants at Thika and Dar es Salaam, and these turn out cans worth over £2 million a year, using tinplate from South Wales. Cans for vegetable oil and kerosene are also produced in two small plants at Jinja. Other factories produce steel drums, window-frames, nuts and bolts and razor blades. These are concentrated in Mombasa and Dar es Salaam, where imported raw materials are readily available, but there are also some factories of this type in Nairobi. Large quantities of corrugated iron sheeting have long been imported, and plants have recently been set up at the coast to undertake the final stages of production of these.

The most widely dispersed metal-using industry is the manufacture of cooking utensils and similar products from imported aluminium. The largest factories are located in Mombasa and Dar es Salaam, but there are smaller concerns in several other towns, including Kampala. Another enterprise in the Kampala area produces enamelware products.

Although very little machinery or transport equipment is manufactured in East Africa, what is imported has to be maintained and repaired. These servicing industries employ over 25,000 people and from this point of view are much more important than the metal industries considered above. The scale of these activities varies greatly, from the huge railway workshops in Nairobi with a labour force of 6,000 to the motor mechanic working on his own, but nearly all the enterprises are labour- rather than capital-intensive.

This group of industries, mostly linked with one another or with other industries and greatly affected by external economies, is heavily concentrated in Kenya. That country accounts for 70 per cent. of the total employment, and the value added by these industries there is estimated at over £10 million a year. Within each country the large concerns are nearly all located in the main cities, but vehicle repair and light engineering works are widely scattered, and form the chief activities in the 'industrial area' of many small towns.

REFERENCES

1 For a general discussion see A. B. Mountjoy, *Industrialization and Under-developed Countries*, Hutchinson, London, 1966. A valuable survey of the African situation is A. F. Ewing, *Industry in Africa*, Oxford U.P., London, 1967. Fuller discussions of East African industry are D. S. Pearson, *Industrial Development in East Africa*, Oxford U.P., 1969; E. J. Stoutjesdijk, *Uganda's Manufacturing Sector*, E. A. Publishing House, Nairobi, 1967; K. Schadler, *Manufacturing and Processing Industries in Tanzania*, Weltforum Verlag, Munchen, 1969; R. B. Ogendo, *Inudstrial Geography of Kenya*, E. A. Publishing House, Nairobi, in the press.
2 J. K. Nyerere, *Freedom and Socialism*, Oxford U.P., Nairobi, 1968, p. 241.
3 E.g. G. Wagner, *The Bantu of Western Kenya*, Oxford U.P., London, 1970, Vol. II, pp. 8–18.
4 E.g. M. Trowell and K. P. Wachsmann, *Tribal Crafts of Uganda*, Oxford U.P., London, 1953. The only major economic study of crafts so far made is K. Schadler, *Crafts, Small-scale Industries and Industrial Education in Tanzania*, Weltforum Verlag, Munchen, 1968.
5 Full details on the structure of industry are provided in annual surveys, the latest available at the time of writing being Tanzania, *Survey of Industrial Production 1966*, Dar es Salaam, 1969, and Uganda, *Survey of Industrial Production 1967*, Entebbe, 1969. Comparable Kenya surveys are summarised in the annual *Statistical Abstract*, but the last to be published in full was that for 1963.
6 National Christian Council of Kenya, *Who Controls Industry in Kenya?*, E. A. Publishing House, Nairobi, 1968.
7 Kenya, *Development Plan 1970–1974*, Nairobi, 1969, Ch. 10; Tanzania, *Second Five-Year Plan 1969–1974*, Dar es Salaam, 1969, Vol. I. Ch. 4; Uganda, *Work for Progress, Uganda's Second Five-Year Plan 1966–1971*, Ch. 5.
8 Tanzania, *op. cit.*, pp. 67–68 & 74.
9 D. M. S. Coles, *The Vegetable Oil Crushing Industry in East Africa*, Oxford U.P., Nairobi, 1968. Studies of the pattern and prospects of many other individual industries in East Africa have been made by the U.N. Economic Commission for Africa, and circulated in mimeographed form.

CHAPTER 11

Power and Transport

Power and transport are both examined in this book from two points of view. In this chapter the production of electricity and the movement of goods and people are discussed as economic activities contributing to the income of East Africa. In Chapter 17 power supplies and transport facilities are considered as factors affecting the distribution of other activities.

ELECTRICITY PRODUCTION[1]

Electricity generation is sometimes regarded as a form of manufacturing, and it is therefore examined here immediately after other forms of manufacturing. The value of electricity produced annually in East Africa exceeds £12 million, and it contributes more to the income of the region than any industry considered above. As elsewhere, power generation employs relatively few people, but power distribution employs many more, and the whole industry provides work for 6,000 men.

The total installed generating capacity in 1969 was just over 400,000 kw., and electricity production slightly exceeded 1,500 million kwh. In comparison with more advanced areas capacity and production are small: Britain has 60 million kw. generating capacity, Canada 36 million and Australia 12 million. Power production is not hindered by lack of physical resources for, although East Africa has little coal and no oil, the latter can easily be imported from the Middle East, while many opportunities exist for the harnessing of water power. It is limited mainly by the small local demand for electricity. The demand per capita, however, is larger than in many African countries, such as Ethiopia and Nigeria, and is steadily rising. In fact, electricity consumption in East Africa roughly doubled between 1959 and 1969, and therefore power production is among the most dynamic sectors of the economy.

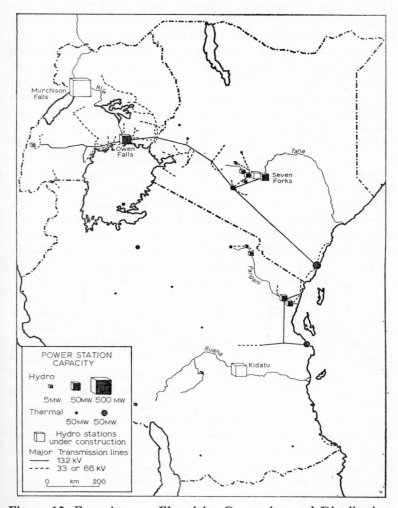

Figure 13. EAST AFRICA: Electricity Generation and Distribution.
The map indicates the situation in 1970. There is a denser network
of 11 kv. transmission lines which could not be mapped.

The location of the main power stations and transmission
lines is shown on Map 13. Uganda contributes the largest
share of the total production, generating 731 million kwh. in

1969, compared with 459 million in Kenya and 358 million in Tanzania. In each country there are also numerous private diesel generators, but their output is very small. Whereas the scale of electricity production has been limited more by demand than by resources, the market has less effect on its location. Although Uganda, with superior resources, is the leading producer, consumption is highest in Kenya. Since 1958 much electricity has therefore been sent from Uganda to Kenya, and this movement now amounts to 200,000 kwh. a year.

Until 1954 most power in East Africa came from thermal stations in the towns, and the distribution of production matched that of consumption very closely. The first plants were built at Nairobi, Mombasa and Dar es Salaam between 1907 and 1909, while ten towns had their own supply by 1939. These three cities are still the main centres of thermal electricity generation. Installations at Mombasa had a capacity of 46,000 kw. in the 1960s, and this was raised to 90,000 kw. in 1970–71. The city is well placed for importing oil, and is far from any site within Kenya suitable for hydro-electricity generation. Dar es Salaam was also entirely dependent on thermal power until hydro-electricity reached it in 1964, and this is again of increasing importance, since the 17,500 kw. capacity there was supplemented by a further 32,000 kw. in 1968–69. Consumption in the Nairobi area is much greater than around Mombasa or Dar es Salaam, and oil is also still used in power stations there, although hydro-electricity satisfies most of the demand. Thermal stations cost more to operate there since fuel must be brought from the coast, and they are used only at times of peak demand or of low water in the rivers. A thermal station supplies the needs of Zanzibar, and smaller thermal plants serve many Tanzania and Kenya towns which are far from sources of water power; but in Uganda most thermal plants have been closed down as hydro-electricity satisfies virtually all requirements.

Hydro-electricity provides most of the power generated in East Africa today, for costs of production are substantially lower than at most of the thermal stations. The outstanding source is the Owen Falls power station, opened in 1954 at Jinja in Uganda. It is located just where the Nile flows out of Lake Victoria. The potential of the site was recognized long ago, the value of the falls being much enhanced by the vast natural reservoir provided by the lake. As Churchill observed in 1908, 'it is possible that nowhere in the world could so enormous a mass of water be held up by so little masonry'.[2] A relatively small dam now retains a volume of water larger than that held behind the huge Boulder Dam in the United States. Not only were physical conditions particularly favourable, but Owen Falls is also situated in the heart of the zone of greatest potential demand for electricity within Uganda. Unlike many power sites it lay beside a road and railway, and was well placed for the assembly of construction materials and the recruitment of labour.

The main factor discouraging development before the 1950s was the size of the market, and the construction of the dam and power station became economically attractive only when industrial development began in Uganda and when technical advances in power transmission permitted sales to Kenya. The 500 km. from Jinja to Nairobi is now within the maximum distance that power can be moved economically, and about one-third of that generated at Owen Falls is exported by 132 kv. transmission line to the Eldoret, Kisumu, Nakuru and Nairobi areas of Kenya. Despite vigorous efforts to expand sales, including the provision of 8,000 km. of transmission line within Uganda, internal consumption at first rose more slowly than anticipated, and the power station was brought to its full capacity of 150,000 kw. only in 1968. Industry accounts for three-quarters of the Uganda consumption, and must remain the main market since the highly dispersed settlement pattern, as well as low income, hinders domestic sales.[3]

In south-west Uganda a small plant on the Kagera has long supplied electricity to local tin mines and now provides a public supply for Ankole, while an even smaller station serving Kabale was opened in 1964. The larger Mobuku power station in Toro supplies only Kilembe mine.

Hydro-electricity was produced in both Kenya and Tanzania before Owen Falls was developed. Map 13 shows several plants on rivers north of Nairobi, which have supplied power to central Kenya for many years. These were supplemented in 1968 by the first stage of the Seven Forks scheme further downstream on the Tana river, in the form of a dam and a

40,000 kw. power station at Kindaruma. Construction costs were relatively high but the site is conveniently located within 200 km. of Nairobi. This development is also to some extent the result of Kenya's wish to make fuller use of its own resources, and to decrease its dependence on supplies from Uganda, so political considerations are joining physical and economic factors in guiding the pattern of power production. The rapid flow of the Pangani river and a substantial demand for electricity in north-east Tanzania encouraged the establishment there of a power station in 1936, later enlarged to 17,500 kw. capacity. In 1964 another, of 21,000 kw. capacity, was built near-by at Hale, mainly to supply the growing needs of Dar es Salaam by a 220-km. transmission line, in preference to the installation of additional thermal plant in the capital at that time; and in 1968 an 8,000 kw. plant was opened at Nyumba ya Mungu, higher up the river, to supply Moshi and Arusha.

These developments have still hardly touched the water power resources of East Africa, and further projects are now in progress and planned.[4] The total potential of the Nile between lakes Victoria and Albert is estimated at about $1\frac{1}{2}$ million kw., and this provides the obvious source for Uganda's increased power requirements of the 1970s. Suitable sites exist at Bujagali, 7 km. downstream from Owen Falls, and at both Karuma Falls and Murchison Falls further north on the Bunyoro-Acholi border. The main demand for electricity is still found in the Kampala-Jinja-Mbale zone of the south-east, and in the short term the Bujagali site might have been the most economic; but for supplying the whole country with electricity Murchison Falls is suitably complementary to Owen Falls, and in the hope of spreading development more evenly over the country this site was selected. The power station there is due to have an initial capacity of 105,000 kw. in 1972, rising later to 150,000 kw., and finally to 600,000 kw.

Meanwhile work is proceeding to make fuller use of the potential at Seven Forks, by building a dam and a 50,000 kw. power station at Kamburu, 24 km. above Kindaruma. Eventually a third project should raise the capacity provided by the whole scheme to more than 250,000 kw. Tanzania also has much unused potential, and attention has turned to the

Ruaha and Rufiji rivers. A dam under construction at Kidatu on the Ruaha should allow the establishment of a power station there by 1973, with a capacity of 50,000 kw., rising later to 200,000 kw. The costs there are relatively high, but are off set by other benefits in the form of flood control and irrigation. The same would apply to the larger scheme proposed for Stiegler's Gorge on the Rufiji, where 600,000 kw. might be generated.

Concurrently with these undertakings the transmission grid within each country is being extended. For instance, the Mombasa thermal plants and the hydro stations in central Kenya have now been linked into a single system, while Owen Falls and Murchison Falls will be similarly connected. It will be to East Africa's advantage if the existing link between Kenya and Uganda is also retained, and perhaps extended to Tanzania, especially if transmission technology improves. This should ensure that each area is supplied with electricity at the lowest possible cost, whatever changes in the pattern of supply and demand may occur.

TRANSPORT

Transport, unlike electricity generation, is not a form of production, but it is an important economic activity. Official estimates place its contribution to the Gross Domestic Product of East Africa at £85 million, which is 7 per cent. of the total and little below that of manufacturing, and this excludes the large amount of transport undertaken within the subsistence sector of the economy. The carrying of water, for instance, occupies much of the energy of many households. Even discounting this, transport is an extremely widespread activity, providing employment in every corner of the region; but there are marked variations in its importance. Nationally, this is greatest in Kenya and least in Uganda, since most of Uganda's overseas trade moves only a short distance within the country but travels a long distance across Kenya and is transferred to and from ships there. Thus about 45,000 people are employed in transport and communications in Kenya, compared with 30,000 in Tanzania and 10,000 in Uganda. Within each country there is heavy concentration in and around the capital city. This is especially clear in Tanzania, where Dar es Salaam

N

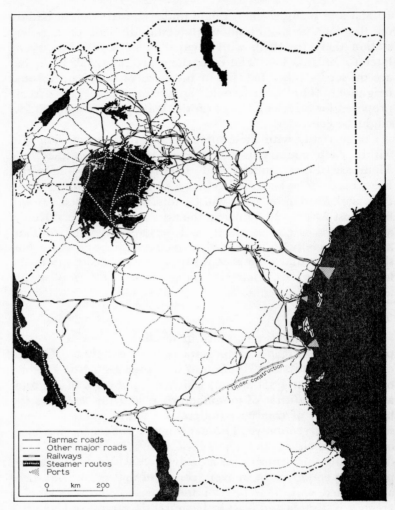

Figure 14. EAST AFRICA: Transport Network
The transport routes shown are those existing in 1970. A dense
network of minor roads also exists in many areas. The port symbols
are drawn in proportion to the volume of cargo handled in 1969.

is also the chief port and thus accounts for almost half of all
employment in transport, but even in Uganda the equivalent
figure for Kampala is over 40 per cent.

Road Transport

Road and rail transport are probably roughly comparable as sources of income in East Africa, although they differ greatly in structure. Road transport is operated mainly on a very small scale; but there are so many small operators that the number of people earning a living in road transport is very large. Motor vehicles came into general use in the 1920s, but the greatest expansion of road transport came thirty years later. Today there are many more vehicles per head of population than in Nigeria or even Egypt, and the number rises each year. As Table 9 suggests, the majority are private cars, but the figures for vans, lorries and buses understate the volume of commercial road transport, since much takes place in private cars. A large proportion of the cars on many East African roads are used, legally or otherwise, as taxis, providing many people with a good income. This is especially well developed in Uganda, and helps to explain the small number of buses there.

TABLE 9

ROAD TRANSPORT IN EAST AFRICA, 1953–1968

	Kenya	Tanzania	Uganda
Thousand vehicles 1968	110	75	45
Private cars	60	31	26
Commercial vehicles	34	30	13
Lorries	12	13	5
Vans	20	14	7
Buses	2·1	3·1	0·8
Thousand vehicles 1963	87	53	42
Commercial	19	21	11
Thousand vehicles 1953	44	22	18
Commercial	9	8	6

Chief sources of data: Kenya, *Annual Vehicle Statistics;* Tanzania, *Annual Vehicle Statistics;* Uganda, *Statistical Abstract;* EAC, *Economic and Statistical Review,*

Within each country, road transport activity is heavily concentrated in the most prosperous areas, especially around the capital. Almost two thirds of the vehicles imported into Kenya are registered in Nairobi, although registration may take place in ten other towns. In Uganda in 1957 Buganda accounted for 56 per cent. of lorry ownership, Eastern Region for 27 per cent., and Western and Northern Regions for only 10 per cent. and 6 per cent. respectively,[5] and there is no evidence to suggest much change since then. Vehicles may of course move far from the town where they are registered, or where their owners live, but traffic counts show a far greater intensity on roads in and around Nairobi, Mombasa, Kampala, Jinja, Dar es Salaam and Tanga than elsewhere.

The overall importance and the areal pattern of road transport are both affected by the nature of the road network.[6] Road building has been assisted by the character of the earth in many areas, simple earth (murram) roads serving very well for light traffic. Although few roads are tarred (Map 14) the road network is much better than in countries such as Sudan and in much of East Africa is adequate for the demands made upon it. Some areas are without roads, notably in central and western Tanzania, and in others many roads are impassable in the wet season, but the distribution of road transport activity is related mainly to factors other than the roads themselves.

The pattern reflects both density of population and incomes, transport being particularly active in such heavily settled and relatively prosperous areas as Buganda and the Kenya highlands. This relationship is particularly close since road transport is essentially local in nature, rarely involving long hauls across poor and lightly settled areas. These are largely the preserve of rail transport, partly because it is cheaper and partly because of restrictive licensing of long-distance movements by lorry in Kenya and Tanzania. Licensing may have limited road haulage somewhat, although paradoxically, Uganda, which has no restrictive licensing, has many fewer lorries than either Kenya or Tanzania. This may be due to the predominance in Uganda of very short hauls on good roads, for which light vans are suitable. Another factor affecting the distribution of road transport is the cost of fuel, for retail petrol prices in 1970 ranged from under 1/– per litre in Mombasa to 1/50 in the extreme south-west of Uganda.

The availability of alternative forms of transport naturally affects the amount of road transport undertaken. Thus it is more important in southern Tanzania, where there is no alternative, than in other areas where population density an incomes are comparable. There, in fact, the railway adminstration operates its own bus and lorry services. Even where rail or water services are available, however, road transport is now expanding at their expense, especially as the roads are steadily improved. In East Africa road transport is generally faster than rail, and this encourages transference to road of both passengers and goods, even though costs are normally greater.[7]

Rail Transport

In spite of competition from the roads, the railways of East Africa still undertake most long-distance movement of bulk loads. All the services are operated by the East African Railways Corporation on behalf of the three governments, although the Tanzania system was developed separately and amalgamated with the remainder only in 1948. Rail transport provides employment for 40,000 people, and the revenue earned annually by the railways is about £24 million. Passengers provide less than 10 per cent. of this sum, freight being far more important. The total length of track in 1970 was 7,000 km., of which 2,900 lay in Tanzania, 2,700 in Kenya and 1,400 in Uganda. In proportion to the size of the country the Tanzania figure is small, for much land there is insufficiently productive to justify railway construction; but in proportion to population it is high, for lines linking well settled zones cross long stretches of empty country. Even in proportion to population, however, the Kenya figure is higher, the European settlement of the highlands having provided a greater stimulus for railway building than peasant agriculture, which dominated the other countries more completely.

The first line to be built, leading inland from Tanga, was started in 1893 but did not reach Moshi until 1911 and Arusha until 1929. The line from Mombasa to Kisumu was built between 1896 and 1902, and the branch into Uganda reached Kampala in 1931. The third main line, from Dar es Salaam to Kigoma, was started in 1905 and completed in 1914. The Tanzania lines were built by the Germans primarily with political motives, and were operated at a loss for many years. That built across Kenya was also partly political in purpose, but was also intended to assist the supression of the slave trade and to tap the productive Lake Victoria basin. It quickly developed substantial freight traffic, and the Kenya-Uganda system has normally operated at a profit.[8]

Several branch lines were built between the wars, most to

assist European settlement in Kenya but some to provide outlets for other areas with a surplus of agricultural produce. Mineral deposits have provided less stimulus than in many countries but were responsible for the early branch to Magadi and the post-war lines to Mpanda and Kasese. The most recent branches are those to northern Uganda, which replaces an outdated water service, and to Kidatu in Tanzania, which should tap the large tracts suitable for agricultural development in the Kilombero valley.

The main line across Kenya is much the most important, carrying over 4 million tons of freight a year, although this is still insufficient to justify either electrification or doubling of track. The equivalent figures for the Tanga and Tanzania Central lines are only ⅓ million tons and 1 million tons. The dominance of the main Kenya-Uganda line reflects both its handling of almost all the exports and imports of Kenya and Uganda, and also the large volume of internal Kenya traffic handled. The Tanga Line does little more than move sisal to the coast, especially since much of the trade of Moshi and Arusha passes through Mombasa. The Central Line handles all the export and import traffic of central and western Tanzania, but since these are poor areas the volume is small. The two longer lines both carry some transit traffic, for they provide the main outlets for Rwanda and Burundi and serve parts of Congo, but this is only a small proportion of the total of 3,500 million ton-km. of freight handled annually in East Africa.

It can be argued that Tanzania's size and Uganda's distance from the sea make these countries more dependent than Kenya on rail transport. But it is of greatest importance as an economic activity in Kenya, which has, for example, 60 per cent. of all people employed in rail transport in East Africa. It generates the greatest volume of freight traffic, and in addition the Uganda traffic handled within Kenya is greater (in ton-kms.) than that handled within Uganda itself. The railway headquarters and the main workshops are located in Nairobi, while Nairobi and Mombasa-Kilindini are the two most important stations on the system in both employment and traffic handled, and even Nakuru is as important as either Dar es Salaam or Kampala.

A new development that will change fundamentally the

pattern of rail transport in East Africa is the construction of a completely new line from Dar es Salaam south-westwards to link up with the Zambian system (Map 14). Proposals for such a line were made many years ago, but traffic prospects were too poor until UDI in Rhodesia forced Zambia to turn to the Dar es Salaam route for its overseas trade. The railway is being financed and built by China, the cost being estimated at £170 million, and completion is planned for 1975. The volume of freight handled could exceed 2 million tons a year if the greater part of Zambia's exports and imports used this route. It was originally intended that the Kidatu branch should form the starting point for such a line, but unfortunately there will be no direct link with the E.A.R. system, at least initially, partly because of a difference in guage.

Inland Water Transport

East Africa has few navigable rivers, but its lakes offer excellent opportunities for transport. Many small enterprises ferry passengers and goods from place to place around the lake-shores, but large scale operations are undertaken only by E.A. Railways. In 1961 this organization owned 12 ships, 9 tugs and 80 lighters, which served 75 ports on lakes Victoria, Kyoga, Albert and Tanganyika, and on short sections of the Nile. Subsequently some services were withdrawn, mainly because of declining traffic, and since 1965 only 35 ports have been served, all on lakes Victoria and Tanganyika.

Lake Victoria has always had most traffic because of its size, the dense population and the high level of production around its shores, and the close links between the countries which border it.[9] About 300,000 tons of cargo are now handled annually. The importance of the lake to its borderlands has declined since 1920, when it provided the only outlet for Uganda and parts of Tanzania; but lake transport is still very valuable to Mara and West Lake, for which a long haul on poor roads is the only alternative. Many goods are also moved across the lake between the Kisumu, Mwanza and Kampala-Jinja areas. Even on Lake Victoria many small ports have closed down, but water transport between the main centres still has an important role to play, as the introduction of train ferries in 1966 clearly demonstrates.

The Lake Tanganyika service is vitally important to the communities near the shores, but these are small and provide little traffic. The main movement on the lake is between Kigoma and Burundi or Congo. The distance from Kalemie to Dar es Salaam is only 1,500 km., compared with 3,200 km. to the Atlantic at Matadi, and although traffic was cut sharply after Congo independence it may expand again in future. For Burundi the incentive to use the Kigoma route has increased now that it is no longer linked politically to Congo.

Sea Transport

East Africa has two small shipping companies, one of which, the Eastern Africa National Shipping Line, built up a fleet of four 5,000 to 10,000-ton vessels between 1967 and 1970. Most of its overseas trade, however, is still carried in the ships of other nations. The volume of coastal traffic is small, and tends to decrease as roads along the coast are improved, apart from the important flow between Dar es Salaam and Zanzibar. The Arab dhows, for which the coast was once famous, have declined in importance, though a few may still be seen, notably at Lamu.

Sea transport as an economic activity concerns East Africa mainly through the employment of 12,000 people at the ports of Mombasa, Tanga, Dar es Salaam, Mtwara and Zanzibar.[10] Deep-sea ships make almost 4,000 calls at these ports annually, loading or unloading 8 to 9 million tons of cargo, of which Mombasa alone accounts for 5 to 6 million.

The dominance of Mombasa is clearly related to the extent and nature of its hinterland. It is the only ocean port for Kenya and Uganda, and also handles some Rwanda, Congo and Tanzania traffic. The site provides an excellent natural harbour opposite a gap in the coral reef; and it is a very old port, although the old harbour has been little used since the establishment in 1912 of the deep-water harbour of Kilindini, where there are now berths for 14 ocean-going vessels. The importance of the port made Mombasa the obvious terminus for the Uganda Railway, and this then enhanced its importance so that today it has no rival on the Kenya coast.

Dar es Salaam has long had a hinterland as large as that of

Mombasa, but much less productive and therefore providing much less traffic. Bagamoyo was formerly the main port on this coast, but the Germans found that Dar es Salaam harbour was both deeper and more sheltered. The entrance is narrow and ships over 180 metres long cannot pass through, but apart from some oil tankers such ships do not normally serve this coast. In the mid-1960s there were still only three deep-water berths and four lighterage wharves, and the volume of cargo handled was about one-third of that at Mombasa; but since Rhodesia's UDI much Zambian traffic has been handled, and partly for this reason three new berths were opened in 1970. As the new rail link is expected to bring even more Zambian traffic to Dar es Salaam construction has now begun on two further berths and also an offshore oil tanker terminal.

Tanga has a less satisfactory harbour since goods must be moved by lighter between ship and shore, and the railway leading inland is much shorter than those terminating at Mombasa and Dar es Salaam. Mombasa draws much northern Tanzania traffic because of the superior facilities there, and Tanga depends very largely on the production of sisal within 150 km. of the port. It will handle much more cargo in the future, however, following the construction of a large fertilizer factory and especially the later establishment of a sisal pulp mill, and therefore a new jetty is to be built in 1971.

There is a close relationship between the three main ports and the three main railways of East Africa. The establishment of a fourth port at Mtwara must be seen in relation to the railway which served it until financial losses forced its closure. Mtwara was planned as the port for the largest section of the Groundnut Scheme, but when this was abandoned it was hoped that the port might assist other forms of development. The harbour is good, with two deep-water berths, and its importance is limited mainly by the poverty of its hinterland. Until recently it suffered competition from the older but poorer port of Lindi, but this has now been closed to ocean shipping.

Zanzibar has only a lighterage port, but this handles all the trade of both Zanzibar and Pemba. In the past it undertook much transhipment for the mainland, but this function declined with the eclipse of the dhow trade and the changes brought about by the revolution.

Air Transport

The role of air transport in the economy is still small, for it caters only for the most affluent passengers and the most valuable goods. Its contribution to employment, for instance, is very slight. Nevertheless, as in most African countries, it is expanding at a rapid rate, especially for international movements.

The region's own airline, East African Airways, was established as a public corporation in 1946 to provide domestic services, and now also operates flights to other African countries, to Asia and to Europe. It carried 450,000 passengers and 9,000 tons of freight in 1969, the total revenue of £15 million for that year comparing with £3 million ten years earlier. In addition the number of other airlines serving East Africa has risen from 10 in 1963 to 20 in 1970.

The largest share of the income from air transport accrues to Kenya. Nairobi provides the main base for East African Airways, and has the busiest airport, receiving 11,000 commercial flights in 1969. Dar es Salaam and Entebbe are on the routes of fewer airlines, and are used for fewer tourist charter flights, and they each received 7,000 flights in 1969. A development which may change the pattern somewhat is the building of a new international airport between Arusha and Moshi in northern Tanzania, due to be open in 1971.

One outstanding feature of air transport in East Africa, reflecting the close co-operation amongst the three countries, is a greater frequency of flights between Nairobi and Dar es Salaam, and between Nairobi and Entebbe, than between any other African capitals. On the other hand air transport is used for internal movement less than in many poor countries, partly because other transport media are better developed in East Africa. In this respect its role is greatest in Tanzania, where scheduled services call at 20 airports, compared with only four each in the other two countries. The large size and peripheral population distribution of Tanzania make internal movement by air more appropriate there than in Kenya or Uganda.

REFERENCES

1 For a full discussion of electricity production, see H. Amann, *Energy Supply and Economic Development in East Africa*, Weltforum Verlag, Munchen, 1969.

2 W. S. Churchill, *My African Journey*, Hodder & Stoughton, London, 1908, p. 120.

3 This is one of the points emphasized in G. Wilson, *Owen Falls*, E. A. Publishing House, Nairobi, 1967, an intensive study of electricity production and consumption in Uganda.

4 H. Amann, *op. cit.*, pp. 44–57 and Appendix Map 1.

5 E. K. Hawkins, *Roads and Road Transport in an Underdeveloped Country*, H.M.S.O., London, 1962, p. 38. This study examines in detail the pattern of road transport in Uganda.

6 The growth of the road network is examined in E. W. Soja, *The Geography of Modernization in Kenya*, Syracuse U. P., 1968.

7 Road/rail competition is one of the main themes of A. Hazlewood, *Road and Rail in East Africa*, Blackwell, Oxford, 1964.

8 M. F. Hill, *Permanent Way*, E.A.R. & H., Nairobi, Vol. I 1950, Vol. II 1958. This is an official history of the railways of East Africa.

9 Transport on Lake Victoria up to 1952 is covered very fully in V.C.R. Ford, *The Trade of Lake Victoria*, E.A.I.S.R., Kampala, 1955.

10 For a detailed study of the ports, see B. S. Hoyle *The Seaports of East Africa*, East African Publishing House, Nairobi, 1967.

CHAPTER 12

Tourism

East Africa is perhaps now best known overseas as a place for holidays, and the tourist industry is of steadily increasing importance to the region. Visitors from abroad can substantially increase local economic activity through their demands for goods and services, and can be especially significant as a source of foreign exchange.[1] This chapter is concerned mainly with holiday visits by people from outside East Africa, but visitors on business also provide some revenue. Tourism is not entirely an export industry and visits by people resident within the region also assist the local economy in particular areas. The tourist industry affects mainly the hotel trade, and there are now about 200 officially recognized hotels, with a total of over 15,000 beds. These employ at least 14,000 people, and have receipts of some £12 million a year. The influence of tourism is also felt though the demand for souvenirs and for specialized transport services, as well as for the regular transport services discussed in the last chapter.

The total number of visitors to East Africa in 1967 was over 150,000, including 75,000 on holiday, 18,000 on business and 55,000 in transit but staying for at least one night. The number of holiday visitors has risen each year since 1958, when it was only 14,000, and by 1970 it certainly exceeded 100,000. Their average length of stay is two to three weeks. The contribution of all these visitors to the national income is extremely difficult to assess, but by 1970 it had probably reached £20 million a year, representing about 12 shillings per head of the population. This figure is very low compared with that in many other countries. Equivalent figures for Israel and Cyprus as long ago as 1959 were 56 shillings and 72 shillings respectively.[2] This, however, is in part a reflection of the generally low level of economic development in East Africa. The contribution of the tourist industry to the economy is indicated more clearly by a comparison of invisible exports in the form of expenditure by visitors, with total visible and invisible exports. On this basis the importance of income from visitors to East Africa is clear. In some exceptional countries, such as Austria, this source of revenue accounts for a quarter of all export earnings, but for most it contributes less than 2 per cent. The figure for East Africa in the late 1960s was about 9 per cent.

No data of any sort are available for revenue from internal tourist travel, but until recently residents of East Africa accounted for the greater part of the clientele of the hotels of the region. They must certainly be taken into account when the importance of tourism in different parts of the region is considered, for the pattern of their movements is not the same as that of visitors from abroad.

Although the tourist industry of East Africa is comparatively small, it is more developed than in many other African countries, and it is perhaps appropriate to consider why this is so. There is much fine scenery, and many parts of the region enjoy a very pleasant climate, but although East Africa has an advantage in both respects over countries such as Sudan, many other countries are equally well favoured. These considerations are more important for local people than for visitors from overseas, and in this connection the great local variation in both scenery and climate is of some significance. There are strong incentives for residents who can afford it to spend a substantial part of their income on travel within the region.

The main attraction which East Africa offers to visitors from abroad is undoubtedly its animal life. This is examined at greater length in Chapter 15, but it should be pointed out here that there is probably no other part of the world which has such a variety of wild life in areas accessible for the visitor yet in no way resembling zoological gardens. Visitors to East Africa can be sure of seeing elephant, buffalo, deer, zebra, hippopotamus and many other wild animals without leaving roads suitable for saloon cars. On the other hand they are to-day not likely to be attacked by lions or snakes while sleeping in their beds. The National Parks and Game Reserves of Kenya, Tanzania and Uganda are of great importance, for they occupy areas where game is particularly abundant and

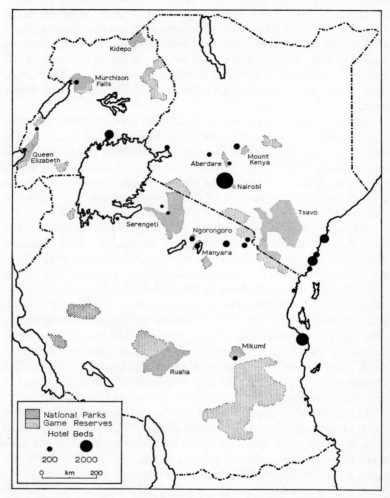

Figure 15. EAST AFRICA: Hotels and Game Parks, 1970

they afford it some measure of protection from hunters and poachers.[3] Within the National Parks, which occupy a total of over 50,000 square km. (Map 15), much has been spent on making roads and tracks, and providing accommodation for visitors, thereby greatly encouraging tourism.

The National Parks also attract the residents of East Africa and are a major inducement for travel within the region. Among the people staying at the lodges in the Uganda National Parks half come from overseas, rather over a quarter from Uganda and rather under a quarter from Kenya and Tanzania. In terms of money spent within the parks, however, these areas have to be heavily subsidized, and their economic value lies mainly in drawing foreign visitors to East Africa.

Hotels and lodges were generally adequate for the needs of visitors until the boom conditions of the late 1960s, and much investment is now being made in increasing the accommodation available. Thus over 1,000 new beds were provided in Nairobi alone in 1969–70. There is little evidence that lack of facilities of this type, or lack of capital to provide them, is likely to hinder the development of the tourist industry in the long run. Similarly transport facilities appear to have been quite satisfactory in many, if not all, parts of the region. Some of the National Parks are still rather inaccessible, but there are sufficient places well served by road and air to satisfy most visitors. Considerable efforts have been made to improve transport facilities for tourists, one example being the tarring of the main road through the Queen Elizabeth Park in western Uganda.

One factor affecting the attraction of the area for foreigners is the prevailing political situation. For many years this has discouraged many potential visitors, sometimes because of political problems within East Africa, but more often because of the widespread view in Europe and North America that the whole of Africa is in a state of upheaval. Since 1960 the proximity of the region to the Republic of Congo has accentuated this feeling. Nevertheless, many have noted in recent years that political conditions have been more favourable in most of East Africa than in some other parts of the continent, and this has assisted the tourist industry. Zanzibar has for some years been an exception.

Political conditions vary from year to year: other factors influencing the importance of tourism are much more permanent. One is the location of East Africa in relation to the parts of the world in which many people can afford holidays. Although most Americans are extremely wealthy by East African standards, few can afford to travel 10,000 km. for their holidays. The number of visitors from North America is therefore extremely small. More come from Europe, but even from there the distance to East Africa is 5,000 to 6,000 km., and a vital factor in the recent growth of tourism has been the organization of package tours at prices well below the standard air fares. In most countries the majority of visitors are from neighbouring lands, but there are few potential visitors from Ethiopia, Sudan, Congo or Zambia, and East Africa will have to depend increasingly on visitors from far away. The contribution of local residents to the tourist industry is naturally severely limited by the small number of people who can afford holidays.

Within East Africa Kenya benefits most from the tourist industry. It has more than half the hotels in the region, and about two-thirds of the hotel beds. In 1966 about 6,000 people were employed in the hotel trade in Kenya, the receipts of which amounted to over £6 million. These figures include the returns of some hotels for semi-permanent residents in Nairobi, but most of the establishments depend to a large extent on tourists. Both employment and receipts must have risen substantially since then, for several large new luxury hotels have been opened, both in Nairobi and at the coast.

The official figures for the number of holiday visitors entering each country from overseas in 1967 (the last year for which truly comparable data are available) were 51,000 for Kenya, 10,000 for Tanzania and 14,000 for Uganda. More of those entering Kenya moved on to one of the other countries than vice versa, but on the other hand the average length of stay was longer in Kenya than elsewhere. Furthermore, the firms engaged in organizing everything from simple sightseeing tours to elaborate hunting safaris are mainly based in Kenya, even though their clients may be taken beyond its borders. Thus of the £20 million a year now spent by overseas tourists, about £13 million probably accrues to Kenya, compared with £4 million to Tanzania and £3 million to Uganda. This concentration in Kenya is perhaps related in part to the facts that Kenya is better known than its neighbours in the rest of the world, and that it is served by more international air services. Some of its attractions are very accessible, notably the Nairobi National Park, in which game is abundant within the boundaries of the capital, and there are excellent opportunities for holidays combining game parks and sea beaches. Because of the central location of the country within East Africa, as well as its position on air routes, almost every visitor to East Africa spends some time in Kenya, whereas few go to both Tanzania and Uganda.

Many of the visitors in transit are spending a short time ashore while travelling by ship along the coast. Kenya has more of this tourist traffic than Tanzania, for more ships call at Mombasa than anywhere else on the coast and normally stop much longer than at Dar es Salaam, Tanga or Zanzibar. One estimate of the expenditures of the passengers and crews of calling ships in 1960 was £308,000 for Mombasa, £124,000 for Dar es Salaam, £46,000 for Zanzibar and £37,000 for Tanga.[4] A 1967 estimate for Mombasa was £1·4 million.[5]

Kenya also has most holidaymakers from within East Africa. More residents of Kenya than of the other countries are able to take expensive holidays, and the country can satisfy most of their demands within its borders. The sea shore attracts those who live inland and the cool highlands suit those who live at the coast. The city of Nairobi attracts those who live deep in the country while there are vast stretches inhabited only by game to provide a change for the city dweller. In addition, both the cool highlands and the coast draw visitors from Uganda.

On a more local scale the main centres of the tourist industry in Kenya are the capital, the Aberdare, Mt. Kenya and Tsavo National Parks and the coast.[6] Of the 1½ million nights spent by all guests at Kenya hotels in 1968, about 700,000 were spent in Nairobi and 500,000 at the coast. The parks are particularly important for foreign visitors, who form the majority of guests at the hotels and lodges within them. On the other hand some small hotels in the highlands, and more around Mombasa, cater primarily for East African holidaymakers. Malindi, about 120 km. north of Mombasa, was sufficiently dependent on these visitors to be described as a small scale holiday resort, even before it was chosen as one of the bases for package-tour holidays from Europe.

Tanzania offers essentially the same attractions as Kenya,

o

and its government is determined to capture a larger share of the tourist market, but it has suffered from the long distances between places of interest within the country, and from the poor accessibility of some of the areas where most game are found. The main tourist attraction of the country is certainly game, and the places where this can best be seen are in the north, notably the Ngorongoro Crater and Serengeti Plains, so that the main centre of the tourist industry is Arusha. Since this town is far nearer to Nairobi than to Dar es Salaam, much of the tourism in Tanzania is organized from the Kenya capital. The new international airport between Arusha and Moshi is intended to rectify this situation, especially by attracting charter flight operators to land visitors there rather than at Nairobi. The Tanzania coast has as much to offer as that of Kenya, but until recently most visitors to Dar es Salaam were either there on business or had come ashore briefly from calling ships. It is now emerging as the second centre of tourism in the country, however, and visitors from Europe and North America in 1968 made 36 per cent. of their bookings there, compared with 60 per cent. in the Arusha-Moshi area, and only 4 per cent. elsewhere in the country. The beaches north and south of the city are being developed, and several large hotels were under construction around 1970, for Tanzania aims to encourage much larger numbers of visitors to combine a week by the sea with a week in the northern game area. The island of Zanzibar has a distinctive character, and tourism might now be rather more important there if political disturbances had not intervened.

Uganda has more to offer the tourist than its very small share of East African income from this source would suggest. The Uganda Development Corporation has invested heavily in hotels and in park lodges, and the standard of accommodation available was until recently higher than in Tanzania. It perhaps fell behind in the late 1960s, but now several new hotels are under construction or planned, both in Kampala and in the National Parks. The two major National Parks are not inaccessible, but they are quite distant from the capital and are in the part of the country furthest from Kenya, where most visitors to East Africa arrive. Uganda suffered for some years from its location, and especially from the location of its National

Parks, close to the Congo, for this appeared to discourage a substantial number of potential visitors. Indeed, in several ways the location of the country has been an important factor affecting the tourist industry in Uganda, for it cannot offer beach holidays (bilharzia prevents lake bathing), while it is less well placed in relation to the present pattern of air routes.

However, both Tanzania and Uganda are now increasing their share of visitors from abroad, as they come to be better known in the rest of the world: and in all three countries it is expected that the importance of the tourist industry will increase very rapidly in the future. The Tanzania 1969–74 Plan anticipates that the number of overseas visitors will treble in five years,[7] while the Kenya 1970–74 Plan assumes a continued 20 per cent. annual increase, and allows for 3,000 extra hotel beds at the coast, and 1,500 in game park lodges, to accommodate the increased numbers.[8] International tourism is clearly likely to be of increasing value to East Africa; and although much of the benefit will accrue to the capital cities, perhaps it could also help to spread income to some of the relatively poor parts of the region, Undoubtedly, its economic impact not just at a national, but also at a local level, should offer a fruitful field of study.

REFERENCES

1   F. Mitchell, 'The Value of Tourism in East Africa', *Eastern Africa Economic Review*, Vol. 2, No. 1, 1970, pp. 1–21.
2   F. C. Wright, *Tourism in East Africa*, cyclostyled report for Department of Technical Co-operation, London, 1962, p. 25.
3   A useful discussion of the National Parks may be found in D. N. McMaster, 'East Africa: Influences and Trends in Land Use', in R. M. Prothero (ed.), *A Geography of Africa*, Routledge & Kegan Paul, London, 1969, pp. 229–234.
4   F. C. Wright, *op. cit.*, p. 38.
5   F. Mitchell, *op. cit.*
6   Interesting maps of tourist attractions and tourist regions are provided in J. P. B. M. Ouma, 'Evolution of Tourist Regions in East Africa', *East African Geographical Review*, No. 8, 1970, pp. 75–77, to be followed by J. P. B. M. Ouma, *Evolution of Tourism in East Africa*, E. A. Literature Bureau, Nairobi, in the press.
7   Tanzania, *Second Five-year Plan 1969–1974*, Dar es Salaam, 1969, p. 144.
8   Kenya, *Development Plan 1970–1974*, Nairobi, 1969, pp. 428–436.

CHAPTER 13

Internal Trade

Trading is an extremely important economic activity, even though it is not itself productive. By redistributing goods it increases their value, and it provides much employment in the process. Yet trading is sometimes omitted in studies in economic geography, partly because of paucity of data on the subject. There is very little data on internal trade in East Africa, but the main trading patterns of the region may be outlined.

Trade plays a smaller part in East African life than in that of more highly developed regions, where people's wants are greater and where they satisfy few of their own requirements. It is less important even than in West Africa, where it forms the main interest of an enormous number of people. Most East Africans produce their own food and cannot afford to buy many other goods. Nevertheless, some goods are now sold in every part of the region and the proceeds are used to buy goods produced elsewhere. Commerce is thought to contribute about 10 per cent. of the Gross Domestic Product of East Africa and to provide 7 per cent. of all paid employment. This commerce has mainly been introduced since 1900, but it has been superimposed on a traditional pattern of small-scale trade which has not been entirely superseded.

TRADE WITHIN THE TRADITIONAL ECONOMY

Trade was carried on in East Africa long before the Europeans, or even the Arabs, penetrated the region. When someone produced more of any commodity than he needed, he tried to exchange it for goods which someone else could supply. Such barter trade continues today, although more often cash is now involved. It sometimes takes place between neighbouring tribes which differ in their way of life. Gulliver has described how the Masai supply the Arusha with meat, milk and skins, in return for grain, tobacco and honey, although he also notes a decline in the trade as the Arusha have adopted cash crops.[1] In Kenya the Kisii provide the neighbouring Luo with grain in exchange for fish. The Bagisu on Mount Elgon send bananas down to the plain below, obtaining millet in return; and in north-west Uganda the Madi supply fish to the Lugbara, often receiving goats in exchange.

Much local trade also takes place between members of one tribe wherever some specialization of production has developed. Beer and livestock are probably the most important elements in such trade. It is officially estimated that beer sales within rural areas in Uganda are worth £6 million a year. In most areas regular cattle markets take place, and while some animals are sold to town butchers, others are sold to rural dwellers. Fishing is often a specialized activity, but many fishermen are dependent on local sales rather than distant markets.

There have always been some members of the community who have not produced their own food, and even within rural areas the number is now rapidly increasing. Grain, fruit, eggs, meat and milk are all sold in local markets to the teachers, policemen, bus drivers and others who have the cash to buy them. Whereas most people traditionally produced not only their own food but also their houses, furniture and clothes, there has grown up a class of joiners and tailors who provide these services and who must often buy their food. The weekly rural market is now a feature of most settled parts of East Africa, although the volume of trade taking place is much higher in areas such as central Kenya than in western or southern Tanzania.

This type of trade is rarely a full-time occupation, but a few people are entirely dependent on it for their livelihood. Around the lakes there are fishmongers who buy fish on the shore and take it to sell in the surrounding countryside. Others are occupied mainly as cattle traders and butchers, and spend much time travelling from one market to another.

One form of trade which has grown out of the traditional economy, rather than been superimposed upon it, is the supply of food to the towns.[2] This provides a full-time occupation for an increasing number of people around the largest towns. Nairobi, Mombasa, Dar es Salaam and Kampala cannot be supplied with basic foodstuffs by farmers bringing in their own produce and selling it. Traders now tour the surrounding country buying produce at the roadside, and sometimes then sell it to other traders well-established in the town markets. Trade in other commodities needed in the towns, such as charcoal, has also developed.

Although local patterns of trade can be described, insufficient information is available to assess the importance of such trade in each part of the region. It certainly could not be mapped in the present state of knowledge, whereas the introduced pattern of trade can be analysed geographically to a considerable extent.

THE INTRODUCED PATTERN OF TRADE

The importance of trade in East African life has greatly increased through the development of new forms of exchange which involve selling goods for cash and buying goods produced far away. Originally such trade consisted almost entirely of sales for export overseas and the purchase of imported goods, but today an increasing volume of sales are to other parts of East Africa, and many of the commodities purchased have been produced within the region.

This type of trade has provided the main basis for urban development. Both the large cities and the small towns of the region owe much of their present importance to their trading function, even though many originated as administrative stations.[3] Within most rural areas the settlement pattern is highly dispersed, and the clusters of buildings which are sometimes termed 'villages' usually consist mainly of shops. Most of these small trading centres grew up to handle the import and export trade, although many now also serve as markets for local trade.

Before examining the spatial distribution of trading activity the structure of the export and import trade can be outlined.[4] At one end of the scale there are firms concerned entirely with the sale of East African produce in overseas markets, and with the import of goods from overseas. Many are foreign companies with headquarters in Europe or India, and some are engaged in trade in many countries. Some specialize in one commodity, the oil companies being among these, while others handle a

wide range of goods. Most have branches both at the ports and
in the larger inland towns. In addition there are many smaller

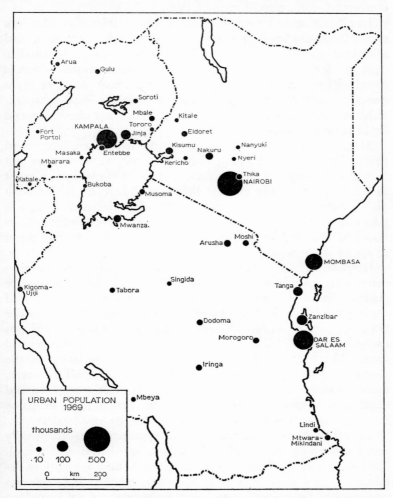

Figure 16. East Africa: Population of Towns, 1969
The information for Kenya and Uganda is drawn from the 1969
Census, that for Tanzania is based on the Census of 1967.

firms, registered locally, most Asian-owned, which operate
from one establishment in either Mombasa or Dar es Salaam.

Some of the larger merchants in the inland towns organize their own imports, but most depend on others, while specialist concerns handle almost all exports.

In all the large towns there are many wholesalers who buy goods from the importers and from local manufacturers, and sell them to retailers either in the same town or in smaller centres. Some also handle local agricultural produce which is supplied by small traders from the rural areas. Most of these concerns are Asian, and consist of a single establishment, although they often have close links with firms elsewhere run by other members of the family.

Most of the Asian shops in every town are concerned primarily with retail trade, although many customers in fact take goods away to sell in minute quantities elsewhere. Except in the cities, most are general stores, each in competition with all the others, and the lack of specialization limits the range of goods available in the small towns. Nearly all are individual or family concerns, and only two firms have a chain of retail shops in six or more towns.

Despite the domination of trade by the Asian community, more Africans than Asians are engaged in the activity, for African shops are scattered throughout all rural areas, and during the 1960s the Asians withdrew from many of the smaller trading centres. There are also increasing numbers of African-owned shops in the large towns though rarely in the central area. Although trading is often the chief occupation of the proprietors most of the rural shops have a very small turnover, mainly from sales of kerosene, soap, textiles, salt, sugar, tea and cigarettes. These are obtained from the larger town shops or from lorries sent round the rural areas by the wholesalers.

The main items sold throughout the countryside but usually not handled by the small shopkeepers are drinks and petrol. Bars form a specialized type of rural trade and are very wide-spread: petrol stations are often erected by the oil companies and rented by a local man, and these are not so abundant except around the town fringes.

Most traders handle more imports than exports mainly because of the existence of other channels for the export of produce. Primary marketing is increasingly undertaken by co-operative societies and, after processing, several products are passed on to the exporting firms by government marketing boards. In addition, some export crops produced on a large scale, and commodities such as timber and minerals, are sold direct to the exporters without the assistance of middlemen. Since independence the structure of trade has begun to change once again, for although the structure just described persisted throughout the 1960s this in turn is having a new system superimposed upon it as the governments begin to play an increasingly direct role in trade. The marketing boards are now relying less upon private exporting firms and more often selling direct to overseas customers, while new bodies have been set up to undertake both importing from abroad and the distribution of imported and locally-produced goods. In Tanzania, for instance, the State Trading Corporation has handled a rapidly increasing share of the country's imports since its establishment in 1967, and it has now opened branches in many of the larger towns. This development may have a significant impact on the geographical pattern of trade during the 1970s, but meanwhile the pattern is essentially that produced during earlier decades.

THE DISTRIBUTION OF TRADING ACTIVITY

The information available on the distribution of shops and of employment in trade is very limited. Most of the cities and towns of the region are so similar, however, in terms of the importance of trade amongst their functions, that Map 16 gives an indication of the distribution of the main centres of this activity.

Nairobi

Much the most important centre of trade in East Africa is Nairobi. Administration, manufacturing and commerce are the three main functions of the city, and are all of comparable importance, each employing almost 30,000 people. The 1966 Survey of Distribution recorded 740 wholesalers in Nairobi, out of a total for Kenya of 2,260; and it recorded 1,380 retail establishments, compared with a similar number in the next nine towns of the country together. The value of all sales by these Nairobi traders in 1966 was £196 million out of a national total of £367 million.

The great importance of Nairobi as a trading centre is related to the fact that it performs trading functions at several levels. In some fields it serves the whole of East Africa, and in more it serves Kenya, Uganda and a small part of Tanzania. Many firms operating throughout the region have their head offices in Nairobi, while merchants in Kampala or Arusha often obtain their supplies from the larger Nairobi wholesalers. Almost half the goods imported into Uganda from overseas are obtained through trading concerns in either Nairobi or Mombasa. The city is the supply centre for most of Kenya for an even wider range of goods, merchants in such towns as Nyeri and Meru being very much dependent on Nairobi firms. It is also the focus of much of the country's export trade, despite its inland location. It is, for example, the marketing centre for coffee and tea.

In retail trade Nairobi serves a large area, parts of which are relatively prosperous, and its pre-eminence has probably hindered the growth of neighbouring towns such as Limuru and Ruiru as shopping centres. Even Thika, 45 km. away, is more important in manufacturing than in trade. Much of the retail trade of Nairobi, however, is dependent on the purchasing power of the ½ million inhabitants of the city. Many people obtain a living by supplying the needs of the administrators, industrial workers, and even other traders. One interesting recent development has been the establishment of groups of up to 20 shops at various points throughout the higher-class suburbs, very much on the British pattern.

The importance of Nairobi in trade is related to its function as the capital of Kenya and in some respects as an administrative centre for East Africa. There is a close net of inter-relationships in which its importance in such fields as banking and insurance are also involved. Its position in each activity enhances its role in the others. Two other factors which favour Nairobi more than possible rivals, such as Mombasa, are its centrality in both Kenya and East Africa, and its location on the eastern edge of the most prosperous part of the region. No town is better placed to serve the whole of Kenya, or to serve all three countries, especially since means of communication have become focused on Nairobi. The country south and west of the city is sparsely populated, but in that to the north and east much purchasing power is concentrated. There is found both a substantial, very affluent, European population, and dense African settlement which is of increasing significance as cash incomes rise. In relation to overseas imports and exports Nairobi clearly enjoys the position of 'gateway' to this area.

Mombasa

Mombasa is not only the leading port in East Africa but also a major centre of trade. The first function has led to the second, and the two together have enabled it to become the second city of Kenya, with a population of 250,000. Although many importing and exporting firms have headquarters in Nairobi, and their goods are consigned directly to or from the port, many others have offices in Mombasa and have warehouses in the industrial area of the city. Some large firms and many smaller ones are based in Mombasa, and compete successfully for the trade of a large part of East Africa. Most traders in Moshi, for example, and many in Kisumu or Kampala, obtain supplies through Mombasa importers. The export trade provides much employment outside the port area for, apart from private firms concerned mainly with exports, the Uganda Coffee and Lint Marketing Boards have large warehouses in Mombasa.

Mombasa is the chief centre of trade for Coast Province of Kenya, but although there is no other major town within 200 km., and none in Kenya within 500 km., Mombasa's function in retail and local wholesale trade is small in relation to its size. Its sphere of influence is inevitably reduced by its coastal location, while much of its immediate hinterland is arid and sparsely populated. The ships calling at the port provide extra trade, for they generally take on some supplies and their crews and passengers often spend some time ashore: but this is of small importance in comparison with the import and export trade.

Dar es Salaam

In some ways Dar es Salaam combines the functions of Nairobi and Mombasa, since it is both the capital and the leading port of Tanzania. Each of these roles encourages trade, and the city is much the most important centre of trade in the country. On the other hand it does not dominate the whole country as much as Nairobi and Mombasa together dominate Kenya, for both the north and the south have only limited commercial connections with it. Arusha and Moshi have close trading links with the Kenya cities and with the port of Tanga, Bukoba has close ties with Uganda and Kenya, and Mtwara Region is often linked physically with the capital only by sea and it is therefore commercially independent to some extent. Dar es Salaam also plays a smaller role than Nairobi and Mombasa in serving other countries. Only goods moving to and from Burundi are normally handled by its traders, although since 1966 they have also supplied some goods to Zambia.

Although Dar es Salaam is thus far less important than Nairobi and Mombasa combined, it has a population of over 300,000, and its inhabitants are very much dependent on its trading functions. It is the main centre of import, export and wholesale trade for an area of 800,000 square km. and a population of 10 million. It is also the centre of small-scale wholesale and retail trade for Coast Region, while the purchasing power of the city population is sufficient to support a wide range of specialized shops.[5]

Kampala

Kampala is comparable to Dar es Salaam in size and importance, and is very clearly the commercial capital of Uganda. Several of the major importing and exporting firms of East Africa have branches there, and many Asian merchants import goods direct through the port of Mombasa. Many of the traders, however, are middlemen who buy from Nairobi or Mombasa wholesalers and who often sell to other wholesalers in smaller towns. Kampala controls most of the trade of Buganda and western Uganda, but less of that of the east and north. Thus whereas much sugar is consigned direct from Kakira to northern towns, little is despatched to towns in the west, for these obtain their supplies through Kampala dealers. But although location and the communications pattern limit Kampala's role as a distribution centre for Uganda, Kampala merchants have extended their sales area in the west beyond the borders of Uganda to Bukoba and to Rwanda.

The role of Kampala in retail and local wholesale trade is relatively large on account of the density of population and prosperity of its surroundings. The total amount of purchasing power within Buganda must be considerably greater than that within 150 km. of either Mombasa or Dar es Salaam. Trade is sufficiently well developed for small but distinctive commercial zones to exist within the city, so that on one street there are a dozen cycle and electrical goods dealers in a row, and on another a similar number of hardware dealers.

Other Towns

It is not possible to examine the trade of every town in East Africa, but some further features of the distribution of trade might be noted. Zanzibar city is remarkably important as a commercial centre in view of its small hinterland. There is a long tradition of trade rather than self-sufficiency in Zanzibar, most people being concerned with production for sale, and many having to buy basic foodstuffs. It has also long engaged in a substantial re-export trade between the East African mainland and the Far East. One third of the population of Zanzibar island lives in the city, and trade is the most important occupation there.

Nakuru and Eldoret are somewhat distinctive in that they developed as trading centres for the European farming population of the Kenya highlands. They are notable for the large scale of trading activity rather than the large number of shops, and concerns such as the Kenya Farmers Association, selling agricultural machinery and fertilizers, are particularly important in both. Kisumu, serving a large area of dense African settlement, has a larger number of traders, and is of increasing importance as the commercial centre of western Kenya, although the nature of trade there is more similar than that in Nakuru to the nature of trade in smaller towns.

Jinja stands out on the map of urban population partly because of its manufacturing function. The area for which it is the centre of trade is relatively prosperous, but is small. Trade is better developed in Tanga, for although it suffers competition from Mombasa its port function has drawn several importing and exporting firms. It is also the focus of wholesale trade for one of the most heavily settled and productive regions of Tanzania.

Most other towns marked on Map 16 are local administrative centres, and their trading function has developed from this. Although they differ considerably in size, many are almost identical in functions and are also very similar in appearance. In addition to administration these towns provide services such as hospitals, and they have generally become foci of local communications. These features tend to enhance their role in trade. The size and importance of these trading centres is generally related to the size, population and prosperity of the areas they serve, often roughly corresponding to an administrative unit. In Tanzania, for example, Mwanza, Moshi and Arusha, headquarters of regions with a substantial total purchasing power, all have a population of between 30,000 and 40,000 and about 400 shops. Tabora and Dodoma, headquarters of poorer regions, have a population of around 25,000 and about 200 shops. Singida and Shinyanga, centres of newly-created regions, are comparable to most district headquarters in Uganda and Kenya, many of which are strikingly similar.[6] Examples include Lira and Fort Portal in Uganda, and Meru and Fort Hall in Kenya. These have a total population of between 6,000 and 8,000 of whom 500 to 800 are Asians, and have rather more than 100 shops, most along a single main street. All are retailers, but many also sell goods to traders from the countryside and buy some local agricultural produce.

Other trading centres are scattered throughout East Africa, varying in both size and frequency with the density of population and the local level of income.[7] In Buganda and Busoga several are quite large, but in much of Tanzania trading centres between district headquarters are both small and far apart. Throughout the rural areas African traders have established themselves, often in groups of ten or twelve shops around a cross-roads, although the extent of such development also varies greatly from place to place. It has progressed furthest in the area of Kikuyu settlement north of Nairobi, where a group of shops is found every few km. along most roads. It is much less important in western Uganda or southern Tanzania where population is less dense and much less cash is circulating.

OTHER FORMS OF COMMERCIAL ACTIVITY

Banking and insurance do not occupy many people in East Africa, but each plays a very important role in the economy. The most striking features of these activities for the geographer are the dispersion of the former and the concentration of the latter. Although until recently all the nine foreign commercial banks operating in the region had their local head office in Nairobi, thereby adding to the pre-eminence of that city within East Africa, most of them also had branches in Mombasa, Dar es Salaam and Kampala, while three had branches scattered throughout all three countries. Today the main banks in Uganda are no longer controlled from Nairobi, while in Tanzania all banking was nationalized in 1967. In each case new banking facilities have been provided where none existed before, so that more than 80 towns have a full branch of one bank, and a further 60 have agencies operating one or two days a week. Insurance is much more concentrated in Nairobi, and to a lesser extent in Dar es Salaam, Kampala and Mombasa. Few offices are found elsewhere, although some companies have appointed local traders as agents in smaller towns.

Many other forms of commerce are represented in East Africa, but there is not space to examine the distribution of each of these here. Many are concentrated in the towns and show a very similar pattern to the activities considered in this chapter. One element in the 'tertiary' sector of the economy which might have been discussed is the building trade, which makes a substantial contribution to the National Income, and an even larger contribution to wage employment since it is relatively labour-intensive. From these points of view, of course, education, health services and administration might all have been considered, for although they have not usually been included in studies in economic geography, they do provide increasing numbers of people with their livelihood, and they are now sometimes regarded as the 'quaternary' sector of economic activity.

As more data become available it will be interesting to see to what extent the spatial pattern of employment in this sector is changing, for it is declared government policy in each country to relate the distribution of these services more closely to the distribution of population, and so to reduce any concentration of them in the more developed areas.

REFERENCES

1 P. H. Gulliver in P. Bohanan and G. Dalton, *Markets in Africa*, North-western U.P., Evanston, 1962, Ch. 16. Chapters 17–20, 22 and 26 also discuss local trade in East Africa.
2 A case study is P. H. Temple, 'Kampala Markets', in *University of East Africa Social Science Conference 1968/9, Geography Papers*, pp. 151–169.
3 A. M. O'Connor, 'The Cities and Towns of East Africa: Distribution and Functions', in H. Berger (ed.), *Ostafrikanische Studien*, Friederich-Alexander-Universitat, Nurnberg, 1968.
4 A comprehensive survey of the early-1960s pattern in one country is H. C. G. Hawkins, *Wholesale and Retail Trade in Tanganyika*, Praeger, New York, 1965.
5 H. De Blij, *Dar es Salaam*, Northwestern U.P., Evanston, 1963, includes much on the spatial pattern of trade within the city. A similar study is H. De Blij, *Mombasa*, Northwestern U.P., Evanston, 1968.
6 D. N. McMaster, 'The Colonial District Town in Uganda', in R. P. Beckinsale & J. M. Houston, *Urbanisation and its Problems*, Blackwell, Oxford, 1968.
7 J. B. Splansky, 'Some Geographical Characteristics of Permanent Retail Institutions in Ankole', *East African Geographical Review*, No. 7, 1969, pp. 61–78. A fuller study, also focusing on Ankole, is C. M. Good, *Rural Markets and Trade in East Africa*, Department of Geography Research Paper 128, University of Chicago, 1970.

CHAPTER 14

External Trade

VALUE OF TRADE

The importance of external trade in the economies of the East African countries was mentioned in the introduction, and may now be examined more closely.[1] The distinction between internal and external trade is not clear-cut in East Africa since movements of goods between Kenya, Tanzania and Uganda are included sometimes in one category and sometimes in the other. Although political developments may change the situation, the most satisfactory approach in 1970 is probably to consider each country as a separate unit, despite their customs union. Sales of sugar from Uganda to Kenya are in fact exports from Uganda, and the external trade pattern of Kenya cannot be understood without reference to its trade with Tanzania and Uganda.

TABLE 10

VALUE OF EXTERNAL TRADE TO SELECTED AFRICAN COUNTRIES, 1969

	Imports £m	Exports and Re-exports £m	Exports per Head £	Exports as % of G.D.P.
Kenya	129	98	9	21
Tanzania	86	90	7	23
Uganda	63	80	8	27
Ethiopia	62	47	2	9
Ghana	126	119	14	18
Malawi	26	19	4	21
Zambia	156	383	90	72

The value of external trade to Kenya, Tanzania and Uganda is compared with its value to various other countries in Table 10. In relation to population the value is much smaller than in some other African countries, reflecting the general poverty of the region. It amounts to only £17 a year per head of the population. Yet in relation to the economy of each country, external trade is of great importance, for the value of exports from each exceeds 20 per cent. of the Gross Domestic Product. Even if movements between the three countries (hereafter termed inter-territorial trade) are excluded, the value of exports from East Africa as a whole is 20 per cent. of that of the G.D.P., whereas the figure for the United States is under 5 per cent., and even that for Britain, so widely known as a trading nation, is only 15 per cent.

The difference between the three countries in the importance of external trade is quite small, for in each the development of the cash economy has been based on the production of goods for export. The contribution of exports to the economy is greatest in Uganda, where cash crop cultivation is particularly widespread, and smallest in Kenya, where the production of goods to supply local markets is most developed. Nevertheless, provided that inter-territorial trade is included, Kenya's export earnings are comparable to those of Tanzania and Uganda. Imports into Kenya are greater than into Tanzania or Uganda, partly because goods required for common services such as the railways and ports generally go in the first instance to Kenya, but also because of the existence there of the largest alien high-income groups, who demand imported goods and can afford to pay for them.

The three countries also differ little with regard to recent trends in the importance of external trade. In each this increased sharply in the early 1960s, as rising export earnings permitted a great expansion of imports. In each the value of external trade per head of population, and its ratio to G.D.P. fell in the late 1960s, the absolute figures for 1969 being almost identical with those for 1966. This reflected their common experience of falling prices for some exports and quota restrictions for others, and common policies of controlling imports and industrialization through import substitution.

DIRECTION OF TRADE

Kenya, Tanzania and Uganda differ sharply from many other African countries in that much of their trade is with their neighbours. About 25 per cent. of the external trade of Kenya is with African countries, whereas the equivalent figures for Ghana and Nigeria are only about 5 per cent. and 1 per cent. respectively. The customs union and the political ties between the three East African countries are largely responsible for this, for the trade within Africa is mainly trade within East Africa.[2] In all three countries industries have been established with the intention of supplying an East African, rather than only a national, market: and each buys certain products from its neighbours rather than from overseas.

In this connection there are marked contrasts between Kenya, Tanzania and Uganda. Kenya sends 30 per cent. of its exports to its East African neighbours, but the figure for Uganda is only 12 per cent. and for Tanzania 8 per cent. Partly as a result of distinctive physical and social conditions Kenya produces a wider range of both agricultural and manufactured goods than Tanzania or Uganda, and it has specialized to some extent in supplying the needs of East Africa as a whole. There is less that these countries can offer to Kenya, and imbalance in inter-territorial trade has recently strained relations somewhat between the three countries. This has led to certain restrictions on trade between them, although the total value of such trade has not fallen significantly.

Trade with other African countries is extremely small (Table 11). Among the main components are re-exports of produce from overseas supplied to Congo, Rwanda, Burundi, Zambia and Somalia. Most countries of tropical Africa can offer few commodities required in Kenya, Tanzania or Uganda, and provide poor markets for East African produce. The incentive to develop trade is therefore small, while even with neighbouring countries good communications are generally lacking. Sudan imports much sugar, cement and textiles, all of which are produced in Kenya and Uganda: but the points of production lie far from the Uganda/Sudan border, and so do the chief consuming areas within Sudan. The market in southern Sudan is very small, and Egypt is better placed than East Africa to supply the north. Similarly Zambia, Malawi and Mozambique all lie adjacent to the least developed part of Tanzania, and the focus of economic life in each lies far from the border. The leading African trading partner for Kenya, Tanzania and

Uganda was for many years South Africa, which required tropical agricultural products and could provide a wide range of manufactures: the disappearance of this trade is due entirely to political differences between East and South Africa. The greater part of the external trade of all three countries is directed towards the most highly developed regions of the

TABLE 11

EAST AFRICA: DIRECTION OF TRADE, 1969

| | Percentage of Imports | | | Percentage of exports and re-exports | | |
	Kenya	Tanzania	Uganda	Kenya	Tanzania	Uganda
East Africa	9	18	26	30	6	12
Rest of Africa	1	1	1	8	8	3
Europe	51	43	43	34	39	30
Middle East	9	8	1	2	2	2
S. & E. Asia	13	14	16	4	25	17
N. America	8	5	3	7	8	24
Others	9	11	10	15	12	12
Commonwealth	46	48	59	57	57	47
Communist Bloc	3	6	3	2	7	5
Kenya	—	16	24	—	5	10
Tanzania	3	—	2	13	—	2
Uganda	6	2	—	16	1	—
United Kingdom	28	23	25	16	24	20
West Germany	8	7	6	8	3	3
Japan	7	8	9	1	5	10
United States	7	5	3	5	7	21

These figures have been calculated from the trade tables in East African Customs and Excise, *Annual Trade Report.*

world. Europe, North America and Japan together take about 60 per cent. of their exports and provide 60 per cent. of their imports. Even Kenya conducts most of its trade with these regions, despite the large contribution of inter-territorial movements to its trading pattern. Apart from the oil producers of the Middle East, the only underdeveloped country playing a large part in East African trade is India. Trade is also clearly oriented towards the Western rather than the Eastern Bloc, for communist countries still account for a very small share of East Africa's trade. Again there has in the past been no significant difference between the three countries in this respect, although the construction of the Tan-Zam railway by China, and the method of payment for this, mean that Tanzania will probably register much more trade with China in the 1970s than will Kenya or Uganda.

For both Kenya and Tanzania the most important trading partner is Britain, but Uganda conducts a roughly equal amount of trade with Britain, the United States and Kenya. The United States takes a larger share of its exports and Kenya provides more of its imports. The long political connection between Britain and East Africa obviously contributes to Britain's importance in the region's trade: but it is notable that its contribution is smaller than that of the former metropolitan power in the trade of most African countries.

COMPOSITION OF TRADE

The major elements in East Africa's external trade have all been noted already, but Table 12 may help to place them in perspective. All three countries are very largely dependent on the export of primary products and the import of manufactures. According to the Standard International Trade Classification both Tanzania and Uganda export manufactures worth several million pounds, but these consisted mainly of diamonds and copper, both products of mining rather than manufacturing industry, until Tanzania began to supply petroleum products to Zambia. Kenya is the least dependent on primary production for its exports, as a result of its sales of many manufactured goods to Tanzania and Uganda, and a few such as cement and petroleum products to other African and Indian Ocean countries.

Not only is Uganda dependent almost entirely on exports of primary products, but most of its earnings are from two commodities since coffee and cotton together represent two-thirds of the total. The economy is not as precarious, however, as that in many countries which depend on a single commodity for two-thirds of their export earnings. Indeed, Uganda exports 9 items to a value of over £1 million. Kenya and Tanzania are exceptional among tropical African countries in the varied nature of their exports. In each case no commodity accounts for more than 18 per cent. of the total, and 16 items are worth over £1 million annually.

The overwhelming importance of manufactures among imports into Tanzania and Uganda is very striking (Table 12), and reflects a high degree of self-sufficiency in primary production. They are slightly less dominant in Kenya, for manufacturing is better developed there. Agricultural imports into

TABLE 12

EAST AFRICA: COMPOSITION OF TRADE, 1969

	Percentage of Overseas Exports			Percentage of Total Exports		
	Kenya	Tanzania	Uganda	Kenya	Tanzania	Uganda
Agricultural Products	67	71	87	50	69	77
Forestry and Mining Products	1	12	9	1	11	8
Manufactures						
Simply Processed*	10	9	3	11	10	4
Other Manufactures	22	8	1	38	10	11
Coffee	24	15	56	17	14	49
Cotton	1	14	18	1	13	16
Sisal	3	10	0	2	9	0
Tea	16	3	7	11	3	6
Diamonds	0	11	0	0	10	0

	Percentage of Overseas Imports			Percentage of Total Imports		
	Kenya	Tanzania	Uganda	Kenya	Tanzania	Uganda
Agricultural Products	2	4	2	4	6	5
Forestry and Mining Products	9	4	1	8	3	1
Manufactures	89	92	97	88	91	94
Transport Equipment	20	13	14	19	11	10
Machinery	15	18	18	14	14	13
Textiles/Clothing	9	13	14	10	12	10
Crude Oil	8	4	0	7	3	0

* E.g. Pyrethrum extract, cotton-seed cake, butter.

Kenya are mainly from Uganda and Tanzania, the largest items being sugar and tobacco. The only primary product imported in large quantities from overseas is crude oil for the Mombasa refinery.

Among the manufactures imported into each country about one-third are consumer goods, one-third are producers' materials and one-third are capital goods. The last are slowly reducing the dependence upon imports for the supply of manufactured goods but, although encouraging developments are taking place, East Africa is likely to depend heavily upon the export of primary products and the import of manufactures for many years to come.

REFERENCES

1 Full details of external trade are provided in East African Customs and Excise, *Annual Trade Report.*
2 Inter-territorial trade and trade with neighbouring countries are both examined in P. Ndegwa, *The Common Market and Development in East Africa,* East African Publishing House, Nairobi, 1968.

CHAPTER 15

Physical Factors affecting Patterns of Activity

LOCATION

Having examined the main forms of economic activity undertaken in East Africa, we may now distinguish various conditions which influence the existence and distribution of these within the region. One fundamental condition is the location of East Africa astride the equator and on one side of a massive and largely underdeveloped continent.

The effect of latitude is felt essentially through climate, which receives attention later in this chapter. The effect of location within Africa has been more direct, for the economy has much in common with that of neighbouring regions, notably a heavy dependence on subsistence production. East Africa lies within a zone little touched by commercial activity until this century and still among the most underdeveloped in the world. It does not lie on any important routeway, and the opportunities for the spread of new ideas and new forms of production from adjacent areas are very limited. While the North Atlantic remains the leading focus of world trade, the location of East Africa places it at a disadvantage in comparison with such tropical regions as West Africa or the West Indies.

One must, however, distinguish between different parts of East Africa, for the coastlands have a much longer history of commercial activity than the interior, having had contacts with the Arab world, Asia and Europe for over 500 years. Although this has left a smaller legacy than might have been expected, the coastlands are more developed economically in relation to their resources than most inland areas, partly as a result of these contacts.

Location in relation to the sea is still of importance today, especially in connection with overseas trade, and both Kenya and Tanzania benefit from their coastal position. Uganda correspondingly suffers from its interior location, although a superior endowment of climate and soils, together with the establishment of transport facilities, has enabled it to keep pace with Kenya and Tanzania in economic development. Railways and roads reduce the effects of location but they do not abolish them. While the distribution of sisal production in Tanzania shows some relationship to the railways, it is related equally closely to distance from the coast. Location has been the main factor limiting sisal to Tanzania and Kenya: only crops of higher value, such as cotton, coffee and tea, can bear the cost of transport from Uganda to the coast. Distance from the sea also affects imported goods, and the effect of high prices for commodities such as petrol is felt throughout the local economy of inland areas. Occasionally, however, distance from the coast assists some local activity: for example, the high cost of imported cement in Uganda encouraged the establishment there of the first East African cement works.

On a more local scale the poorly developed nature of West Nile District of Uganda is a matter more of distance from the sea, and from all *foci* of economic activity, than of lack of resources or even of transport facilities. By contrast, the commercial development of Mombasa, Dar es Salaam and Tanga is obviously related to their coastal location and consequent role as ports for inland areas. Several features of the economic geography of Zanzibar are related to its position as an off-shore island.

The significance of location is not confined to the commercial sector of the economy. There appears to be some connection between the importance of cassava in West Nile, Bunyoro and Toro and the proximity of these districts to Congo, where this is the leading food crop. Similarly the importance of rice in some coastal areas may be related to influence from the East. The traditional millet is certainly becoming increasingly associated with the more remote parts of the region.

RELIEF

The main relief features of East Africa have been mentioned frequently in earlier chapters since they greatly influence the pattern of economic activities. Two aspects of relief may be distinguished, altitude and surface form, both of which are important although in different ways.

The influence of altitude, like that of latitude, is felt largely through climate. Since most of East Africa lies more than 1,000 metres above sea level, it does not experience typically equatorial conditions; and the distinctive economy of the Kenya highlands reflects the existence of much land over twice that altitude. The relationship between height and temperature is so close that many activities take place entirely above or below a certain altitude. Although Mount Kilimanjaro rises to 5,895 metres, the area of land in East Africa too high to be of any use to man is extremely small. Much mountain country is unused (Map 17), but this is sometimes on account of surface form rather than altitude.

The form of the land directly affects patterns of economic activity on both a broad scale and a local scale. Ruggedness limits the opportunities for cultivation in the Aberdare mountains or the Ruwenzori as a whole, but within these mountain masses there are significant local variations. Similarly within areas of generally low relief, such as eastern Uganda or Sukumaland, there are isolated hills with slopes too steep to be cultivated. There are areas such as Kigezi, where, as in Rwanda, steep slopes are used with the aid of elaborate bunding, but cultivation is more often found where slopes are gentle. The thin soils of most steep mountainsides, and their liability to erosion, contribute to their unattractiveness for agriculture. Very often the only economic use for such land is forestry, since trees will grow on steep slopes and they serve to check erosion, and in the Kenya highlands much land of this type has been afforested. Mining may also be affected by rugged relief, as shown by Kilembe copper mine, which lies in mountain country. In some respects this is advantageous, for a deep valley has exposed the ore, which can be mined by means of adits into the valley sides and moved to the concentrating plant by gravity.

Many studies have been made of the influence of relief on transport, and East Africa provides many examples of such influence. The walls of the rift valley hamper communications in many places, while difficult terrain was a factor which delayed the building of a railway to the southern highlands of Tanzania.

By hindering the establishment of communications rugged relief may limit all forms of commercial production, as in the Livingstone mountains in southern Tanzania or the Buhweju

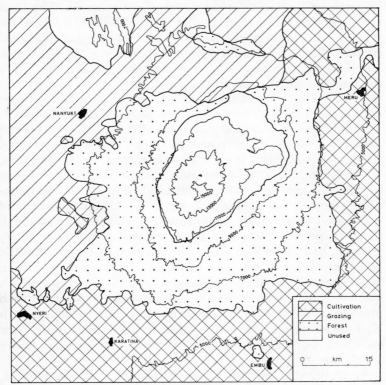

Figure 17. MOUNT KENYA: Relief and Land Use
The map is based upon 1 : 50,000 and 1 : 250,000 topographical maps produced by the Survey of Kenya.

highlands in western Uganda, neither of which are exceptionally high.[1] This problem has even hindered the use of rugged land for timber production, for extensive natural forests on Mount Elgon and Mount Kenya cannot be exploited because of inaccessibility, even though there are markets quite near.

Although steep mountainsides tend to be avoided for cultivation, there is often a concentration of farms on gentle slopes at their foot. The mountains provide a good water supply, but there is sufficient gradient to ensure good drainage. An accumulation of eroded material frequently provides a particularly rich soil there. The fringes of the Usambara mountains in northern Tanzania provide an excellent example. The same situation is repeated on a smaller scale in Buganda, where the typical landscape is an alternation of flat-topped hills and broad valleys. The hill-tops and upper slopes are often used only for rough grazing, while the ill-drained land in the valley floor may also be used for pasture, cultivation taking place mainly on the land in between. A similar relationship between landforms and land use may be seen south of Lake Victoria.[2]

The lowest and flattest parts of the land surface may be as unsuitable for man's activities as rugged mountain country. The greatest problem in such areas is generally poor drainage, which hinders cultivation of most crops. The Athi plains in Kenya provide one example, although rainfall and soil conditions are also of significance there. In Uganda much land is so poorly drained that it is occupied by swamp, and although the swamps can be drained, the expense of doing this is rarely justified. In these two cases the existence of land of little agricultural value has been advantageous in one way: both Nairobi and Kampala have flat land near the city centre which was unoccupied when industrial development began, and which provides suitable sites for factories and railway sidings. In Kampala all but the worst drained parts have now been occupied, but in Nairobi there is plenty of land for future development.

Agriculturally, swampy land is really suitable only for rice, and in many areas little use has been made of this potentiality. There is a marked concentration of sweet potato cultivation, not within the swamps but by their margins; and in central Kenya sugar cane is often planted on damp valley floors. Seasonally waterlogged land may provide good dry season pasture, and many examples of this type of land use may be seen around Kampala: but the many permanent swamps are of very little use to man.

The swamps are possibly a greater barrier to communications than rugged land, especially in Uganda. Many can be crossed only where costly embankments have been built, and some have enforced major detours. The western Uganda railway extension exemplifies the barrier effect where it runs for 30 km. beside a swamp which greatly hinders access to the line from the country to the north. Bugerere County was long cut off from the rest of Buganda by the swamp-filled Sezibwa valley, and an influx of settlement has followed improvement in the swamp crossing, resulting in a great increase in agricultural production.

The tectonic history of East Africa has led to the creation of the many lakes which form a striking feature of the region. Although they are far less productive than the land, they do support a flourishing fishing industry, which forms the chief source of income for many people living near their shores. The size and shape of the lakes is of some significance: since only inshore fishing is practised the waters of small lakes such as Lake George or Lake Rukwa are more fully exploited than those of the larger lakes. Much of Lake Victoria lies too far from a landfall to be touched by fishermen at present. From this point of view the irregular outline of Lake Kyoga is an advantage, although accessibility inland from many landing places is difficult.

The lakes have been of value as routeways. For the first quarter of this century Lake Victoria linked Uganda with the railway from Kisumu to the sea. Trade across Lake Victoria was established much earlier, and the value of accessibility by lake dates from well before the 20th century. The lake has drawn together economically to a certain extent the people of its shores, although as land transport has improved orientation towards the lake has decreased, and it has increasingly become a barrier to be crossed rather than an agent linking the areas around it. This applies even more strongly to Lake Kyoga, on which E.A.R. vessels have ceased to operate: its main effect today is to increase the road and rail distance between Teso and Kampala.

A further value of the lakes is for water supply. Lake Victoria provides 40 million litres a day for Kampala, and supplies other towns such as Kisumu and Mwanza. However, urban development at these places can hardly be attributed to this factor. Similarly, the lake provides irrigation water for Kakira sugar estate, but location away from it has not prevented irrigation on other estates. The lakes could be magnificent sources of water if any large-scale irrigation projects were established in their vicinity, but nothing of this nature has yet been undertaken.

While lakes are extremely important in the geography of East Africa, rivers are a less striking feature of the region. The Rufiji in Tanzania and the Tana in Kenya are the only major rivers flowing to the Indian Ocean, and the only other important one is the Nile, flowing north from Lake Victoria. The rivers are significant for economic geography in much the same ways as lakes. Most are used for fishing, although their contribution to the total catch is small. The Nile was formerly used by E.A. Railways steamers, but these have now been withdrawn. The cotton industry in West Nile at first depended greatly upon the river for transport of seed cotton, lint and seed; and some use is still made of it there, although economic activity in West Nile is increasingly focused on Arua, well away from the river.

The most striking relationship between rivers and economic activity in East Africa lies in their use for power generation. The irregular profile of many African rivers limits their use for navigation, but it provides opportunities for electricity production. Falls and rapids on the Nile confined the steamers to short sections, but they have permitted one of the major hydro-electric developments of tropical Africa, and provide a great potential for the future. The Owen Falls scheme benefits greatly from the fact that Lake Victoria constitutes a vast natural reservoir, enabling a small dam to make a great volume of water available, and ensuring a remarkably constant flow. Any future power stations on the Nile will also benefit from the even river regime, and thereby enjoy an advantage over those on other East African rivers.

Rivers, like lakes, may provide urban water supplies, and Nairobi faces problems in that the river by which it is located is very small, and quickly became inadequate for the town's needs. The value of a river as a source of water, and also as a channel for the disposal of effluent, is evident at Jinja, where both textile factories are sited beside the Nile. Even in rural areas rivers may be important in similar ways, notably for factories processing sisal, which use much water and must dispose of much effluent.

Most irrigation undertaken in East Africa is based on rivers, examples including the Mwea-Tebere scheme using rivers flowing from snow-capped Mount Kenya to irrigate the dry plains to the east, and that on the dry floor of the rift valley in Uganda using streams from the Ruwenzori.[3] Natural irrigation from seasonal floods on the Tana and Galana rivers permits rice cultivation in Coast Province of Kenya despite low rainfall. In the Rufiji basin in Tanzania there is scope for an integrated water development scheme on the T.V.A. pattern. The rivers there are now a liability rather than an asset, for periodic flooding has discouraged settlement anywhere near them. By providing breeding-grounds for insects the floodwaters contribute to the disease problems of the area. A comprehensive survey of the problem and potentialities of the basin has indicated how control of the rivers would facilitate economic development on a large scale.[4]

GEOLOGY[5]

In most countries geology is of some importance in the distribution of economic activities, either directly through opportunities for mineral exploitation, or indirectly through relief and soils. Since East Africa is predominantly an agricultural region, the effects of geology are likely to be mainly indirect. However, except for areas of volcanic rocks, these effects are mainly of only local importance. Geological maps distinguish clearly between the Basement System and more recent rocks, but this distinction is often not clearly reflected on the surface. The schists, gneisses and granites which occupy much of East Africa are broadly similar in their effects on relief and soils, and are often overlain by a thick mantle of weathered material which masks such variations as do exist. Thus in southern Buganda 'the character of the soils does not in general reflect the nature of the underlying bedrock'.[6] Even in southern Tanzania, where Jurassic, Cretaceous and Tertiary sediments are found in close proximity, the soil map, and therefore the pattern of agriculture, shows little relationship to the geological map.

The Tertiary and Recent volcanics of the Kenya highlands form the basis for their high altitude and their fertile soils, both of which affect the nature of agriculture there. Volcanic activity is also reflected in high agricultural productivity on Mount Kilimanjaro and Mount Elgon. Not all volcanic areas are productive, however, for on the Serengeti plains and in northern Kenya climate is dominant and the land supports very few people. Local illustrations of the effects of geology may be seen in western Uganda and north-west Tanzania, where resistant rocks of Karagwe-Ankolean age often give rise to sharp relief features with land unsuitable for cultivation, and quartzites tend to form ridges with very steep slopes and thin soils. By contrast, amphybolites around Lugazi in Buganda produce particularly fertile soils. On Pemba and Zanzibar Islands rock type and soils are closely connected, Miocene sediments and Pleistocene coral limestone being especially significant as will be shown later.

The occurrence of useful minerals offers the most obvious case of the relevance of geology in economic geography. 'Economic geology' is generally concerned primarily with this matter, and in most Geological Survey reports mining is the only economic activity discussed. Investigations made to date suggest that most rocks in East Africa are poor in minerals. In the Basement System many minerals are found, but none in large quantities, so that mining is confined to scattered mica workings in eastern Tanzania and a small kyanite mine in Kenya. Within the zones underlain by other ancient rocks minerals are associated with particular local geological conditions, rather than with rocks of a certain age or type. Thus diamonds occur in kimberlite pipes of limited extent, gold is associated with localized quartz veins in a wide range of rocks, and copper is found at Kilembe in rocks of the Toro System which elsewhere have provided no important minerals.

The existence of rocks of Karroo age in Tanzania is of potential importance, for these contain coal seams there as in southern Africa. Among the younger sedimentary rocks those of most value are coral limestones used for cement production near Mombasa and Dar es Salaam, and Pleistocene and Recent lake beds in the Kenya rift valley providing diatomite and soda ash. The volcanic rocks *in situ* contain no important minerals, except fluorspar which may soon be worked in Kenya's Kerio valley; but in eastern Uganda and northern Tanzania weathered volcanic material has taken the form of apatite, from which phosphate fertilizers are being produced in Uganda. Geological formations in some areas of sedimentary rocks suggest that oil may be found, but as yet drilling has been unsuccessful.

One geological feature of great importance for mining in East Africa is the scattered and broken nature of most mineral deposits. There is abundant wolfram and tin in south-west Uganda, but all in small deposits. If the limited extent of the Kilembe copper deposit had been known in 1953, the mine would probably not have been developed. Mpanda mineral field was once expected to provide a major source of wealth for Tanzania, but it was not mentioned in Chapter 9 as rapid exhaustion of worthwhile deposits has brought mining there to an end. Such experience discourages investment in mining elsewhere in East Africa.

Over much of the region a thick mantle of decomposed material hinders the investigation of the underlying rocks, which may contain more minerals than are known at present even in such accessible and well-populated areas as Buganda. This material itself consists largely of iron oxide and aluminium oxide, both of which are potential sources of useful minerals. Unfortunately there is no prospect of their exploitation in most places because the iron and aluminium content is too low. Nowhere in East Africa is the aluminium content high enough for the decomposed rock to rank as bauxite, while the ferruginous material rarely constitutes workable iron ore.

CLIMATE

Climate has been mentioned very frequently in earlier chapters, for it has probably contributed more than anything else to differences in ways of life between one part of East Africa and another. The complexity of the patterns of economic activity, compared with those in West Africa for example, is to a large extent related to the complexity of climatic patterns. Maps 18A and B, depicting mean annual rainfall, taken from the same source and simplified to a comparable extent, illustrate this contrast. Rainfall provides the most important climatic differences within East Africa, but temperatures are considered first since they affect mainly the character of the region as a whole.

Q

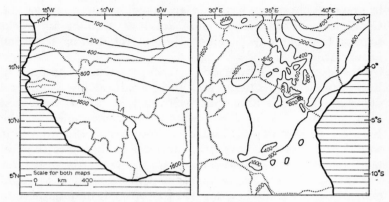

Figure 18A. WEST AFRICA: Figure 18B. EAST AFRICA:
Mean Annual Rainfall   Mean Annual Rainfall

These maps are both taken from Map 28 in B. W. Thompson, *The Climate of Africa*, O.U.P., Nairobi, 1965, and are therefore presumably simplified to a comparable extent. The figures are in millimetres.

Temperature

The position of East Africa astride the equator causes most parts of the region to have high temperatures all the year round, although they are commonly about 5°C. lower than in some equatorial countries since most of the land lies between 800 and 1,800 metres above sea level. Attention is here confined to the direct influence of temperature on economic activities. It is most significant for agriculture, greatly affecting the range of crops on which the region mainly depends.

Most of East Africa has mean annual temperatures between 20°C. and 25°C., has a monthly range of under 5°, and never experiences temperatures below 10°C. Such conditions are more suitable for coffee, cotton and tea, than for cocoa, rubber and oil palm or for the crops of temperate lands. Coffee can withstand neither constant great heat nor seasonal frost, and elevated land near the equator provides ideal conditions. All the major staple food crops, apart from maize, are those largely confined to the tropics. One important consequence of the even temperature regime is the possibility of taking two crops from the land each year wherever rainfall permits.

There are important differences in temperature conditions within East Africa, mainly dependent on altitude. This has contributed to the great variety of crops grown, the number of crops for which suitable conditions cannot be found somewhere in the region being small. The highlands, with mean annual temperatures between 10° and 16°C. permit cultivation of wheat, potatoes and other crops which are found in few parts of tropical Africa. But they are confined to the limited areas above 1,800 metres. Other crops, such as cashew nuts, do well only in hot low-lying country near the coast. The relationships between temperatures and the distribution of specific crops have been indicated earlier. Thus cotton is rarely found above 1,300 metres, where the mean temperature falls below 20°C.; while tea is concentrated in areas where temperatures rarely exceed 30°. For some plants the mean annual figure is significant, for others the extremes are more important.

Temperatures affect livestock in East Africa primarily through the diseases which are prevalent in hot conditions. Exotic cattle will survive even at sea level, but are kept healthy more easily in the cool highlands. Forestry is also directly affected, the importance of softwoods in Kenya and of tropical hardwoods in Uganda and Tanzania being related to the temperatures prevailing in the main forest areas of each country.

One indirect effect of temperature that must be mentioned is the attraction the cool highlands have had for European settlement. This was especially important in the past when health conditions in the hotter areas were much worse than in the cooler zone above 1,500 metres. The distribution of such settlement has in turn greatly affected the pattern of economic activities.

Rainfall[7]

Temperature and rainfall are closely related factors, for high temperatures lead to high evaporation rates which increase rainfall requirements for all forms of agriculture. These requirements are frequently not satisfied, so that rainfall has had profound effects on the patterns of activity in East Africa.[8] Thus over much of northern and eastern Kenya cultivation is impossible without irrigation, and in some places there are no opportunities even for grazing. No land is completely waterless, but some is true desert. Mean annual rainfall at Lodwar is under 150 mm. Such land is economically a liability rather than an asset, and must remain so unless minerals are found there. The tract with a rainfall of between 200 and 450 mm. is the zone of pastoral nomadism, flocks and herds moving long distances in search of water and grazing. There is some correlation between rainfall and the type of stock kept, for only camels and goats are found in the driest parts. Even where rainfall approaches 500 mm. conditions are poor for cattle, and their density is low, but they provide the best of the limited possibilities of such areas.

The limit of cultivation in East Africa generally occurs around the 450 mm. isohyet, although aspects of rainfall other than the mean annual total are also relevant. For the establishment of a cultivating economy it has often been suggested that the figure exceeded in, say, four years out of five, or nine years out of ten, is most significant. The East Africa Royal Commission observed that where less than 750 mm. is received three years in ten 'rainfall is too poor to allow arable farming to be normally possible'.[9] Yet in fact many communities within such areas are largely dependent upon cultivating the land.

Analyses of rainfall probability represent a refinement over mean annual figures, but the latter are still of value. Thus bananas are confined to areas with a mean fall of over 750 mm., while tea is grown only where it exceeds 1,200 mm. Other crops, such as sorghum and bulrush millet are associated with areas of low rainfall, although this is not because they do best there, but because they will survive there and other crops will not.

The highest rainfall, exceeding 2,000 mm. a year, occurs at the northern end of Lake Malawi, on Pemba island, around Bukoba and on the Sesse islands. It is very beneficial for clove cultivation on Pemba, but the other areas are little different in economy from those with 1,300 to 2,000 mm. These include most of those with a dense agricultural population, dependent either on perennials or on multiple cropping with annual plants. Nevertheless the relationship is far from exact, for large tracts of well-watered country between the Uluguru mountains and the southern highlands of Tanzania are hardly used, while areas of dense agricultural settlement around Kampala, Nairobi and Mwanza receive under 1,300 mm. of rain.

Rainfall is of greatest significance for the distribution of economic activities in Kenya. Well under a quarter of Kenya has a mean annual fall of over 750 mm., whereas half of Tanzania and 90 per cent. of Uganda has this amount. This is clearly reflected in the concentration of economic activity into a small part of Kenya, contrasting with the existence of several lesser concentrations in Tanzania, and the more even spread in Uganda.

Within Coast Province of Kenya agriculture is largely confined to the narrow coastal strip which receives over 1,000 mm. of rain. Inland less and less of the land is cultivated, and the last patches of cultivation to be seen on the Mombasa-Nairobi road lie near Mackinnon Road, which has just over 500 mm. Further inland the country supports only goats and game until the Taita Hills are reached. These induce an annual rainfall of over 750 mm., which permits cultivation of various food crops in the hills, and sisal on the adjacent plains. Within the highlands there are numerous close relationships between rainfall and land use. The wet southern and eastern slopes of Mount Kenya are intensively cultivated, but the dry northwestern slopes are used only for extensive grazing (Map 17). Even on the east rainfall decreases sharply away from the mountain, where maize and coffee give way first to bulrush millet and then to pastoralism. Much land within the rift valley has under 750 mm., and is used for ranching rather than crops despite fertile soils: but where rainfall is higher, as around Menengai and Rongai most land is cultivated.

Local differences in rainfall are of great importance in northern Tanzania, where conditions on Mount Kilimanjaro and Mount Meru are similar to those on Mount Kenya. The southern slopes, which face the prevailing winds and receive over 1,100 mm. of rain, support bananas and coffee: but to the north less than 750 mm. falls even on land over 2,000 metres, and little cultivation takes place. Between the two mountains is a zone of intermediate rainfall, unsuitable for coffee but satisfactory for wheat. In Uganda the significance of rainfall is apparent along the road from Kampala to Masindi. As it decreases northwards coffee is replaced by cotton as the main cash crop, and bananas give way to some extent to millet. Where the rainfall is below 1,000 mm. little land is cultivated, but towards Masindi it increases again sharply and more of the land is used, the range of crops again including coffee.

There are certain areas where anomalies which appear when the distribution of economic activity is related to that of mean annual rainfall can be explained by reliability of the rain. In parts of Masaka District of Uganda, and parts of the country around Moshi and Arusha, coffee is grown where the mean fall is under 1,000 mm., but where this is exceptionally reliable. On the other hand northern Kitui and western Narok in Kenya and much of Mbulu District in Tanzania have a mean figure of over 750 mm., but receive less than 500 mm. at least one year in ten. All these areas are primarily pastoral even though the rainfall is usually adequate for crops. Even within southern Uganda periodic failure of the expected rain may be important, possibly contributing to the limited extension of coffee into Busoga, where the mean annual fall is as high as in Buganda.

Rainfall Regime

Agriculture is affected not only by annual rainfall, but also by its distribution over the year. In East Africa there are generally two wet seasons around the equator, gradually merging into a single wet season in the north and south of the region. There are many local variations, however, the most important of which concern the length of real dry seasons.

In much of Buganda there is no dry season at all, for although there are two peaks of rainfall, in April and November, Kampala and Entebbe receive over 50 mm. in every month. This greatly assists banana and coffee cultivation, while it also permits the planting of two annual crops on any plot each year. It enables the sugar estates to harvest and process cane all the year round, and makes possible tea cultivation despite a mean annual rainfall lower than in most tea-growing areas. In eastern Uganda a dry season becomes increasingly distinct away from Lake Victoria, hindering perennial crops, although there are sufficient wet months for two annual crops to be grown each year. The short dry season is felt even on Mount Elgon, but unlike *robusta*, the *arabica* coffee grown there benefits from this. In much of northern Uganda the dry season lasts for four months, and there is only one growing season for crops. The period of enforced idleness lowers productivity, and less cotton is planted there than in the east because farmers must devote most of their attention during the wet season to food crops. The dry season is most severe in Karamoja, most of which has four months with under 25 mm. and another two with less than 50 mm. Even cattle rearing is hazardous there, and the density of stock is limited by lack of grazing at the end of the dry season.

In northern Kenya the distinction between wet and dry seasons is equally clear, and there the latter is the longer. In the highlands the pattern is extremely complicated, with much local variation which is reflected in the agricultural calendar. Most areas occupied by European farmers enjoy a very favourable regime, with over 75 mm. in most months. The African-settled areas north of Nairobi have more distinct double maxima and minima, but the total fall is sufficient for crops to be grown in each wet season. There is no real dry season in most of Nyanza and Western Provinces, but dry spells may occur at any time of year. In general the rainfall regime is much less significant than the total annual fall in relation to patterns of activity in Kenya.

In Tanzania wet and dry seasons become increasingly distinct from north to south. Parts of West Lake Region with an annual fall of 1,000 mm. receive 50 mm. every month from September to May, whereas places with a similar total in the south receive 50 mm. only in the months from December to April. The land just south of Lake Victoria could not support such a high density of cattle if it experienced a long and severe dry season. In the southern highlands the rainfall regime is one factor limiting the development of perennial crops. Because of the concentration of most of the year's rain into 5 or 6 months, a higher total is needed than in Uganda or Kenya if coffee or tea are to flourish. Both these crops, and also the banana, are therefore confined to the wettest parts of this area. The limitation of agricultural activity to part of the year has also hindered cash crop development in Mtwara and Ruvuma Regions.

An evenly distributed rainfall is not always an advantage for agriculture. When the annual total is low, cultivation may not be possible unless it is concentrated into one wet season. If some rain falls in every month there may not be sufficient in any 6-month growing season for any crops. Thus most of the

Katonga valley in western Uganda is unused, partly because the 750 mm. rainfall is too evenly distributed. A similar situation exists in many parts of Kenya which receive 500 to 600 mm. a year.[10] By contrast, the 550 mm. received at Dodoma and Itigi in central Tanzania falls mainly between December and April, and annual crops may be grown during this period.

Rainfall Intensity

The value of the rainfall depends upon how it falls, and in much of East Africa most falls in short but extremely heavy storms, rushes away on the surface and is quickly lost. This problem is especially great in the drier areas, just where water is most needed. Within Uganda, for example, sudden storms account for more of the total rainfall in Karamoja than anywhere else. The situation is illustrated in the following account of an experience there. 'Within ten minutes of the initial downpour the whole surface of the plain for miles around was covered with a sheet of water moving westwards. . . . When the storm had passed I dug into the ground to see how far the rain had penetrated; and nowhere could I find moist soil at a greater depth than 6 inches.'[11] This feature of Karamoja goes far to explain the lack of cultivation despite a fairly reliable rainfall of 600 to 1,100 mm. In southern Uganda more rain falls gently, seeps into the ground and can be used by plants. The sky is more often cloudy than in areas in the north with the same total rainfall, and this reduces evaporation. The 1,100 mm. received at Jinja is thus far more effective than the 1,100 mm. received in parts of Karamoja. A wide range of crops is grown in southern Kigezi, which has a not particularly reliable 900 mm. of rain, for this is very effective. Falls of over 25 mm. in 24 hours are rare, mists frequently occupy the valleys in the mornings, and the average humidity at Kabale at 8.30 a.m. is 91 per cent.

SOILS

Since East Africa is so heavily dependent upon agriculture, the character of its soils is of great importance in its economic geography. In general, 'the soils of East Africa, in common

with those of a large section of the tropical world, are by nature
relatively poor, unproductive and fragile.'[12] In much of the
region the soil has a low nutrient status, is deficient in humus,
is quickly leached, and is easily eroded when exposed to the
rain. The main effect of poor soils is to lower the productivity
of the land, depressing yields per hectare. The low cotton
yields of Uganda and Tanzania compared with most producing
countries may be attributed in part to poor soils. Another
consequence is the need for a long resting period in many areas.
Where land is abundant this only affects the farming system,
but where land is scarce the result is the cultivation either of
less land or of land not really able to sustain crops. The
importance of such crops as sorghum and cassava is related to
their capacity to grow in very poor soils. The situation will
improve when more fertilizer or manure is applied: and the low
level of agricultural productivity is related to natural poverty
of the soils in conjunction with farmers' failure to integrate cattle
and crops sufficieny to apply manure, and inability to pay
for artificial fertilizers.

There are exceptions to this gloomy picture, and differences
in soils within East Africa are of great importance. Whereas
climatic differences are felt mainly over wide areas, significant
contrasts in soils are most often found on a local scale. A
regional physical division of East Africa would depend mainly
upon relief and climate, but within each region soils would
provide local variations in environmental conditions. One
broad zone that must be distinguished, however, is that of
volcanic soils. Throughout the volcanic highlands of Kenya
soils are much more fertile than is common in tropical Africa,
giving high yields even when continuously cultivated. They are
also relatively resistant to erosion. Similar soils permit intensive
cultivation around Mount Elgon and Mount Kilimanjaro.
Within the southern highlands of Tanzania only Rungwe
District has volcanic soils, and only there is the land intensively
used. Ruvuma Region of Tanzania perhaps stands out as a
well-watered area with particularly poor soils and low productivity.

The area of volcanic soils in Uganda is small, yet it has
been said that 'compared with most other places in the tropics
the soils of Uganda are, on the whole, very fertile.'[13] This is

very clear in the Lake Victoria zone, and contributes to the
high level of production there, but there are major contrasts
in soils within the country. Even within Buganda the contrast
between the intensive agriculture of the lake-shore areas and
the low productivity of the north is related to soil as well as
rainfall conditions. Southern Bunyoro has a rainfall of over
1,100 mm. with no real dry season, but its soils are less fertile
than those of most of Buganda, and its contribution to Uganda's
banana and coffee crops is small. On a more local scale there is
a striking contrast between the Masaka shore of Lake Victoria,
where land with a rainfall of 1,200 mm. lies unused because of
the low mineral content and excessive drainage of the coarse
sandy soil, and the country inland with deep soils, retentive of
moisture yet easily worked, where coffee is grown although the
rainfall is below 1,000 mm.

Clear relationships between soil character and cotton
production may be seen in Teso District, where most cotton
is grown on the clay loams of the south-east. The sandy soils
of the north-east give much lower yields, while the soils
fringing Lake Kyoga in the south-west are often waterlogged
and always difficult to work. Most of northern Uganda has
poorer soils than the south, and this contributes to the lower
level of agricultural production there, but again there are
important local variations, notably in West Nile District.

Kenya and Tanzania also provide many examples of the local
significance of differences in soil type. Thus soils play a major
part in the agricultural geography of Zanzibar and Pemba
islands. In the west of Zanzibar deep and fairly fertile 'Changa'
soils are used for clove cultivation, whereas the 'Maweni' soils
of the south, east and north will not support this crop. Indeed
the latter consist only of pockets of soil on coral rock, and are
occupied mainly by bush and scrub. Various intermediate
soils are satisfactory for food crops and for coconuts, but
unsuitable for cloves. Two distinctive soils are 'Pwani', deep
soft sands suitable only for coconuts, and 'Namo' which are
heavy clays, difficult to work but valuable for rice cultivation
because of their capacity to retain water. Soils of sufficient
depth and fertility for cloves occupy a much larger proportion
of Pemba than of Zanzibar, and the crop is more widespread
there. Only the extreme east has 'Maweni' soils of little value.

Certain soil characteristics are important for particular crops, such as the acidity required by tea. In Kenya tea does particularly well on acid soils around Kericho; but further west around Kisii, where soils are more alkaline it is replaced by coffee. Similarly in Nyeri District tea is generally grown at higher altitudes than coffee, partly because it benefits from cooler conditions, but also because the soils at higher altitudes are more acid in nature. Groundnuts are very difficult to grow in a heavy soil, and in all three countries they are associated mainly with light soils, although these are often of low fertility.

NATURAL VEGETATION

Most land in East Africa carries some form of natural vegetation, although this is usually secondary rather than original as a result of disturbance by man. This vegetation may be of direct economic value as a source of wood or of grazing,[14] or may hinder economic activity since cultivation requires its clearance. Some types are more difficult to clear than others, but in East Africa burning is generally quite effective, and in few places can lack of cultivation be attributed to difficulty of clearing the land. Vegetation has certainly presented the farmer with less problems than in the Congo rain forest.

Two ways in which natural vegetation does hinder economic activity in this region are rapid weed growth and the role of woodland and bush as the habitat of tsetse fly. Striga may have kept out cultivation from parts of Sukumaland, while couch grass decreases crop yields in such fertile areas as Buganda. The tsetse fly, discussed further below, is entirely dependent on certain forms of vegetation, and disappears when this is cleared. Thus in Tanzania there is a close association between the fly and the Miombo woodlands of the west and south, while in western Uganda the main weapon used against tsetse is bush clearance.

Forests are the most useful form of vegetation for direct exploitation, and their importance was indicated in Chapter 8. The forests which once covered much of Uganda, and of which small patches remain, contain many species valuable for timber, notably mvule (*Chlorophora excelsa*) and mahogany (*Khaya nyasica*). In the forest of northern Kigezi, however, the predominant species is ironwood (*Cynometra alexandri*) which is of little commercial value. Even where mvule and mahogany occur, they are interspersed with less useful trees, and their frequency within each forest area affects the pattern of timber production.

High altitude forests, found mainly in Kenya, do not include species of such high value, but usually contain more useful trees on each hectare. Nevertheless, although the trees are softwoods, they grow less quickly than those of most high latitude coniferous forests, the main species cut, podocarpus, taking 150 years to mature. Consequently the natural forests are slowly being replaced by plantations of exotic species, and the natural vegetation is providing a decreasing share of the timber cut in Kenya.

Much of the Forest Reserve of Tanzania is occupied by woodland rather than true forest, as indicated on Map 3. This is of limited value for timber, although some of the dominant brachystegia is cut, together with the more valuable, but less abundant, pterocarpus. Much more wood is cut for fuel and for building poles, but over large areas population is so sparse that little use is made of the vegetation even for these purposes. There are, however, some districts within Tanzania, such as the Usambara mountains, where the natural vegetation is very fully exploited for timber, poles and fuel.

Much of East Africa is occupied by savanna or grassland vegetation, the main value of which is in pasture for cattle. In this region livestock rearing depends very largely on the natural vegetation, for animals are only rarely grazed on sown pastures or provided with other fodder. As elsewhere in tropical Africa, the natural grass is often of low nutrient value, and will support neither a high rate of stocking nor animals of high quality. Burning of the vegetation to promote new growth is a widespread practice, and except where it is overdone it improves the grazing somewhat.[15]

There are considerable variations within East Africa in the quality of the natural pasture. It is best at high altitudes, the predominant Kikuyu grass (*Pennisetum clandestinum*) favouring high-grade cattle rearing over most of the Kenya highlands for example. The quantity of pasture available per hectare depends largely on rainfall: thus in Karamoja grass is much less abundant in the east than on the Acholi border, where most of the cattle are concentrated during the dry season. The natural pasture is particularly unsatisfactory in certain areas such as Bukoba District in Tanzania, which has a 'pasturage having one of the lowest nutritional planes in the world'[16] and consequently has very few cattle.

The thicket and scrub of much of northern Kenya are of little value for cattle, and support only goats. Gulliver notes that 'the cause of Turkana nomadism is poverty of vegetation'.[17] In the dry season there is grass for cattle only in the mountains; in the wet season cattle are grazed on the edge of the plains to conserve the mountain pasture; and at all seasons goats are kept mainly far out on the plains since they alone can make use of the scrub there.

Two distinctive types of vegetation found in East Africa are mangroves, which fringe much of the coast, and papyrus, which occupies many inland swamps. The mangroves are exploited commercially, small quantities of poles being exported, notably from the Rufiji delta. The papyrus is of less commercial value, for although it has several potential uses, including the manufacture of paper, to which it gives its name, none appears to be an economic proposition. It is cut only on a small scale for rural handicrafts such as basket-making.

Vegetation is of significance for crop production mainly as an indicator of climatic or soil conditions.[18] Thus land occupied by bracken normally has acid soil suitable for tea, while sugar thrives wherever elephant grass (*Pennisetum purpureum*) is abundant. The vegetation is not itself, however, a factor directly affecting tea or sugar production, for it must be cleared away before these crops are planted.

ANIMAL LIFE

The fauna of East Africa may be justly regarded as a major economic asset, for wild animals provide the region's main attraction to tourists from overseas. They are also a source of food in certain areas, as are fish in most districts. On the other hand animals discourage settlement in some places, and damage crops in many more. Even more significant is the role of insect life in the transmission of disease: in fact this is so important that a separate section must be devoted to it.

Some parts of East Africa have a richer store of animal life than any other part of the world. The most abundant of the larger mammals are various species of antelope, buffalo, elephant, giraffe, hippopotamus and zebra, but lion, leopard, rhinoceros and many others are also found. Although some areas with much game are at present inaccessible, there is a close correlation between the distribution of these animals and that of tourist areas. The numbers of many species have fallen greatly during this century, but now that conservation is government policy, the future of wild life in East Africa seems assured.

Tourism is among the most sophisticated forms of economic activity. The least sophisticated type, hunting, also depends on wild animals: but this is of small importance in East Africa today. This situation reflects the scarcity of game today in most settled areas, and the restriction of hunting wherever animals are sufficiently numerous to attract tourists, rather than an abundance of alternative meat supplies. In northern Uganda small animals that are still common, such as hares, are often hunted, but as much for sport as for food. In the Uganda National Parks hippo are now multiplying rapidly, and controlled cropping has begun, thus increasing local meat supplies.

Hunting elephant for ivory was once a major element in the East African economy. In Uganda, for example, ivory accounted for over half the value of exports in 1904: but although the volume exported was almost identical sixty years later, it has paled into insignificance as other exports have developed. Sales of ivory are now more important in Tanzania than elsewhere and are worth over £300,000 in some years, but even there the number of elephants is quite inadequate to support large scale ivory production.

Fishing is the main form of direct exploitation of animal life in East Africa today, and its distribution is greatly affected by the numbers and types of fish present in various parts of the coastal waters and in each of the lakes. Many illustrations of this have been provided in Chapter 7.

Although wild animals are not found lurking round the corner everywhere in East Africa, there are many areas where they steal chickens and damage crops,[19] and a few where they remain dominant and hinder settlement. It has been possible to schedule some areas National Parks partly because game had discouraged other forms of land use. Parts of the Serengeti plains would have been suitable for pastoralism if lions had not prevented cattle keeping. Damage done to crops ranges from elephants stampeding on newly-planted tea in a sparsely populated part of Ankole to the regular depradations of monkeys in maize plots in the densely populated Maragoli area of western Kenya. In parts of Sebei District of Uganda so much cotton has been trampled down by giraffe that little is now grown. Even the fishing industry is affected by another form of animal life, for it was greatly discouraged on Lake Kyoga by crocodiles, which both ate the fish and fouled the nets, until they were recently cleared away.

Even birds may hinder certain forms of activity, for their attacks on wheat have discouraged this crop in parts of northern Tanzania. The replacement of millet by maize in much of East Africa has been encouraged by its lesser susceptibility to depradation by birds. Locusts have also been a major scourge and, although this problem seems to have been largely overcome, the importance of cassava throughout the region is partly related to their visitations in the past.

Animals as well as insects may assist in the spread of disease. The tsetse fly not only depends on certain types of vegetation for its habitat, but also relies on wild animals for most of its food, carrying trypanosomes from one such animal to another and ultimately to cattle. Tsetse eradication methods have therefore included the destruction of game as well as of bush. In this way the presence of cattle is often related to the absence of game. These measures of course conflict with efforts towards game conservation, and the result is increased regional differentiation, with an increase of wild animals in some areas and a decrease in others. From this follows regional specialization in economic activity, with tourism concentrated in the former areas, and cattle rearing in the latter.

INSECT LIFE

In East Africa, as in most tropical regions, insects are of great significance in economic geography as carriers of disease to men, livestock and crops. The most widespread tropical disease, malaria, is carried from man to man throughout most of East Africa by the *Anopheles* mosquito, debilitating a large proportion of the population and limiting their capacity for work, whether on their own farms or as paid labour. The high density of population in many highland areas, as also in neighbouring Rwanda and Burundi, and the consequent intensity of cultivation, may be related to the absence of the *Anopheles* which does not thrive in the cool conditions above 1,500 metres. But it cannot be established that freedom from malaria makes the people of these areas more industrious than those living elsewhere. On highland margins the significance of malaria is sometimes clear. Thus it discourages migration of people in Kigezi from the overcrowded south to the sparsely-populated north, thereby influencing patterns of activity within the district.

The tsetse fly, which transmits sleeping sickness to man and also trypanosomiasis to cattle, is less widespread than the *Anopheles* mosquito, and far fewer people come into contact with it. It is, however, much more deadly, and where it does occur its impact is often far greater. It therefore contributes much more to regional differentiation within East Africa. In southern Busoga sleeping sickness killed almost 100,000 people in one epidemic early in this century, and forced many more to abandon their homes. This area has since remained officially closed to all settlement, and therefore agriculturally unproductive despite favourable climatic and soil conditions. Even fishing in the adjacent lake waters has suffered, for there are few landing-places along this shore. The same epidemic swept the Sesse islands, and although resettlement began in 1920, the population in 1959 was still only 5,300 compared with an estimated 20,000 sixty years earlier. Many former farm sites lie unoccupied, and the level of economic activity is lower than in most of Buganda, although the islands have some of the best potential coffee land in East Africa.

Sleeping sickness is transmitted mainly by one species of tsetse fly, *Glossina palpalis*, found almost exclusively near open water. But *G. morsitans* and *G. pallidipes*, which spread trypanosomiasis among cattle, are much more widely distributed. They are found over 60 per cent. of Tanzania, 30 per cent. of Uganda and 10 per cent. of Kenya, and throughout these areas they make cattle-keeping almost impossible. There is probably no closer spatial relationship between a feature of the physical environment and an economic activity than that between tsetse infestation and cattle keeping, illustrated on Map 10. Thus in western Tanzania the only areas free of tsetse are the country around Tabora, the Ngara and Kasulu uplands, and the Ufipa plateau south-west of Lake Rukwa: and these are the only areas where cattle are of any importance.

The significance of tsetse infestation is particularly great for Tanzania since low and unreliable rainfall makes much of its land more suitable for grazing than for cultivation. The fly tends to be concentrated in such country, for it can be driven away by clearing for cultivation, and since the land cannot be used for cattle it is not used at all. Even on some cultivable land the tsetse fly rather than man is dominant, for people avoid country where they cannot keep cattle when there is land elsewhere where they can do so.

The tsetse fly is being combatted in many areas, notably in Uganda, where it constantly threatens to spread to areas where cattle are kept.[20] Some success has been achieved, as in Buruli County of northern Buganda where cattle have increased from under 200 in 1945 to over 50,000 today. Often, however, progress has been slow; and there has even been some spread of tsetse both in Uganda and in Nyanza Province of Kenya.

Ticks affect far more cattle than tsetse flies, spreading several diseases including east-coast fever. This is at least partly responsible for the death of over 30 per cent. of the calves in some parts of East Africa. Although it affects livestock rearing over much of the region, it rarely prevents it altogether; but in Karamoja there is clear evidence of its influencing the distribution of cattle.[21] Ticks can be controlled by dipping the animals and then keeping them free from contact with others, and only such control allows the high productivity of cattle on both large and small farms in the Kenya highlands. The flourishing Nyeri dairy industry was made possible only by the local authorities' insisting on dipping. Among other diseases which have affected the distribution of cattle is rinderpest. An epidemic in 1890 killed most of the cattle in Karagwe District of Tanzania, although it is the tsetse fly which now prevents their re-introduction.[22]

Among the many insects which have local effects on agricultural activity is the Mbwa fly, which bites so severely that it

R

long kept settlement out of the country beside the Nile north of Lake Victoria. Much land on the Buganda side is still under forest, but on the Busoga side advantage was taken of the lack of settlement by clearing the land of vegetation, and therefore of Mbwa flies, for the Kakira sugar plantation. A further assault on the fly in the 1950s assisted a rapid spread of cotton cultivation in this area.

There are also numerous insects which attack crops, and although some do so wherever they are grown, others are sufficiently localized to affect their distribution very greatly. The antestia bug has greatly discouraged coffee growing in south-west Uganda and in the Ngara uplands of Tanzania. Stainer bugs discouraged the establishment of cotton in Ankole, and the bollworm has defeated attempts to establish it in southern Tanzania. Even the process of afforestation has been affected by insect damage in certain areas. With the aid of insecticides, however, much is now being done to overcome this problem of the East African environment.

REFERENCES

1 J. C. Doornkamp, 'The Isolation of Buhweju County, Ankole', *East African Geographical Review*, No. 2, 1964, pp. 23–29.
2 P. H. Temple, 'Physical Factors Influencing Land Use in Coastal Sukumaland', *East African Geographical Review*, No. 3, 1965, pp. 17–26.
3 A traditional irrigation system is described in R. F. Gray, *The Sonjo of Tanganyika*, Oxford U.P., London, 1963. Recent developments in Uganda are discussed in I. D. Carruthers, 'Irrigation Development in Uganda', *East African Geographical Review*, No. 8, 1970, pp. 11–22.
4 F. A. O., *Rufiji Basin Survey*, Rome, 1961.
5 The geology of East Africa is outlined by E. P. Saggerson in W. T. W. Morgan (ed.), *East Africa: Its People and Resources*, Oxford U.P., Nairobi, 1969.
6 E. M. Chenery in Geological Survey of Uganda, Report No. 1, *The Geology of Southern Mengo*, Entebbe, 1959, p. 16.
7 J. M. Kenworthy has contributed a valuable study of rainfall in East Africa to R. W. Steel and R. M. Prothero (eds.), *Geographers and the Tropics*, Longmans, London, 1964.
8 L. W. Hanna, 'Climate and Crop Potential of Uganda', in S. H. Ominde (ed.), *Studies in East African Geography and Development*, Heinemann, London, in the press.
9 *East African Royal Commission 1953–1955 Report*, H.M.S.O., London, 1955, p. 254.
10 M. K. Bennett, 'An Agroclimatic Mapping of Africa', *Stanford Food Research Institute Studies*, Vol. 3, No. 3, 1962, p. 201.
11 Quoted in E. J. Wayland, *Soil Erosion and Water Supplies in Uganda*, Entebbe, 1938, pp. 37–38.

12 *East Africa Royal Commission, op. cit.*, p. 262.
13 E. M. Chenery, *Introduction to the Soils of Uganda*, Uganda Department of Agriculture, Kawanda, 1960, p. 32.
14 B. J. Turner, 'Land Use and Ecological Problems in East Africa', in S. H. Ominde (ed.), *op. cit*,
15 B. W. Langlands, 'Burning in Eastern Africa', *East African Geographical Review*, No. 5, 1967, pp. 21–37.
16 J. P. Moffet, *Tanganyika, A Review of its Resources and their Development*, Dar es Salaam, 1955, p. 573.
17 P. H. Gulliver, *The Family Herds*, Routledge & Kegan Paul, London 1955, p. 26.
18 I. Langdale-Brown and others, *The Vegetation of Uganda*, Entebbe, 1964, pp. 92–101, illustrates this point.
19 A. C. Mascarenhas, 'Agricultural Vermin in Tanzania', in S. H. Ominde (ed.), *op. cit.*
20 A. G. Robertson, 'Tsetse Control in Uganda', *East African Geographical Review*, No. 1, 1963, pp. 21–32.
21 V. R. Dyson-Hudson, 'East-coast Fever in Karamoja', *Uganda Journal*, Vol. 24, No. 2, 1960, pp. 253–259.
22 D. N. McMaster, 'Change of Regional Balance in the Bukoba District of Tanganyika', *Geographical Review*, Vol. 50, No. 1, 1960, pp. 73–88.

CHAPTER 16

Demographic and Social Factors

DISTRIBUTION OF POPULATION

The amount of economic activity in any area is in part related to the number of people living there; and this is particularly clear in a predominantly agricultural region where, provided there is land to spare, more hands mean a larger area cultivated. Where mechanization has made little progress, as in most of East Africa, and most farming operations are done by hand, the relationship between density of population and crop production is especially close.

Over East Africa as a whole there are only 21 people to the square km., and the region is underpopulated in the sense that an increase in numbers in the right areas could bring a proportionate, or more than proportionate, increase in production. However, density of population differs greatly from place to place: some areas are uninhabited while others are very densely settled (Map 2). Overall figures are therefore of little value, and attention must be concentrated on particular areas.[1]

In much of northern and eastern Kenya there is less than one person per square km. and virtually no economic activity. There, however, physical conditions are such that no more activity is feasible even if people were willing to move in. In Tanzania, on the other hand, large stretches of country offering a potential for agriculture and stock-rearing are unused because there are few people to engage in these. The Kilombero valley offers the best example, while others are the Great Ruaha valley and the shores of Lake Victoria west of Mwanza. The changes occurring in this last area as settlers move in from Sukumaland indicate the importance of density of population. Even within Uganda there are areas where economic activity is limited by the sparse population. Much of Bunyoro District is quite fertile and well-watered, and the value of agricultural production per head is higher than in most of the country; but in relation to the area of the district the total value is small, and much good land lies idle.

While population density clearly affects the development of particular *areas*, in terms of improving the lot of the *people* its significance is less obvious. Nevertheless, much of Tanzania and parts of Kenya and Uganda could not only support far more people, but would also probably have a higher income per head if they were more densely settled, as a wider range of services could then be provided. Forestry or mining may take place in very sparsely populated areas if the resources are attractive: but even these are often discouraged where sparse settlement results in shortage of labour, limited local markets and inadequate transport facilities.

Most agricultural production of East Africa, and almost all industrial production, comes from a few zones of dense population. In Central, Nyanza and Western Provinces of Kenya, in the Lake Victoria zone of Uganda, and in parts of northern Tanzania, a large proportion of the land is cultivated. Dense settlement enables these areas to produce large quantities of crops. It makes shifting cultivation impossible, and in some places most of the land is in use every year. Density of population also affects the type of agricultural production. Among the food crops of the region cassava, sweet potatoes and bananas which give the highest yields per hectare, are often particularly important where population is dense. Among the cash crops of the highlands, tea and pyrethrum are especially suitable where there is pressure on the land, for they are more demanding on labour than on land.

In some places, such as southern Kigezi in Uganda, the population is so dense that all cultivable land on many farms is required for food crops and there is none to spare for cash crops. In parts of Bugisu the area under coffee cannot ever increase unless that under other crops falls and food is obtained from elsewhere. This appears to be happening in Nyeri District of Kenya, where a density of over 2,000 people per square km. in some locations has not prevented recent expansion of coffee and tea cultivation. The widespread practice of intercropping in central Kenya may be related to density of population, for it gives a high food output per hectare even though it reduces the yield of each crop. Some intercropping occurs everywhere, but it reaches its extreme form where pressure on land is greatest.

Dense population and resulting land shortage often restrict the number of cattle each farmer may keep, and therefore limit their importance in the local economy. This is clear in Bugisu and Kigezi, and also in parts of central Kenya where this factor has encouraged the keeping of pigs which makes less demands on land. Both there and on Mount Kilimanjaro density of population also encourages the feeding of stock on cut grass or banana peelings where grazing is scarce. Occasionally, as in Zanzibar and perhaps in Nyanza, high population density has encouraged non-agricultural activities such as fishing, although there is a notable lack of cottage industry such as is found in many densely populated rural areas in Asia.

Some areas in East Africa suffer from severe overpopulation, despite large-scale emigration to other districts. Unless the economic activities were to change, income per head in Bunyore and Maragoli districts of western Kenya would probably be greater if their population were smaller. But over-population is not a problem characteristic of East Africa as a whole. One of the most important differences among underdeveloped countries is their density of population; and solutions for the problems of poor but crowded countries in Asia may not be applicable to sparsely settled African countries.

It is not only the present distribution of population which is significant in the economic geography of East Africa. The distribution seventy years ago, when the Europeans arrived, has greatly affected the present pattern of economic activities, especially in Kenya. Physical conditions, accessibility and the extent of existing African settlement together guided the occupation of land by European farmers and, therefore, influenced the present distribution of many crops. The Kenya tea industry is centred on what was formerly a sparsely populated no man's land between two tribes, and the main zone of sugar production is similarly located. The coffee and sisal estates between Nairobi and Thika were likewise established on unoccupied land between areas of Kikuyu and Masai settlement.

Some land occupied by Europeans has now been taken over

for African settlement, and there former sparse population has indirectly influenced the present pattern even of African farming. Dairying, for example, is developing in these areas rather than in the long-settled country with a strong tradition of communal grazing. The Kenya resettlement programme offers many opportunities for the study of the significance of population density. Only where settlement schemes are bringing a much increased density of population is there increased intensity of land use. The number of people the land can support is limited, however, and there is considerable disagreement on the optimum density for these schemes.

DEMOGRAPHIC CHARACTERISTICS[2]

The age structure of the East African population is significant, for, as in most underdeveloped countries, a large proportion of the population is not of working age. Children of 14 years or under account for about 45 per cent. of the total, which is comparable with the figure for Nigeria or Brazil but contrasts with under 25 per cent. in Britain. What constitutes working age varies, and in East Africa many children assist in picking cotton or herding cattle. Nevertheless, their productivity is generally far lower than that of adults; and as increasing numbers attend school their contribution is decreasing, although education should enhance their income-earning capacity in the future.

Sharp contrasts in age and sex structure exist within East Africa, generally resulting from migration.[3] In Njombe and Songea Districts in southern Tanzania, about one-third of the adult men are usually away, and so adult males make up a much smaller proportion of the resident population than is normal. The situation is similar 2,000 km. away in West Nile District of Uganda. There males of 16 or over account for only 22 per cent. of the population, compared with the national average of 28 per cent. In Kigezi district less than 20 per cent. were adult men according to the 1959 census. The absence of adult men is even more marked in parts of western Kenya, for they comprised only 17 per cent. of the population of Kakamega District at the 1962 census.

In all these areas the high ratio of children to adults tends to lower the level of economic activity. This is not true of the preponderance of women among the adults, for they generally do more work than men; but the ratio of men to women may affect the nature of economic activity in each area. Women are often responsible mainly for food crops, the production of

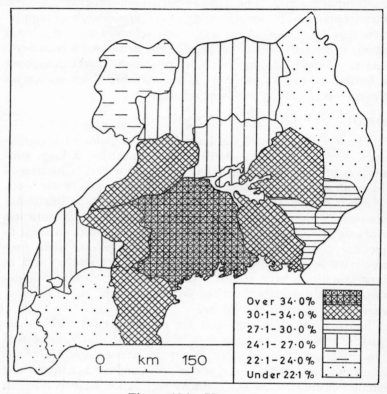

Figure 19A. UGANDA.

Proportion of the Total Population, Males over 16 Years, by District, 1959.

cash crops being the men's concern, and where many men are away cultivation of cash crops is affected. Songea, Njombe, West Nile, Kigezi and Kakamega are all districts in which cash crops are poorly developed (Maps 19a and 19b). In a study of the Ngoni, of Songea District, P. H. Gulliver notes that 'the inroads into cash crop production caused by the continual absence of so large a proportion of men are serious',[4] and observes that within Songea tobacco cultivation is concentrated in areas where least emigration takes place. A similar local correlation occurs in West Nile, where most cotton

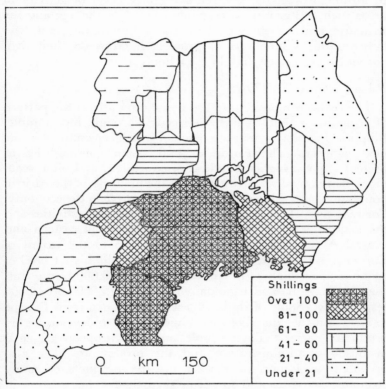

Figure 19B. UGANDA.

Annual Income per Head from Peasant Cash Crops. Average for 1958–60.

is grown in places where the population includes most adult men. A high rate of emigration may itself result from lack of local opportunities to obtain a cash income; and indeed it is often difficult to establish which is cause and which is effect. But the absence of many adult men has certainly limited commercial activity in several parts of East Africa.

Conversely, an unusually high proportion of men of working age has favoured development in some places. This is most evident in the cities, but it also applies to larger areas, such as Buganda or Tanga Region. Other factors must be favourable to attract people, but the relatively high level of activity in areas such as Buganda is certainly related to the age and sex structure, and especially to the numerous immigrant men who either work as labourers or grow cash crops on their own account there rather than in their home area.

RACIAL COMPOSITION

The racial composition of the population affects the pattern of economic activity mainly indirectly, through, for example, supplies of capital or markets, each of which is examined in the next chapter. The European and Asian communities at present enjoy a higher standard of education, and often seem more commercially motivated, than the majority of the African population, and this greatly enhances their role in the economy. For reasons such as these, the range of economic activities and the general level of incomes in the countries of eastern and central Africa still show some relationship to the extent of European settlement. This is illustrated by the higher level of economic development in Kenya, which has 40,000 Europeans, than in Tanzania and Uganda, which have 15,000 and 10,000 respectively. Some of those who went to Kenya from Europe to farm had the education, skills and capital to develop highly productive farms.[5] These people, and the Europeans engaged in business, administration and the professions, have also provided an important market for the products of many economic activities and so encouraged their concentration in Kenya.

Certain activities are particularly closely connected with the European element in the population. Wheat cultivation and dairying provide two examples, for their importance and distribution in Kenya is related not only to climatic conditions but also to the pattern of European settlement. The current spread of dairying on African farms in central Kenya indicates that the relationship is not immutable, but it is still close. Similarly, wheat is grown increasingly by Africans, but whereas around Eldoret and Moiben wheat is the main crop on European farms, in Elgeyo Marakwet with a similar physical environment African farmers depend mainly upon maize.

Over 380,000 Asians live in East Africa, three-quarters of all those living in tropical Africa.[6] They too have played a role out of proportion to their numbers in the economic development of the region, and as half are in Kenya they have contributed to that country's economic lead over Tanzania and Uganda. Asians dominate internal trade, play a substantial part in manufacturing industry, and make some contribution to commercial agriculture. They have helped East Africa to avoid the development of a dual economy in which a European-managed commercial sector and an African subsistence sector exist side by side with little interaction.

The Asians have scattered more widely over the region than the Europeans, bringing with them an expertise in trade which few Africans can yet match. In the most remote parts of the region they have bought the local cash crops and offered goods on which cash might be spent. In this way they have contributed to the wide spread of trade and also of cash crop production, which contrasts with the pattern in countries such as Zambia.[7] Their role has been enhanced by the reluctance of the British to undertake such small scale activity as retail trade in towns of a few hundred people.

Asian firms dominate the sugar industry and play a large part in sawmilling and the building trade. The Asians have been active in establishing manufacturing and own a large proportion of the factories in East Africa. They possess more capital and more technical skills than most Africans, yet they have been willing to set up factories on the small scale that is often most appropriate for East African conditions. Asians also figure very largely in the road transport industry which is of increasing importance throughout East Africa. Their role in the distribution of economic activity, however, has undoubtedly been greatest in wholesale and retail trade.

DIFFERENCES WITHIN THE AFRICAN POPULATION

Since Africans account for an overwhelming majority of the total population the differences between one group and another must be noted, despite the disagreement which exists on the exact nature of these differences. It is uncertain, for example, to what extent language forms an appropriate basis for classification into broad groups, while the use of the term 'tribe' for smaller groups is sometimes challenged, although no satisfactory alternative is offered.[8] Undoubtedly, sharp contrasts exist between tribes, although they are now decreasing in importance while differences between individuals within each group are perhaps of increasing significance.

A distinction is commonly made between Nilotic, Nilo-Hamitic, Hamitic and Bantu peoples,[9] although the validity of this is increasingly being questioned.[10] All except the last are by tradition pastoralists, with a strong attachment to livestock, especially cattle. The Hamitic (or Cushitic) peoples, of whom there are relatively few in East Africa, still live a pastoral life, and often undertake no agriculture. The Galla and Somali of northern Kenya are two examples, but since they occupy country which receives only 250 mm. of rain a year their pastoral life may be related more to the physical environment than to their Hamitic character. The significance of ethnic origin is clearer in the Bahima of western Uganda, who occupy a less hostile environment and show their lack of interest in cultivation by seeking employment elsewhere as herdsmen if they have no cattle of their own.

Some Nilo-Hamites, such as the Turkana and many Masai, also despise cultivation; but most do some tilling of the soil, and for the Iteso, the Kipsigis and several other Nilo-Hamitic tribes it is the dominant occupation. The Nilotic people of northern Uganda and western Kenya have turned even further to cultivation, and while they retain an emotional attachment to cattle, most do not own great numbers and make little economic use of those that they have. While other groups have turned from pastoralism to cultivation, most Bantu peoples have added livestock keeping to their occupations and some now have as many cattle per head of population as the Nilotics. The Wasukuma of Tanzania are an outstanding example. Although the distinctions between these ethnic groups are less important than formerly, they cannot be disregarded entirely. The use of cattle by the Iteso as beasts of burden and as a major source of income is related to the fact that these people are Nilo-Hamites; and the small extent of cultivation in the well-watered Nandi country of Kenya results in part from its occupation by another tribe of this group.[11]

Distinctions between these ethnic groups are not confined to attitudes towards livestock and cultivation. Several writers have observed that most Nilotic and Nilo-Hamitic peoples offer more resistance to any form of change than most Bantu, with important implications for their economy.[12] Ethnic differences may affect the nature of agriculture. In Uganda there seems to be some association of the banana and the sweet potato with the Bantu, and of millet with the Nilotics and Nilo-Hamites. The association has, however, been blurred by increased contacts between peoples, and especially by the introduction of maize among all groups. These processes have advanced further in Kenya than in Uganda, and little difference can now be seen between the agriculture of the Bantu Baluhya of western Kenya and that of their Nilotic Luo neighbours.

Some economic activities seem more closely associated with certain tribes than with broader ethnic groups. The banana is not important to all Bantu peoples in East Africa, but is dominant wherever the Baganda, Bahaya, Bagisu, Wachagga or Nyakyusa form the main element in the population. The crop has spread from the Baganda to the Basoga and Banyankole, and from the Wachagga to the Warusha, and is equally important to these groups; yet it is unimportant among most Bantu tribes of Kenya, some of whom occupy land with suitable environmental conditions. The spread of the banana in Uganda is related to the prestige attached to it by the Baganda and to their influence over other tribes. The efforts of the Uganda government to discourage maize cultivation have been assisted by the fact that no such prestige attaches to this crop as it does among many Kenya tribes. Over most of Kenya and much of Tanzania maize is now the food of all 'respectable' people. This difference in attitude has contributed to the adoption of maize by the Luo, when most of the Lango and Acholi of Uganda, to whom they are related, still adhere to millet as their staple crop.

Cassava is disliked by many tribes yet is the main food of others. The Baganda grow little, and are reluctant to buy it even when prices of bananas and sweet potatoes soar high. By contrast, cassava is extensively grown by tribes ranging from the Digo, near the coast between Mombasa and Tanga, to the Lugbara, in north-west Uganda, apparently from preference. The significance of tribal attitudes rather than the physical environment is suggested by studies of urban expenditure patterns. The Batoro, Banyoro and Lugbara living in Kampala buy more cassava than people of other tribes, while most immigrants from Kenya spend much of their income on maize meal.

The relationship between economic activities and certain tribes is not confined to agriculture. The Luo are more interested in fishing than most tribes, and urban expenditure patterns show that they spend more on fish than most people. The intensity of fishing in Nyanza is related to this interest, while the development of fishing in parts of Uganda awaited immigration of Luo. Most Banyoro, on the other hand, are reluctant to eat fish, and they make little use of the fish resources of Lake Albert. Similarly, some tribes show more interest in local trade than others.

One difference between tribes of some significance for the economic geography of East Africa is the attitude towards individual enterprise. Among some tribes there is a strong resistance from the group as a whole towards the economic advancement of the individual. This may restrain the individual from increasing his income since most of the reward for his efforts will have to be distributed among his neighbours if he wishes to avoid hostility. This situation is particularly evident among some Nilotic tribes, as illustrated by Luo resistance to land consolidation, and has probably contributed to the low level of economic activity in Nyanza and northern Uganda.

The Baganda place less emphasis on conformity, and the social system has encouraged the emergence of an affluent class. Much of the coffee on which the economy of Buganda depends has been planted by these people, while the humbler members of the tribe have subsequently followed their example on their own smaller plots. Individual enterprise perhaps reaches its peak among the Kikuyu. Their farms are now mostly enclosed, and even livestock, which are communally grazed almost everywhere in East Africa, are kept in paddocks so that diseases will not spread to them from neighbours' stock. The Kikuyu are standing out increasingly as an economically progressive group, in contrast to the tribes who adhere rigidly to custom and among whom new developments cannot take place until they have been agreed by all.

Individual enterprise is not synonymous with economic development: a strong communal tradition may be an advantage where co-operative development is the answer to the problem of poverty. The Lango and Acholi work some of their land communally, and therefore one man cannot double his area under crops without placing an extra demand on the community. However, the communal cultivation of large blocks of land, even when parts of each block are held by individual farmers, provides an excellent opportunity for the introduction of mechanization. Tractors can be used which peasant farmers could not afford and which could not be employed economically on small holdings. This, unfortunately, is of significance more for the future than for the present economic geography of East Africa.

Land Tenure

One notable difference between tribes is that of land tenure systems. Most commonly all land is the property of the tribe, or of some section of it, and the individual has exclusive rights only over any land he is cultivating. The significance of this for crop production is sometimes exaggerated, for virtual security of tenure normally exists; but land cannot be bought and sold. Thus many farmers cannot obtain credit for the development of their farms since they have no title to the land and therefore cannot offer it as security. Farmers also have less incentive to improve their land when they hold it by customary right than when they own it individually. Land tenure may affect agriculture in other ways: much land in Nyanza could be irrigated, but this has proved difficult because of the local customs of tenure and inheritance. Customary tenure systems are of greatest importance for livestock rearing. Since grazing land is generally communal there is little possibility of farmers' planting improved grass or keeping their stock free of infectious disease.

In some parts of East Africa different tenure systems exist. Many Kikuyu appear to have bought land outright from the Wandorobo even in the 19th century, and land consolidation is

extending individual ownership over much of central Kenya.
The establishment of titles is assisting the provision of rural
credit and is encouraging farmers to take more interest in their
land. The most striking effect on economic activity has been
the development of dairying on peasant farms. In Kiambu
District small paddocks of grazing land are now the rule, and
little communal pasture remains.

Near the coast freehold ownership is common, probably
because of Arab influence; and some land is also held freehold
in Buganda. There is some apparent relationship between such
tenure and the establishment of tree crops such as coconuts,
cloves and coffee. In Uganda, however, 'the type of agriculture
practised and the uses to which the land has been put have been
but little influenced by the systems of land tenure. Rather the
opposite, in that in those areas where soil and climate were
suitable for the production of perennial crops their cultivation
on a large scale had a profound effect on the traditional
systems of tenure.'[13]

LABOUR SUPPLY

Labour, perhaps an economic factor, is so closely tied to
other aspects of population that it is considered here, providing
a link with the next chapter. Most peasant farmers do not
employ labour and even at the busiest season have assistance
only from their children. It is doubtful whether a large un-
satisfied demand for paid labour in small-scale agriculture exists
anywhere in East Africa, for most farmers could not pay men to
work for them even if such men were available. Indeed, it is
often suggested that underemployment is a feature of much of
the region, many farmers having little incentive to use their
energies to the full. Nevertheless, at least seasonally and in
areas where the prospects for selling surplus produce are good,
lack of labour may be a major factor limiting farm production,
and wherever labourers are employed productivity is greatly
increased.

The areas with most paid labour in small-scale agriculture
are Buganda, where there are probably 100,000 employees on
African farms, and the Central Province of Kenya. Many
Baganda farmers have two or three labourers, often Banyar-

wanda, and some also employ a Muhima to herd their cattle. This custom developed gradually as cotton provided a cash income, and it then greatly assisted the spread of coffee cultivation. The availability of labourers from south-west Uganda and from Rwanda has certainly been an important factor in the relative prosperity of Buganda.[14] Employment of labour is developing rapidly among Kikuyu farmers, and this both assists and is assisted by the establishment of cash crops. There labourers are generally local people, who have become landless as pressure on the land has increased.

Most of the paid labour in East Africa is employed in large scale agriculture, industry or services. The numbers involved are about $1\frac{1}{2}$ million out of an adult population of 17 million, so either the demand or the supply must be small. In fact supply generally outstrips demand, and urban unemployment has become serious in recent years. The total supply of unskilled labour is adequate, and it is not markedly confined in its distribution. The mobility characteristic of many African peoples applies to many East African tribes, such as the Luo, the Lugbara and the Ngoni. More workers at the Jinja textile mill, for example, come from West Nile and Tanzania than from the local area: and almost 90 per cent. of the workers on the Uganda sugar estates come from more than 300 km. away. Similarly in Tanzania sisal estates in sparsely populated country rarely suffered from shortage of labour, even before the slump in prices caused many to be laid off, since men will travel far to seek work.

As noted earlier, the flow of labour away from some districts has hindered the improvement of peasant agriculture there. The significance of the age and sex structure in Songea or Maragoli lies in the local shortage of adult men to provide labour on their own farms. Thus the gain of one area has been the loss of another, and many parts of East Africa would benefit if those unable to find employment in the towns returned to work on the land in their home areas.

Although unskilled labour is not scarce in East Africa, a shortage of skilled labour and of people to fill managerial posts is restricting economic development. Employers needing many skilled workers must generally undertake costly training programmes, and the transient nature of much of the labour

s

force militates against this. The high turnover rate of short-term migrants often makes training impracticable. The number of people with sufficient education to set up commercial concerns of their own is so small that entrepreneurship is in even more short supply than skilled labour. This situation is gradually improving, but the problem will be felt for many years; and for all the foreseeable future both skilled labour and entrepreneurship will be more readily available in the major cities than in the poorer parts of the region, thus tending to accentuate the spatial disparities in development.

REFERENCES

1   I. D. Thomas, 'The Relevance of Population Density', *University of East Africa, Social Science Conference 1968/9, Geography Papers*, pp. 5–15. A case study is I. D. Thomas, 'Population in the Southern Highlands of Tanzania', in S. H. Ominde (ed.), *Studies in East African Geography and Development*, Heinemann, London, in the press.

2   B. W. Langlands, *The Demographic Condition of Uganda*, Department of Geography, Makerere University College, Occasional Papers, No. 9, 1970, outlines the characteristics in one country.

3   A detailed study of both demographic patterns and migration is S. H. Ominde, *Land and Population Movements in Kenya*, Heinemann, London, 1968.

4   P. H. Gulliver, *Labour Migration in a Rural Economy*, E.A.I.S.R., Kampala, 1955, p. 34.

5   The Europeans of Kenya are discussed at length in N. S. Carey Jones, *The Anatomy of Uhuru*, Manchester U.P., 1966.

6   D. P. Ghai (ed.), *Portrait of a Minority*, Oxford U.P., Nairobi, 1965, especially Ch. 4.

7   G. Hunter, *The New Societies of Tropical Africa*, Oxford U.P., London, 1962, p. 145. There is much in this book on social factors which affect economic development in East Africa.

8   A full discussion of the tribe as a cultural grouping may be found in P. H. Gulliver (ed.), *Tradition and Transition in East Africa*, Routledge & Kegan Paul, London, 1969, especially the introductory chapter.

9   This distinction is accepted by Ominde, *op. cit.*

10   E.g. J. E. G. Sutton, 'The Settlement of East Africa', in B. A. Ogot & J. A. Kieran (ed.), *Zamani*, E. A. Publishing House & Longmans, Nairobi, 1968.

11   J. C. D. Lawrence, *The Iteso*, Oxford U.P., London, 1957 and G. W. Huntingford, *Nandi Work and Culture*, H.M.S.O., London, 1950.

12   E.g. H. K. Schneider in W. R. Bascom and M. J. Herskovits, *Continuity and Change in African Cultures*, Univ. of Chicago Press, 1959, pp. 144–167.

13   G. W. Anderson in W. T. W. Morgan (ed.), *East Africa: Its Peoples and Resources*, Oxford U.P., Nairobi, 1969, p. 202.

14   A. I. Richards, *Economic Development and Tribal Change*, Heffer, Cambridge, 1954.

CHAPTER 17

Economic Factors

INTERNAL MARKETS

In many ways internal markets are governed by the distribution and characteristics of the population considered above, but their significance should be examined separately. The location of markets influences the distribution of many activities, while the total size of the East African market affects decisions on whether to establish certain industries within the region.

The introduction of a cash economy has created a local market for numerous agricultural and industrial products, but since incomes are generally very low the demand is often still small. The volume of production of many commodities is severely limited by the size of the market. Low incomes have least effect on the consumption of staple foods and, therefore, the production of these dominates the economy; but as so many people provide their own requirements the commercial market for such crops is small. In many rural areas grain can be sold only when needed for beer to celebrate a birth, marriage or death. Among cash crops, tobacco and sugar are the most strongly affected by the size of the East African market, although the problems of the coffee growers would be eased by greater local consumption of this commodity. The local market for some products fluctuates considerably. The timber industry suffered greatly from the slackness of the building trade between 1959 and 1964, when sawmills throughout the region had either to work far below capacity or to close down. The cement industry was similarly affected, the Tororo factory working below half capacity for several years.

The size of the internal market is particularly significant for activities which can be undertaken only on a large scale. The market within each country is now large enough to support textile mills, but the customs union between Kenya, Tanganyika and Uganda, giving free access to a market of over 25 million people, was an essential factor in the establishment of the first mill in Uganda in 1956. The common market assisted the development of several other industries, such as shoe production, steel rolling and asbestos-cement manufacture, in which one factory was built initially to supply all of East Africa.

Even the common market, now of 35 million, is too small to support all forms of activity, for although larger in numbers than say, the Australian market, it is far smaller in terms of income. Where the average annual cash income is only £25 per head and, perhaps more important, where the number of people earning over £100 per year is extremely small, it is uneconomic to establish manufacture of cars or refrigerators. An efficient integrated iron and steel works must sell four times as much steel as is now consumed annually in East Africa.

For some goods, such as sugar or cotton cloth, the market is widely spread over East Africa, although it never corresponds exactly with the distribution of population. For others it is much greater in one country than another, and this has often affected the distribution of production. The market for maize is much larger in Kenya and parts of Tanzania than in Uganda, and the pattern of production for sale clearly reflects this. There are many more people with a high income in Kenya than in Tanzania or Uganda, and this has certainly contributed to the greater development of manufacturing there. In addition a factory in Kenya is generally better placed to supply the whole East African market than one in Tanzania or Uganda.[1]

Proximity to markets may also be important on a more local scale. Within Kenya the greatest concentration of purchasing power is found in and around Nairobi, and this is one factor favouring the location of many industries there. Other areas providing substantial markets for manufacturing are Mombasa, Dar es Salaam, Moshi-Arusha and Kampala-Jinja, all of which have attracted industries. Some forms of manufacturing are always market-oriented, notably brewing and baking: others originally established near sources of raw material are migrating towards their markets, sawmilling providing the clearest example. As manufacturing becomes more diversified inter-industry linkages become increasingly important, so that one industry provides the market for the products of another. This is clearly illustrated by the development of the packaging materials industry, especially in Nairobi.

The distribution of agricultural production has been influenced less than that of manufacturing by the location of markets, yet several examples of such influence may be found. Large-scale sugar production in Uganda is concentrated in the zone where demand for sugar is greatest. The demand for bananas in and around Kampala supports some production for sale in Buganda; but in Ankole the commercial market is so small that most bananas surplus to subsistence requirements go to waste. Most large towns have some effect on agriculture in the vicinity through the market for foodstuffs which they provide. Around Nairobi large quantities of fruit and vegetables, including many popular mainly among Europeans and Asians, are grown for sale to the urban dwellers. Vegetable production in the Taita hills is favoured by their position as the nearest high land to Mombasa, and Dar es Salaam provides the market for such production in the Uluguru mountains. On Zanzibar island there is a marked concentration of food crop production for cash in the immediate vicinity of Zanzibar city.

In these and many other ways internal markets influence the pattern of commodity production in East Africa, and as the region reduces its dependence on subsistence enterprise and on overseas exports, and more production for local sale develops, this influence will become stronger. Internal markets are of course equally important for the distribution of many service activities, such as retail trade, banking, insurance and road transport, whose role in the whole economy is tending to increase. In so far as new economic activity is attracted to markets, which are themselves a function of relatively high incomes, this factor is clearly playing a critical role in the process of widening the gap between the richer and poorer parts of the region.

EXTERNAL MARKETS

As East Africa is heavily dependent on overseas trade at present, external markets for its produce are of great importance to the economy. The region benefits greatly from the existence of a large demand for coffee, cotton, sisal and tea in countries which are unable to produce these. In recent years, however, it has suffered from a swing in world terms of trade against exporters of primary products. This has been particularly serious for Uganda, the economic health of which is closely related to the world price of coffee, and for Tanzania, which has been especially hard hit by the slump in sisal prices. Kenya, which is less dependent on overseas exports of primary products, has suffered much less.[2]

Both present and past world market situations have affected the present pattern of export production. The demand for cotton and coffee earlier in this century encouraged the establishment of these crops, while favourable market conditions assist the current expansion of tea cultivation. World markets may also be a negative factor. Sunn hemp grows well in East Africa, but traders are unable to find overseas buyers for it. Rubber was important until Malaya and Indonesia captured the bulk of the market.

External markets clearly greatly affect the nature of economic activity in East Africa, but the size of the world demand for any commodity does not normally affect the distribution of production. Nevertheless the total size of the market may in some instances be significant for this. Limited markets for coffee, and consequent imposition of export quotas, have tended to freeze the pattern of production: if no such problems had arisen, Kenya would probably now be producing a larger share of the East African coffee crop, and African farming areas a larger share of the Kenya crop.

The location of external markets is of great importance to East Africa. Neighbouring countries provide markets for some commodities: sales to Mauritius and Seychelles have assisted the cement industry, while Rwanda, Burundi and Somalia provide small but useful markets for other manufactures. In general, however, proximity to external markets is not a characteristic of East Africa, which suffers from its distance from the countries offering the best markets for its products. The situation has improved following some shift of the direction of trade from Europe to Asia; but the main demand for East African produce still lies within the North Atlantic region.

The significance of proximity to both local and external

markets depends upon the transport facilities linking points of production to them, and these must now be considered.

TRANSPORT FACILITIES

The transport facilities discussed in Chapter 11 have played an important part in shaping the pattern of economic activity in East Africa, being indispensable to all forms of commercial production. Unless some means of overcoming the problem of distance exists there is no alternative to a subsistence economy, and this situation still prevails in a few parts of the region. Most places, however, are now within reach of a road which widens horizons beyond those of local self-sufficiency (Map 20), although there are great contrasts in the type of transport facilities available in different areas.

It is ocean transport that has overcome the problem of distance between East Africa and the rest of the world; and the establishment of ports and their use by major shipping lines have been essential to economic development. For 70 years ships have been bringing people who have contributed greatly to such development, but today their major role is the transport of goods to and from East Africa. For the export of coffee, cotton and sisal, and for the import of oil and machinery, there is no alternative to ocean transport. In the 1950s port facilities became inadequate, and long delays at Mombasa and Dar es Salaam harmed the East African economy: but following major improvements they now meet all normal requirements. The only recent example of an activity discouraged by inadequate facilities is phosphate production for export. The rates charged by the shipping companies of course affect East Africa, and in this respect the closure of the Suez Canal has provided a setback.

Ocean transport has affected the local pattern of activities mainly by encouraging a concentration of trade and industry near the ports. Most of the 250,000 inhabitants of Mombasa depend indirectly on the port for their livelihood, for it has brought the warehouses, the trading firms, the industries and even the railway, which together provide most of the town's employment. Similarly many activities taking place in Tanga and Dar es Salaam are related to their port functions although,

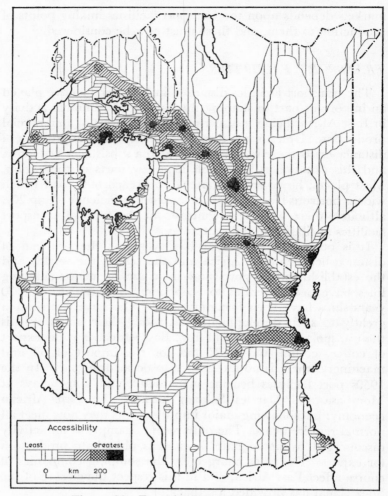

Figure 20. EAST AFRICA: Accessibility

The map is based upon an index which incorporates scores for proximity to ports, rail junctions, railways, road junctions, roads of different quality, and airports.

the limited development of Mtwara indicates that port facilities alone are not enough.

Water transport on the lakes has also assisted the expansion of economic activity and influenced its location. Steamers were operating on Lake Victoria by 1900, and they helped the lakeshore area of Uganda to take a lead in economic development, which it has never lost, by linking it with the railhead at Kisumu. The parts of Tanzania near the lake have also been assisted, although politics limited trade through Kisumu until 1918. The Mombasa-Kisumu railway greatly enhanced the value of lake transport, but the subsequent extension of railways and roads has cut the importance of Lake Victoria steamers. To-day they provide the main outlet only for the Bukoba and Musoma areas, and their main function is to facilitate trade between Kenya, Tanzania and Uganda. The trade which they handle is small in relation to the whole East African economy but is increasing. Lake Tanganyika steamers still improve the accessibility of the small settlements near the shores, but those on Lake Kyoga have been withdrawn, although they have influenced the present economy by their role in assisting the establishment of cotton earlier in the century.

Many local illustrations of the former significance of lake transport may be seen around Lake Victoria. Small ports drew traders to such places as Mjanji and Bukakata in Uganda, but few remain at either, for Mjanji was by-passed by the railway in 1927, and road transport drew so much traffic away from Bukakata that the port has been closed. In Nyanza an old Asian trading centre at Asembo, on the lakeshore, has been superseded by a new trading centre at Bondo on a main road a few kilometres inland.

Railways have a much greater influence on the pattern of activities in East Africa than inland water transport. They handle most of the region's exports and imports, as well as much internal freight traffic, and make possible many forms of production which could not otherwise take place. Their importance was especially great before road transport provided an alternative, and the early establishment of cotton and coffee production would have been impossible without rail transport. Even today haulage is cheaper by rail than by road, and the railways continue to play a vital role in many agricultural, mining and manufacturing activities. Without them Uganda in particular would suffer much more from its inland location, but even in Kenya less movement of such low-value commodities as maize could take place.

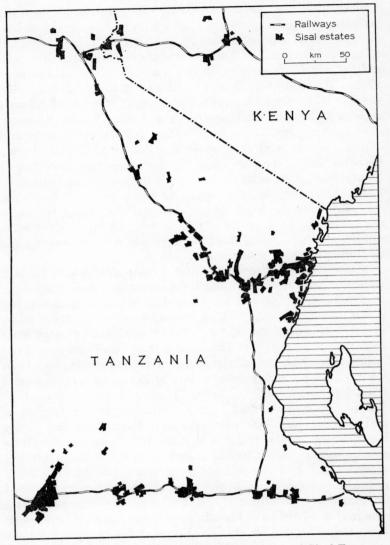

Figure 21. NORTH-EAST TANZANIA: Railways and Sisal Estates

The map is based primarily upon 1 : 50,000 topographical maps. It represents approximately the maximum extent of estates, before the contraction of the late 1960s. Note that the north-south rail link in Tanzania was opened only in 1963.

The impact of rail facilities on the distribution of many activities within the region is clear. Map 21 indicates the close relationship between railways and sisal estates, while the pattern of large-scale agriculture in the Kenya highlands has been equally closely guided by both main and branch lines there. The mining of soda ash and copper were made possible only by rail construction, although its role in assisting mining has been smaller than in many parts of Africa. Railways have also affected the pattern of trade and, although some towns have grown up far from them, the four largest in Kenya all lie along the original line from Mombasa to Kisumu.

However, the influence of the railways is often exaggerated, for they do not automatically stimulate development wherever they are laid. Their effect on the local distribution of activities varies both in space and in time. It has been greater in Kenya and Tanzania, where much agriculture is undertaken by people or firms that operate on a sufficiently large scale to make direct use of rail transport and have also chosen a specific location, than in Uganda where peasant farmers have had little choice of location and grow coffee and cotton which must be sent away for processing before being railed to the coast. In Uganda there is a concentration of activity in the broad zone that has been served longest by rail, but not along the lines themselves.

The railways built before 1930 have had much more impact on the present distribution of production than those built more recently, for they 'opened-up the country' in a way that is not possible now that motor transport is widespread. The Western Uganda Extension, completed in 1956, has had much less effect on the surrounding country than was anticipated: and the Southern Province Line in Tanzania stimulated so little activity that it had to be closed. As the writer has argued at greater length elsewhere, railways were essential to the establishment of a commercial economy in East Africa and still play a vital role to-day, but they now affect the distribution of economic activities less than is commonly supposed and new construction is unlikely to stimulate their expansion very greatly.[3] Even the Tanzania-Zambia line is likely to have little local impact unless positive measures are taken to make use of the opportunities which it presents.

Road transport has done much to spread commercial

agriculture far beyond the immediate vicinity of the railways, and now contributes greatly to its dispersed pattern. The density of the road network in each area affects the intensity of cash crop production, for farmers are naturally reluctant to carry produce a long way to the nearest road. Buganda benefits from a dense network, whereas distance from any road hinders coffee production in parts of Bugisu, and cotton growing in parts of Acholi and West Nile. The areas suffering most from inaccessibility are in southern Tanzania, where crop marketing poses great problems. Intensity of fishing effort in the lakes also depends greatly upon whether the landings are served by roads, and around Lake Kyoga rapid expansion of fishing has followed road construction in several places.

Throughout East Africa settlement is now to some extent concentrated along roads, so that they have even affected the location of subsistence cultivation: but the building of new roads has not generally changed the spatial pattern of the rural economy as much as, for instance, in southern Nigeria. The effects of new major highways are sometimes less obvious than those of new minor roads, for although they assist economic developments by speeding transport between major centres they may have little local impact. The Dar es Salaam-Morogoro highway illustrates this, for little settlement has been drawn to it, while its impact on either of the two towns is very difficult to assess. The Mombasa-Nairobi road has recently been improved, but it is doubtful whether this will greatly affect the distribution of economic activity in Kenya.

The direct effect of air transport upon the pattern of activities is very small, for few depend upon it for the movement of goods. Its main role has been in the extension of markets for such perishable goods as meat and butter, and if it became cheaper it could assist production of and trade in these goods very greatly. At present it contributes more to the East African economy by the movement of executives or administrators, and by assisting the development of the tourist trade.

One general feature of the transport pattern that is perhaps significant is the emphasis on port-interior routeways inherited from the colonial era. Although lateral internal links and links with neighbouring countries are gradually being improved, these are often still much less satisfactory, and this tends to perpetuate the overseas orientation of much commercial activity. Nevertheless, physical communications between the three countries are much better than those between most neighbouring African states, and this assists the relatively high degree of economic interaction which takes place in East Africa.

POWER SUPPLIES

In a predominantly agricultural region such as East Africa power supplies are less important than the other economic factors considered here, for their influence is felt mainly in manufacturing. They affect agriculture only in relation to crop processing and transport. Power supplies merit some attention, however, not only because power-intensive activities have begun to develop, but also because this is one factor often regarded as contributing to the limited economic development of the region.

Coal and oil provide most of the world's energy, and neither is produced within East Africa. No activities, therefore, have been attracted by availability of fuel: but probably none have been kept away on this account either. Imported coal is very expensive and hardly any is used, but oil can be imported more easily. The Middle East oilfields lie only a short distance away by sea, and a satisfactory distribution system exists to supply oil to all inland centres. The cost of moving it inland is quite high, however, and prices in some places are double those at the coast. This directly affects the distribution of some activities, favouring Mombasa and Dar es Salaam as locations for cement production in which fuel consumption is exceptionally high. Oil is especially important for the transport industry, as it is used by the railway and steamer services and by all road vehicles: and high fuel prices indirectly affect many activities by increasing local transport costs in all up-country areas, especially those far from an oil depot.

Outside the field of transport, most energy consumed in East Africa is in the form of electricity. The easy import of oil assists thermal production, while there are opportunities in several areas for the development of hydro-electric power. These opportunities have been seized, and some industrial development thereby assisted. Electricity production appears to satisfy present demands, and there is little evidence that inadequate supplies have discouraged any form of activity.

Electricity production is greatest in Uganda, but consumption is higher in Kenya, indicating that local availability of power has not always influenced the location of power-consuming activities. The town of Jinja has experienced much industrial development since 1954, and this is generally attributed to the location there of Owen Falls power station. The relationship is not as close as it might appear, for power lines extend from Jinja to other towns where electricity is readily available. Standard rates are applied everywhere in Uganda, and a small manufacturing concern loses nothing by being located 300 km. from the source of power. The largest consumers have negotiated special tariffs, however, and power has been made available to them at lower rates in Jinja than elsewhere. In this way the location of the textile mills, the copper smelter and the steel mill at Jinja has been encouraged, whereas more small factories have been established in Kampala.

Apart from the large concerns mentioned above, the supply of power from Owen Falls has not encouraged industries to develop in Uganda rather than elsewhere, for its cost to the consumer is no lower than in Kenya and Tanzania. Indeed, electricity has been supplied to Kenya at a lower rate than that charged within Uganda, in order to make use of surplus capacity: Owen Falls power has thus assisted industrial development in Nairobi. Nowhere else in East Africa has power generation attracted other economic activities. None have sprung up, for example, around the sites on the Pangani river, all the electricity produced there being sent to consumers some distance away.

Although the location of power production has had little effect on the location of other activities, it might be expected that the availability of public supplies is of some importance, and that districts provided with electricity would be better placed than those without it. The level of economic activity is generally highest in the areas supplied with electricity, but this may be because electricity has normally been provided wherever there is sufficient demand for it. This applies especially to thermal stations but, even in the case of water power, sites near to potential consumers have been developed in preference to those in districts with little local demand.

Power is required for agricultural processing industries, sawmills and mines, often in isolated rural areas, as well as for factories in towns. But the establishment of these is nowhere prevented by the absence of public power supplies, for any enterprise can generate its own electricity. There are in fact numerous small private generators scattered over the region, most dependent on oil fuel, and the majority of cotton ginneries, sisal factories and maize mills are powered in this way. Sawmills and sugar factories often use their own waste materials as fuel, but for most enterprises a public power supply is cheaper than operation of a private generator using oil, and they therefore connect to the main system if it is extended to their locality. But the difference in cost is rarely sufficient to determine whether an activity takes place or not, or to influence its location. The provision of a public power supply in towns such as Nyeri, Soroti and Bukoba has been of value to traders and small industrial enterprises, but it has had no visible effect in stimulating new forms of activity.

In countries where industrial development is more advanced than in East Africa, and also in those which have some resource such as aluminium which can be fully exploited only with the help of great quantities of electric power, electricity supplies may be of great significance in the local economic geography. The wide distribution of power on a national grid has had great influence in Britain; the development of hydro-electricity has had important consequences in the Tennessee Valley in the United States: and power from the Volta River has made possible an aluminium industry in Ghana. A report on Uganda stated: 'There is ample evidence that power supplies are far more than a *sine qua non* of economic development; they are in fact its major stimulus'.[4] As far as East Africa is concerned this seems an exaggeration. Provision of power supplies has been of great value to the region, assisting economic development in many ways: but there is little to suggest that they have stimulated it.[5] Similarly, they have affected the location of some activities within the region, but in these under-developed and primarily agricultural countries other factors are of much greater significance.

CAPITAL

Most economic activities require some capital, although the amount required varies greatly, and is not normally proportionate to the income obtained. The farmer growing cotton needs very little, but tea production demands a large outlay. All industrial enterprises require capital for plant and equipment, although these range from a simple carpentry workshop to a £6 million oil refinery. Fishing is one of many activities which may be undertaken on either a capital-intensive or a labour-intensive basis, but all fishermen must make some investment in the form of boats and nets. Capital is also essential for the establishment of the infra-structure upon which a modern cash economy can be built. Such investment is frequently undertaken by government, and very large sums may be involved. Thus East African Railways represents an investment of over £100 million.

On a world scale differences in the availability of capital have greatly influenced the pattern of economic development. The production of surpluses and the accumulation of capital have enabled Europe and North America to forge ever further ahead, while other regions remain caught in the vicious circle of poverty. In East Africa very little capital accumulation has so far taken place, while only limited supplies have been available from external sources. This has restricted the extent of advance beyond subsistence production, and has affected the nature of the commercial activities which are undertaken, discouraging some more than others.

The capital used in East Africa comes from a variety of sources. A little lies in the hands of the African population and is used for agricultural development or for starting small businesses. This has accrued mainly from cash crop sales and is widely but thinly spread through the community. The situation is different from that in such regions as the Middle East, where there is a small class of very wealthy people able to make large capital investments. The co-operative movement is now bringing together the small resources of numerous individuals to finance the construction of cotton ginneries and coffee works and other similar projects. But the membership figures of most societies are more impressive than their financial strength. The Asian community includes some people with sufficient capital to form the chief source of private investment from within the region. Some was brought from India, but most has been accumulated locally over the past sixty years. The outstanding example is the Madhvani concern, which began as a small sugar estate near Jinja and has ploughed back profits into greatly expanded sugar production and also into industrial activities ranging from confectionery to steel which spread over Uganda, Kenya and Tanzania.

The role of the East African governments in providing capital for economic development has been great. Much of this is of local origin, such as funds obtained from export taxes and import duties, although they also handle funds from external sources. Most government expenditure is on services essential to the economy such as communications, education and administration. The amount of money available for such services influences the type of economy which can develop in any region. Governments sometimes also provide capital for productive activities, the role of the Kenya Tea Development Authority providing one illustration, that of the Uganda Development Corporation, discussed in the next chapter, providing another.

If East Africa were entirely dependent on local sources of capital, many of the present elements in the economy would be absent. It has benefited from much investment from overseas, especially from Britain. Money brought by private individuals has played a vital part in the establishment of large mixed farms in Kenya, and the largest sisal and tea estates have required the financial resources of foreign companies. Foreign capital has been especially important for the development of mining and manufacturing, many countries contributing to these. A Canadian company financed Kilembe copper mine, and an Italian firm provided much of the capital for the Dar es Salaam oil refinery.

No overseas companies play such a great role in the region's economic life as the United Africa Company does in West Africa, or certain Belgian concerns do in Congo. But some 500 firms registered outside East Africa do business there, and their investments are of great importance. Special mention should be made of British and Indian banks, which provide

T

finance for many activities in Kenya and Uganda, though no longer in Tanzania since all foreign banks there were nationalized in 1967. In general, the relative importance of foreign private capital is now decreasing in all three countries, for while it brings undoubted commercial benefits the governments realize that excessive dependence on it could hamper long-term development, in the broad sense of the term.

Overseas governments have provided funds as both grants and loans, for strengthening the infrastructure of public services and for productive enterprises. Most was formerly provided by Britain, but many other countries are now also contributing either directly or through agencies such as the International Bank.[6] The reduction of the economic gap between East Africa and the more developed countries of the world now depends in part upon the amount of capital made available by these countries.

The relative importance of capital compared with other factors affecting the level of economic activity is a much-debated question. The International Bank mission to Uganda saw 'a pressing need to infuse capital into the peasant economy'[7] yet according to one economist 'it would seem to be a tenable view that even in Buganda there is much more capital than enterprise can effectively use'.[8] There is evidence that the slender resources of most peasant farmers in East Africa limits their productivity. The amount of cotton planted by each farmer is largely governed by the area he and his wife can cultivate with no mechanical equipment. When a cotton spraying programme was started in Teso few pumps and little insecticide were sold until government loans were provided. Shortage of capital may therefore both limit the area cultivated and reduce the yields obtained from that area. It is rash, however, to assume that an infusion of capital would necessarily bring great changes in peasant agriculture. It has been argued that the witholding of some income from coffee growers in Uganda when prices were very high retarded economic development by reducing the amount of capital in the farmers' hands.[9] But it is uncertain whether the extra income would have been used mainly for investment or for conspicuous consumption or, as one writer put it, an accumulation of bottle-tops. Certainly some income that was received was spent on imported cars which were used for a while but are now rusting between the coffee trees.

The provision of capital is likely to have most long-term effect on peasant agriculture if it is combined with developments in such fields as land tenure and marketing. The resettlement schemes in the Kenya highlands offer the best examples of this. Government loans have been especially important in the planting of tea on small farms, for this costs about £250 per hectare. The Kenya highlands clearly illustrate the significance of capital for present farming patterns, much of the area being farmed in ways quite different from those in most of East Africa partly because it was settled by people with the capital to establish large-scale production. Wherever African farmers with little capital are taking over land formerly owned by Europeans of considerable means the system of agriculture must change.

The Kenya highlands demonstrate how capital availability can assist the development of activities in one area rather than another. Likewise within Uganda cotton cultivation brought money to farmers in Buganda which assisted them to invest in coffee on a much larger scale than farmers in Western Region. In general, however, capital supplies affect the level of activity in East Africa as a whole much more than the distribution of activity within the region. Shortage of capital among the fishermen of East Africa, for example, has hindered large-scale fishing enterprise: but this has applied equally to those in each area, except that in some places outboard motors are becoming common. A greater supply of local capital in Kenya than in Tanzania or Uganda may have assisted the concentration of manufacturing there, but most concerns have been willing to invest in the part of East Africa where other conditions are most favourable.

It is doubtful whether shortage of capital has been a major factor influencing the level of industrial development in East Africa. There are few forms of manufacturing that would clearly have been undertaken if more capital were available. The same is true of mining. The agricultural opportunities, however, which could be taken up if farmers had more capital are very great. Bauer and Yamey suggest that whereas the problems of under-developed countries were once thought to be caused mainly by lack of capital, 'more recent events and developments have made it clear that, even though increased capital may be a necessary concomitant of economic growth, it is not a sufficient condition for it'.[10] Nevertheless, injected among the right people, and alongside other changes, increased capital could greatly affect the pattern of economic activities in East Africa as a whole, and could also affect their distribution.

REFERENCES

1   An extremely useful discussion is A. Hazlewood, 'An Approach to the Analysis of the Spatial Distribution of the Market in East Africa', *Bulletin of the Oxford University Institute of Economics & Statistics*, Vol. 31, No. 4, 1969, pp. 243–261.

2   World market prices are a major theme of Y. Kyesimira, *Agricultural Export Development*, E. A. Publishing House, Nairobi, 1969.

3   A. M. O'Connor, *Railways and Development in Uganda*, Oxford U.P., Nairobi, 1965.

4   Economist Intelligence Unit, *Power in Uganda*, London, 1957, p. 151.

5   The economic consequences of electricity provision are examined in H. Amann, *Energy Supply and Economic Development in East Africa*, Weltforum Verlag, Munchen, 1969, and in G. Wilson, *Owen Falls*, E. A. Publishing House, Nairobi, 1967.

6   See, for example, R. Clark, *Aid in Uganda—Programmes and Policies*, ODI, London, 1966, and H. Mettrick, *Aid In Uganda—Agriculture*, ODI, London, 1967.

7   International Bank, *The Economic Development of Uganda*, Entebbe, 1961, p. 112.

8   J. L. Joy, 'Some Agricultural Aspects of the East African Royal Commission Report', *East African Economics Review*, Vol. 2, No. 2, 1956, p. 114.

9   D. Walker and C. Ehrlich, 'Stabilisation and Development Policy in Uganda', *Kyklos*, Vol. 12, 1959, pp. 341–353.

10 P. T. Bauer, and B. S. Yamey, *The Economics of Under-developed Countries*, Cambridge U.P., Cambridge, 1957, p. 127.

CHAPTER 18

Political Factors

Frequent reference has been made to the influence of government action on the pattern of economic activities, for this influence has been very strong in East Africa. For fifty years a government department in each country has been responsible for assisting each type of activity, and these have frequently influenced the present pattern by providing more encouragement in some areas than in others. Since independence government involvement has in many respects increased, and although none of the three countries has a planned economy in the Soviet sense, all have prepared comprehensive Five-year Plans to guide the pattern of development. In this field controversial issues quickly arise, and the writer would point out that he intends neither to justify nor to condemn government actions, but merely to examine their spatial consequences.

THE FORMER COLONIAL ADMINISTRATION

Before the advent of the British and Germans there were few exceptions to a general pattern of subsistence production, and economic change was very slow. No-one knows what economic development would have taken place in the absence of colonial administration, but there is little doubt that its presence assisted the establishment and rapid spread of commercial forms of production. The details of how the British and Germans encouraged economic development are best left to the historian:[1] but some aspects of East Africa's economic geography which are a legacy of the colonial regimes must be noted here.

One legacy common to most ex-colonies in Africa is a heavy dependence on overseas trade, and an economy largely complementary to those of European countries. These cannot produce coffee, cotton, sisal, or tea and so encouraged their production in their colonies. Less attention was given to production of goods for local sale and, although suggestions that the colonial powers prevented the establishment of industries because they wanted to sell manufactures to Africa are open to question, national self-sufficiency was not a major aim as it is today. The importance of former colonial status should not be overstressed, however. The role of overseas trade in the economy is larger in East Africa than in Ethiopia, but no larger than in many Latin American countries which have been independent for 150 years. Colombia, Ecuador and many others are heavily dependent on exports of commodities required in temperate lands and imports of goods produced there.

The attachment of East Africa to Britain rather than to any other country has had little obvious effect on the present pattern of activities, except perhaps favouring the production of tea. The link with other British territories in addition to the mother country was of some significance. Cotton was established in Uganda when Britain was anxious about supplies, but during the main phase of development most was sold to India: and much East African sisal is used in Canada and Australia. The clearest consequence of the link with Britain is the orientation of overseas trade, although Britain dominates East African trade far less than the United States dominates that of many countries which it has never administered.

Other legacies of British control are the substantial number of British people producing goods or providing services within the region, and the much larger number of Indians and Pakistanis who play such an important role in the economy. British firms still operate in many fields, banking providing one clear example; and more ships and aircraft from Britain than from anywhere else serve East Africa.

Detailed study of contrasts across the Uganda/Congo or Tanzania/Burundi borders might reveal other differences in economic life related to different former regimes, but in general the economic impact of British and Belgians seems to have been quite similar. Likewise few features of Kenya, Tanzania and Uganda appear related to their having been a colony, a trust territory and a protectorate respectively. One exception may be the encouragement of British settlement on the land in Kenya, and its discouragement in Uganda: and it can be argued that Britain invested less in Tanzania during the 1920s and 1930s because its administration might only be temporary.[2]

The fact that all three countries were administered by Britain for forty years certainly contributed to the present inter-related nature of their economies. The British government established several organizations which served all three, including a single customs and excise department, and many British firms operate on an East African basis. In this case the contrast with Rwanda and Burundi is clear: if they had been handed over to Britain rather than Belgium in 1919 their present economic ties with Tanzania would be much stronger, and those with Congo much weaker.

PAST AND PRESENT GOVERNMENT INFLUENCE

While the influence of former colonial status is largely a matter of conjecture, the effects of particular aspects of government policy are more certain. The colonial governments participated in some activities, but more often they exerted pressure on individuals or firms undertaking them. Since independence the pressure has generally been increased, in some cases involving total nationalization of formerly private enterprises, in others the acquisition by the state of a large shareholding. Today, as in the past, government policy may also be significant at local as well as national level, for each district has agricultural and other officers, whose decisions may affect the local distribution of activities.

Government policy has contributed to the contrasts in the whole structure of the economy between Kenya and Uganda. In Kenya Europeans were strongly encouraged to settle and develop large-scale agriculture upon which the commercial economy now rests very heavily. Even since independence its importance is recognized, and government policy still favours the existence of much large-scale agriculture under European management, although not on such privileged terms as in the past. In Uganda there have been severe restrictions on occupation of land by non-Africans for the past fifty years and, although Uganda would probably never have become a major European farming area, the restrictions have limited the extent of plantation agriculture. Plantation production can now expand rapidly only under African control; and in view of the lack of private capital it must take the form of government enterprise, thus adding further to the role of government. In Tanzania colonial policy generally stood midway between that in Kenya and that in Uganda, alienation of land being permitted rather than encouraged.

Today perhaps the contrast of greatest significance for economic activity is that between Kenya and Tanzania in their interpretation of the philosophy of African Socialism. Throughout the late 1960s Tanzania favoured more government intervention in the economy than Kenya, and took less pains to attract foreign private investment. Emphasis on maximizing economic growth was greater in Kenya, that on spreading it more widely among the population was greater in Tanzania. The Kenya government was more willing to accept both the temporary alien control of certain sectors of the economy, and the establishment of an African bourgeoisie: Tanzania endeavoured to resist both, possibly sacrificing some material gains in the process. In these respects Uganda has occupied a midway position.

Throughout East Africa official policy has limited somewhat the commercialization of the peasant economy. Tanganyika officials observed that 'the tendency to swing from food crops to cash crops has continually to be watched, and sustained propaganda is necessary to prevent this swing from going too far'.[3] Kenya has long prohibited the movement of food crops between districts, except under strict marketing board control. This attitude was severely criticized in the 1953–55 Royal Commission report.[4] If it had not prevailed, more farmers in East Africa would have concentrated their energies on cash crops, and in some areas production of food crops for sale would have developed further.

Government influence is apparent in the distribution of most major crops. That of maize cannot be understood without reference to the discouragement of the Uganda Department of Agriculture[5] and the contrary policy adopted in Kenya. The importance of cassava in many districts results largely from official insistence that it should be planted as a famine reserve. The importance of cotton in Uganda, despite poor returns in relation to effort involved, is related to seventy years of vigorous government encouragement.[6] This has taken forms ranging from pressure by local chiefs to free distribution of seed and insecticide. The emphasis on cotton rather than coffee in Busoga District can be understood only in relation to the policy of the Department of Agriculture.

In Kenya the government greatly affected the pattern of coffee cultivation by prohibiting it on African farms everywhere until 1935, and in Central Province until 1954. The withdrawal of the restrictions permitted a wider extension of coffee cultivation but, although the present Kenya government is anxious to increase peasant incomes, new planting has had to be banned because of marketing problems. Similarly the expansion of pyrethrum cultivation in Kenya and Tanzania has been limited by necessary government action.

Governments have influenced the local distribution of crop production by promoting settlement schemes or by providing such facilities as water supplies. Official work in the latter field has assisted the extension of cotton and food crop cultivation in Geita and Maswa Districts of Tanzania. The role of the Department of Settlement in changing the whole cultural landscape of the Kenya highlands, and thus also the pattern of economic activities, is especially significant (Map 22).

Government restrictions have affected trade in cattle, and timber production, as a result of very proper concern with disease control and forest conservation. Compulsory destocking has taken place in some areas, although the recommendation of one veterinary official that cotton cultivation should be prohibited in southern Teso so that people would meet their cash needs by selling cattle was not implemented! It is sometimes suggested that mining has been hindered by unrealistic regulations and excessive taxation.[7] Official policy has probably limited the scale of rural trade by forbidding non-Africans to trade outside gazetted trading centres. The role of governments in stock-rearing, fishing, forestry, mining and trade has not, however, been mainly restrictive. An afforestation programme, the stationing of a fisheries officer or some geological survey work in a particular area has often assisted the development of timber production, fishing or mining there.

The distribution of many activities shows some relationship

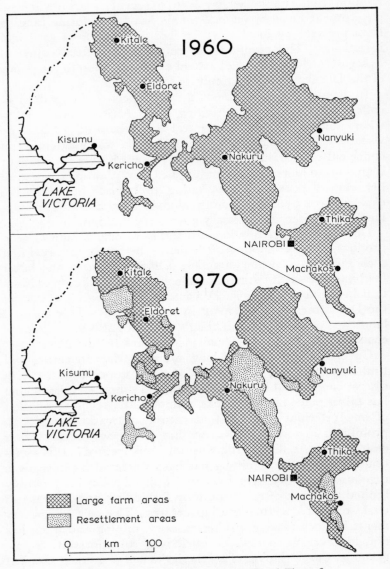

Figure 22. KENYA HIGHLANDS: Land Transfer

to the distribution of government officers working in the field. The successful cultivation of tea on small farms in central Kenya owes much to very close government supervision. In Uganda the concentration of prosperity in Buganda and the east is in part related to the longer period and greater intensity of government activity there than elsewhere. In Tanzania the south has suffered from receiving less attention than some other parts of the country. This relationship has now been recognized in all three countries, and some dispersal of economic activity may result from present efforts to assist the poorer parts of each by, for example, spreading agricultural assistants more evenly.

A final example of government influence on the pattern of economic activities is the encouragement given to them by imposition of high tariffs or quantitative restrictions on imports. Wheat cultivation and textile manufacture are among the activities which depend most heavily upon such assistance. Similarly, any decision on the establishment of an iron and steel industry must depend in large measure on the degree of tariff protection provided against imported steel.

GOVERNMENT PARTICIPATION IN ECONOMIC ACTIVITY

In some countries most economic activity is under direct government control but, except in Zanzibar, there is no sign of this situation developing in East Africa. However, even in the United States, with its firm attachment to private enterprise, government has sometimes taken part in economic activity, as in the Tennessee Valley. Likewise in East Africa there are some state-owned agricultural and industrial concerns, and governments organize the marketing of several commodities.

One activity undertaken exclusively by the state is rail transport, of which there would certainly be less if it had been left to private enterprise. It is difficult to envisage any private company building and operating railways anywhere in Tanzania; and although the Kenya-Uganda line is now profitable, the British government took a financial risk in building it which no business concern could take. Most air transport and large scale inland navigation in East Africa is also operated by government enterprise. In Uganda electricity generation has long been undertaken by a government corporation, and this may have contributed to the higher level of production than in Kenya and Tanzania. Owen Falls provided an ideal site, but it is uncertain whether any private company would have risked developing it.

Government participation in both agriculture and industry developed earlier in Uganda than elsewhere, mainly through the Uganda Development Corporation, set up in 1952. The U.D.C. has established several important enterprises, and has contributed to other largely private concerns, providing advice on technical matters, a useful link with government and some capital. By developing new tea estates, the Corporation has assisted the expansion of this crop where people are strongly opposed to alienation of land for estate agriculture. It also pioneered the field of cattle ranching, even though with only limited success as yet. It has assisted the tourist industry by building the majority of the larger hotels in the country including lodges within the National Parks. The greatest contribution of the U.D.C. has been to the development of manufacturing, for it owns the cement works and one textile plant, and is a shareholder in the fertilizer and steel factories. It is doubtful whether all these industries would be found within Uganda if the government had not participated in their development. Such participation certainly encouraged the location of the first East African textile mill in Uganda rather than Kenya.

Similar development corporations have recently been established in Kenya and Tanzania, and in the latter the N.D.C. has expanded its activities very rapidly. It has played a major part in the recent growth of manufacturing, and it moved into several other fields, such as tourism, before these hived off as separate entities within the 'Parastatal' sector. The Tanganyika Agricultural Corporation was set up in 1955 to take over land cleared for the Groundnut Scheme; and, although for some years its work was mainly experimental rather than commercial, its direct contribution to the pattern of economic activity, under the new name of National Agricultural and Food Corporation, is now increasing steadily.

In general, government participation has been significant for the spatial pattern of economic activity only on a national, rather than local, scale. The Tanzania government has a large investment in Mwadui diamond mine, but this is intended to associate the people of the country with an already flourishing industry and has not affected its size or location. The participation of government in the meat canning industry has assisted its development in both Tanzania and Kenya, reducing over-stocking at the same time by providing an outlet for surplus cattle. It is unlikely that meat would make such a large contribution to East African exports in the absence of such government participation. There is, however, no evidence that it has affected the location of meat canning within these countries.

In each country the government has considered directly influencing the distribution of productive activities by setting up manufacturing industries in the more poorly developed areas: but little has been achieved as yet, except perhaps some decentralization from Dar es Salaam in the case of N.D.C. enterprises, and the location of the new Uganda cotton-spinning mill at Lira in the north.

Governments have participated in the economic activities of East Africa more in the field of marketing than in anything else. The Uganda government buys all the country's cotton and most of its coffee through marketing boards, and then sells them both directly and through private exporters. Cotton is also handled by marketing boards in Tanzania and Kenya, as is all maize that is moved legally between districts. Many other crops are also marketed in this way in both Tanzania and Kenya. There is much disagreement among economists about the effects of such government activity. The purchase of coffee in Uganda at prices below world levels around 1954 probably seriously limited the area planted, with long-term effects on production since coffee is a perennial crop. The effects of price stabilization policies on annual crops such as cotton are not so long lasting, and the announcement of a guaranteed minimum price before the planting season has probably encouraged cotton production considerably. Where a crop is bought regularly at a price above world levels, this is bound to favour its cultivation, and this applies to maize in Kenya.

The operation of the marketing boards has also affected the

distribution of crop production within each country, especially where a uniform price is paid to growers everywhere. This is clearly seen in Uganda, where cotton cultivation was in the past more favoured in the south than in the north since extra transport costs resulted in lower prices to growers in the north. Today the West Nile farmer receives the same price for his cotton as the farmer in Bukedi, 500 km. nearer to the coast, and in this way government policy has in a sense counteracted 'the facts of geography'. Likewise on a more local scale a farmer living near a buying centre 100 km. from a railhead is in no worse position than one whose farm is beside a ginnery and a railway station. The Lint Marketing Board has thus assisted a spread of cultivation into the less accessible districts, and away from the major transport routes even within these districts. The situation is similar in Tanzania, where cotton growers near Dar es Salaam now have no advantage over those near Mwanza, and the latter have no advantage over those in remote Biharamulo.

The Maize Marketing Board in Kenya never adopted the same policy, partly because it was dealing with a much more bulky product than cotton, although a standard price is often offered at all markets within one district. Government market-ing policy has probably not assisted maize production more in one area than another, except in so far as the price structure prevailing up to 1963 may have favoured the European farmers more than farmers in areas of African settlement.

In all three countries governments have participated in stock marketing, as well as organizing markets for private traders. The Kenya Meat Commission and the Tanzania government's share in Tanganyika Packers have been mentioned already. The Kenya and Uganda governments have set up livestock marketing organizations serving the more remote parts of each country, thereby contributing to destocking where this was thought necessary, controlling movement to markets to avoid spreading disease, and providing a source of income in areas where a commercial economy is little developed. The African Livestock Marketing Organization has encouraged cattle sales in the part of Kenya north of the highlands, with the aid of an annual £100,000 subsidy. In Uganda the Karamoja Cattle Scheme made it possible for many cattle to be sold at the peak of the dry season, although they must then remain in quarantine until they are required in Jinja or Kampala: no private trader could operate on this basis. The scheme has met much criticism, but there is little doubt that the somewhat paternalistic role of even the present government has assisted the expansion of the cash economy in Karamoja.

On both broad and local scales, government policies have greatly influenced the distribution of economic activities in East Africa, directly, indirectly and even sometimes unintentionally. But political factors are not confined to internal government policies: they also include the external relationships of each country.

RELATIONSHIPS BETWEEN THE EAST AFRICAN COUNTRIES

The ties established between Kenya, Tanzania and Uganda under British administration have remained since independence and continue to affect patterns of economic activity. The common railway, airways and postal systems, customs and excise, and various other services, formerly the responsibility of the East Africa High Commission, were taken over first by a new East African Common Services Organization in 1962, and then by the East African Community which was set up under the Treaty for East African Co-operation in 1967.[8]

The customs union between Kenya and Uganda dates from 1917, and Tanganyika joined it in 1924. Its effects have therefore been felt over a long period, and this is reflected in the volume of trade passing between these countries. Each exports much more produce to the other two than to any other neighbouring country, apart from Tanzanian exports of oil products to Zambia; and the trade between Kenya and Uganda is quite exceptional among the countries of tropical Africa. The customs union has been a particularly important factor in the pattern of Kenya's exports, and thereby in the nature of the Kenya economy; but its significance for the external trade of both mainland Tanzania and Uganda is also great. Zanzibar was not incorporated in the customs union until 1968, and as a result it still undertakes little trade with Kenya and Uganda.

The role of the customs union in assisting the development of industries by widening markets was noted earlier. It has also influenced the distribution of economic activity within East Africa. There is little doubt that Kenya has benefited most, for most forms of enterprise serving all three countries are located there. It is even sometimes suggested that Tanzania, and possibly also Uganda have lost more than they have gained from the customs union, although there is little evidence that they would have experienced greater development if they had been less closely linked to Kenya. It certainly would not follow that they should withdraw from the customs union, especially since various measures have now been taken to ensure that its benefits are spread more evenly.

The distribution of many economic activities would probably be different in the absence of a customs union and other close links between these countries. Kenya would perhaps be growing more sugar, and Uganda growing less, while Kampala might not be dependent mainly on Kenya for its milk supply. Close political relationships are an essential factor in the production of steel in Uganda using mainly Kenya scrap and supplying mainly Kenya markets, and in the import from both Tanzania and Uganda into Kenya of tobacco, much of which later returns in the form of cigarettes. They have also enhanced the importance of Mombasa and Nairobi as centres of trade for Uganda and Tanzania as well as Kenya. If the customs union did not exist Uganda traders would import more goods directly from overseas, and either Tanga or Dar es Salaam would handle more Moshi and Arusha trade.

The common railway administration also assists the movement of goods to and from Moshi, Arusha and Bukoba through Kenya. Nevertheless, its existence has been advantageous to Tanzania for the rail services there are to some extent subsidized by Kenya and Uganda.[9] They carry so little traffic, and cross so much unproductive country, that the rates charged would have to be higher if they were not operated on an East African basis. They were, in fact, much higher than those in Kenya and Uganda until the systems were amalgamated in 1948.

The close ties between the three countries have greatly assisted the growth of Nairobi. The city provides many administrative services for the whole of East Africa, and has been chosen by many companies in such fields as banking and insurance, as well as commerce and industry, as the centre from which to serve the whole region. These activities might be more evenly distributed if no such political links existed. Until recently Nairobi also housed most of the administration of the common services themselves, but since 1967 a policy of decentralization has been adopted, thus providing more employment opportunities elsewhere. The posts and tele-communications headquarters, for instance, is now in Kampala, while the Community secretariat is located at Arusha.

Nevertheless Kenya, Tanzania and Uganda are still separate countries, and some features of their economic geography reflect this fact. Free trade is not permitted in all commodities, and restrictions on movements of maize between Uganda and Kenya may have discouraged greater production in the former. The wish for greater national self-sufficiency is a force of considerable importance, and this lay behind the establishment of a cement works and an oil refinery in Tanzania at a time when Kenya was able to supply all that country's needs. The same political factor is encouraging expansion of sugar pro-duction in Kenya, wheat cultivation in Tanzania and dairying in Uganda. One attempt to overcome the problems which might result from an increasing concentration of manufacturing in Kenya was the 1965 Kampala Agreement, which largely failed but which did encourage such firms as British American Tobacco and the Bata Shoe Company to increase their pro-ductive capacity in Tanzania and Uganda rather than in Kenya. Subsequently, the Treaty for East African Co-operation adopted a system of transfer taxes which at present give a slight advantage to Tanzania and Uganda as locations for new factories in various industries. In these circumstances the significance of political factors in the distribution of economic activities becomes particularly clear.[10]

EXTERNAL POLITICAL RELATIONSHIPS

The significance of external political relationships for the economic geography of East Africa lies mainly in the direction of its overseas trade. Membership of the Commonwealth is particularly important, for Britain is still the leading trading partner of all three countries, and all conduct half their trade with Commonwealth countries (Table 11). In the absence of this link trade with Australia, Canada and India, as well as with

U

Britain, would probably be much smaller. The non-aligned status of the East African countries in relation to the great power blocs might appear to be less significant, for trade with countries of the Communist bloc is still small. Nevertheless its volume is much greater now than it was during the colonial period.

One special instance of the political factor in economic geography is the break of all relations with South Africa. This has had severe repercussions on industries such as soda ash working at Magadi, which depended very largely on the South African market. The break has also involved the diversion of all South African airways services from East African airports.

Conversely, strenuous efforts are now being made to establish closer ties with other African countries. It is frequently argued that these could greatly assist the process of economic development, and the experience of integration within East Africa gives some support to this view. In general, the feeling of brotherhood with other tropical African states has so far been of limited economic significance for East Africa, but an exception is provided by the degree of re-orientation of Zambian trade that has occurred in recent years. Increasingly close political ties have played a part not only in the expansion of trade between Tanzania and Zambia, but also in the decisions to proceed with first an oil pipeline, then a tarmac highway, and finally a railway between the two countries.

Economic integration with neighbouring states could also be significant for the geography of East Africa through its effects on the comparative advantage of different locations for economic activity. Closer relations with Zambia, for instance, are already improving the economic prospects for the southern highlands of Tanzania. By 1970 Burundi, Ethiopia and Somalia, as well as Zambia, had all sought formal association with the East African Community, but no action had been taken to formalize this, and so integration on a wider Eastern African scale remained mainly a factor of potential rather than of actual importance.

Although continued dependence on the more prosperous countries of the world is in many respects an unfortunate aspect of East Africa's external relations, friendly relations with many countries have brought to East Africa much financial aid, which is greatly assisting economic development. In general this is too recent to have had much impact, but the rapid progress of resettlement in the Kenya highlands owes much to British aid, while the construction of the Tanzania-Zambia railway reflects China's interest in cementing ties which were previously largely a matter of words. In most cases, of course, it is the volume and terms of the aid, rather than its source, that are of direct significance for the pattern of economic activities. Furthermore, with regard to most aspects of foreign aid there is no striking difference between East Africa and most underdeveloped regions, or between Kenya, Tanzania and Uganda. Therefore, while it is a subject of great importance, it perhaps lies within the fields of economics and political science rather than economic geography.

REFERENCES

1 There is much on this subject in K. Ingham, *A History of East Africa*, Longmans, London, 1962, and in V. Harlow and E. M. Chilver, *History of East Africa*, Volume II, Oxford U.P., London, 1965.

2 C. Leubuscher, *Tanganyika Territory, A Study of Economic Policy under Mandate*, O.U.P., London, 1944.

3 Tanganyika Department of Agriculture, *Annual Report for 1950*, Dar es Salaam, 1951, p. 4. *The Tanganyika Five-Year Plan 1964–1969*, Dar es Salaam, 1964, pp. 19–20 indicated a change in attitude.

4 *East Africa Royal Commission 1953–1955 Report*, H.M.S.O., London, 1955, pp. 65–66.

5 E.g. Uganda Protectorate, *Crop Production Programme 1961*, Entebbe, 1961, p. 4.

6 The role of government policy in cash crop development is evaluated in D. N. McMaster, 'Uganda: Initiatives in Agriculture', in *Institute of British Geographers, Special Publication No. 1*, 1968.

7 International Bank, *The Economic Development of Uganda*, Entebbe, 1961, pp. 209–210.

8 The most comprehensive account is P. Robson, *Economic Integration in Africa*, Allen & Unwin, London, 1968, Ch. 4. See also A. Hazlewood, *African Integration and Disintegration*, Oxford U.P., London, 1967, Ch. 3; P. Ndegwa, *The Common Market and Development in East Africa*, E. A. Publishing House, Nairobi, 1968, Ch. 6 & 10; and various essays in C. Leys and P. Robson (ed.), *Federation in East Africa*, Oxford U.P., Nairobi, 1965.

9 A. R. Roe, 'The Impact of the East African Treaty on the Distribution of EACSO Benefits', *East African Economics Review*, Vol. 3, No. 2, 1967, pp. 39–52.

10 A fuller discussion is A. M. O'Connor, 'Geography and Economic Integration in East Africa', in S. H. Ominde (ed.), *Studies in East African Geography and Development*, Heinemann, London, in the press. See also W. A. Hance, *African Economic Development*, Praeger, New York, 1967, Ch. 6.

CHAPTER 19

Conclusion

The preceding chapters have been concerned to break down the complex pattern of economic activity in East Africa into its component parts, and to single out some of the factors that have most clearly influenced the pattern. Before closing the discussion it may be appropriate to put the pieces together again, and to consider briefly the composite picture, for although the various sectors of the economy can be examined individually there is much interaction amongst them. Economic activity can in fact be viewed in terms of a single scale such as 'prosperity', or (given certain assumptions) 'development'. It can even be considered along with various other phenomena in terms of 'modernization'. None of these concepts is very precise, but all undoubtedly have a spatial expression which it is the geographer's task to investigate. This has recently been demonstrated in the case of modernization by Soja for Kenya[1] and by Gould for Tanzania,[2] each using a wide range of variables brought together by principal components analysis.

No such statistical analysis is undertaken here, but an attempt is made to map both economic activity, in terms of absolute income, and also prosperity, in terms of income per head. Neither map can be regarded as definitive, for the data upon which they are based consist largely of very rough estimates, but they do indicate the very real differences between areas of relatively intense development and others lacking any form of economic activity. The pattern that emerges from Map 23 is one of islands of high income standing out from a sea of extreme poverty. In these islands a very large proportion of the most productive forms of activity is concentrated. They focus upon the towns, but also include certain rural areas such as the highlands of Kenya, the Lake Victoria zone of Uganda and the slopes of Kilimanjaro in Tanzania. Such variations in the

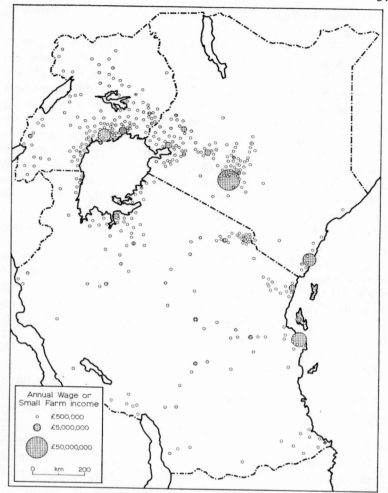

Figure 23. EAST AFRICA: Household Income

This map indicates the approximate distribution of income from wage employment and from crop, livestock and fish sales by the self-employed.

intensity of development are of course found in every country, and may be no greater in East Africa than in many other areas; but in this region the distribution of income does not match the distribution of population at all closely, so that variations in income per head (Map 24) are far greater than at least in most of the more highly developed parts of the world.[3]

The picture provided by both maps is unfortunately a static one, whereas the patterns are in fact constantly changing. Ideally these changes should also be mapped, but the necessary data are not at present available. Clearly there are various examples of development spreading from one area to another, and more studies of such diffusion in East Africa are urgently needed; but there is some reason to believe that more development tends to take place in the areas which are already relatively prosperous, and that the gap between the more affluent and the poorer parts of the region is widening. This is undoubtedly occurring at the extremes along the scale, for all the most highly developed areas are experiencing further growth while in some of the poorest areas no change is taking place at all.

It should not necessarily be assumed that development is always a good thing: this is even more evident in the case of modernization, especially when this means much the same thing as westernization. The current rapid rate of urban growth in East Africa, for example, gives some cause for alarm. But even if it is not to be sought at any price, all would agree that the raising of living standards in general, and income in particular, is an urgent need throughout the Third World. Indeed the governments of Kenya, Tanzania and Uganda have all dedicated themselves to the elimination of the poverty from which their countries suffer. They are also committed to African Socialism, and therefore to encouraging the equitable distribution of income amongst the whole population. From this point of view the contrast between islands of development and great tracts where incomes are extremely low presents one of the greatest practical problems facing these governments. Indeed, the whole issue of promoting economic development can be viewed spatially as a matter of increasing the extent of these islands, or of establishing new ones, so that they eventually accommodate the entire population of the region.

The significance of the spatial pattern of development in relation to economic planning is increasingly appreciated in all three countries. Contrasts at the international level at one stage threatened to break up the close links between these

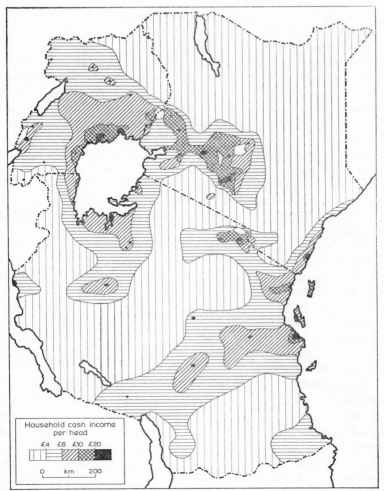

Figure 24. EAST AFRICA: Household Income per Head
This map indicates the pattern of poverty and prosperity, in terms
of cash income from wage employment and from crop, livestock and
fish sales by the self-employed.

countries, and within the framework of the East African
Community measures to spread development more equitably
amongst them have been put into effect. It has been shown,
however, that the contrasts within each country are of a much

greater magnitude, and it is encouraging to note that close attention is now being given to these.[4]

The principle of economic planning was accepted in all three countries as they became independent, and comprehensive development plans were quickly prepared. But although these indicated what type of activity was to be encouraged, and when each item of investment should be undertaken, they had little to say on where development was expected to take place within each country.

Subsequent plans have in general become more explicit about the spatial pattern of development. The existence of great inequalities has been clearly acknowledged, and each government has declared its wish to reduce these wherever possible, although they differ in the degree of priority accorded to this aim.

The Second Tanzania plan aims 'to redress the regional imbalance by promoting an economically effective regional division of labour, which incorporates a much more positive role for regions neglected in the past',[5] and includes a separate volume on 'Regional Implications'.[6] The second Kenya plan devotes less attention to the question, but it notes 'the problem of securing a satisfactory balance between developments in different districts', and declares 'a concern to ensure that some districts do not continue to lag behind'.[7]

Both plans give explicit attention to regional development policies largely in the context of urban development. In Kenya the attempt 'to plan a national framework or strategy for the location of capital investments'[8] involves the designation of seven major and numerous minor 'growth centres'. The Tanzania plan proposes 'a vigorous policy of urban decentralization',[9] and specifies nine towns as 'growth poles', all of which are expected to grow at a faster rate than Dar es Salaam.

The second Uganda plan, covering the period from 1966 to 1971, gave little more attention to spatial patterns than the first, 'Regional Aspects of Planned Development' being relegated to a single-page appendix.[10] More recently, however, much more discussion of the subject has taken place in Uganda, and the third plan is expected to indicate measures for reducing regional disparities in income in that country also.

While this concluding chapter is concerned mainly with the

spatial pattern of economic activity in general, it must be noted that as efforts are made to incorporate the spatial dimension into economic planning attention has to be given to regional variations in each sector of the economy. Just as the present nature of economic activity differs from one area to another, so does the nature of the new development which can most appropriately be encouraged. It is therefore suggested that effective regional planning of this type requires a thorough understanding of the economic geography of the area.

This book has hardly begun to explain the patterns of economic activity, but it should at least have indicated the diversity of both land and livelihood which exists within the region. East Africa has zones with heat and cold, high rainfall and aridity, fertile and infertile soils, dense and sparse population, good and bad transport facilities and many other contrasting characteristics in innumerable combinations. It is therefore not surprising that man makes his living in many different ways and, since most of these zones are small, there is a very intricate pattern of economic activities on the ground.

The diversity of environment and of economic response within a small area, which sets East Africa apart from much of the continent, presents the geographer with great opportunities and also a great challenge. The challenge is particularly great because the contrasts are found not only within the region as a whole, but often on a local scale also. East Africa is not easily studied at a simple level, for there are no broad physical zones each with its characteristic economy. West Africa or the Congo lands likewise should be studied at a more advanced level, when earlier oversimplifications quickly become apparent: but one might almost say that East Africa can only be studied at this level.

There is rarely a simple explanation of the distribution of any form of activity. Many factors are generally involved and, if one wishes to discover why things happen where they do, all these have to be considered. Similarly, there is rarely one all-important reason why things are not happening in any particular area, which is perhaps more often the question of concern to the practical politician. Just as there is no single panacea for the great problem of poverty in East Africa, so also there is rarely a single panacea for any area within the region which is in an even worse position than others. All the contributory factors must be studied, and where possible either altered or countered.

It is hoped that the inadequacies of this book, the numerous questions which it has left unanswered, may serve to indicate lines of research for others. The geography of East Africa is still an almost untouched field, offering unlimited scope for study. In addition, this is a region in which the applications of geography to very real practical problems are particularly apparent. It is undoubtedly one of the most fascinating parts of the world in which a geographer could live and work.

REFERENCES

1 E. W. Soja, *The Geography of Modernization in Kenya*, Syracuse U.P., 1968.
2 P. R. Gould, 'Tanzania 1920–63: The Spatial Impress of the Modernization Process', *World Politics*, Vol. 22, No. 2, 1970, pp. 149–170.
3 Patterns in Uganda are examined in B. W. Langlands, 'On the Disparity in the Distribution of Economic Activity in Uganda', *University of East Africa Social Science Conference 1968/9 Geography Papers*, pp. 209–228.
4 A valuable review of work in progress is M. Safier (ed.), *The Role of Urban and Regional Planning in National Development of East Africa*, Milton Obote Foundation, Kampala, 1970.
5 Tanzania, *Second Five-Year Plan 1969–1974*, Vol. I, Dar es Salaam, 1969, p. 9.
6 Tanzania, *Second Five-Year Plan 1969–1974*, Vol. III, Dar es Salaam, 1970.
7 Kenya, *Development Plan 1970–1974*, Nairobi, 1969, p. 14.
8 Ibid., p. 81.
9 Tanzania, *Second Five-Year Plan 1969–1974*, Vol. I, p. 179.
10 Uganda, *Work for Progress*, Uganda's Second Five-Year Plan 1966–1971, Entebbe, 1966, p. 171.

Index

(Figures in italics refer to maps only)